POETRY'S DATA

Poetry's Data

DIGITAL HUMANITIES AND THE HISTORY OF PROSODY

MEREDITH MARTIN

PRINCETON UNIVERSITY PRESS
PRINCETON & OXFORD

Copyright © 2025 by Princeton University Press

Princeton University Press is committed to the protection of copyright and the intellectual property our authors entrust to us. Copyright promotes the progress and integrity of knowledge created by humans. Thank you for supporting free speech and the global exchange of ideas by purchasing an authorized edition of this book. If you wish to reproduce or distribute any part of it in any form, please obtain permission.

Requests for permission to reproduce material from this work should be sent to permissions@press.princeton.edu

Published by Princeton University Press
41 William Street, Princeton, New Jersey 08540
99 Banbury Road, Oxford OX2 6JX

press.princeton.edu

PSR Authorized Representative: Easy Access System Europe - Mustamäe tee 50, 10621 Tallinn, Estonia, gpsr.requests@easproject.com

All Rights Reserved

Library of Congress Cataloging-in-Publication Data

Names: Martin, Meredith, 1976– author.
Title: Poetry's data: digital humanities and the history of prosody / Meredith Martin.
Description: Princeton: Princeton University Press, 2025. | Includes bibliographical references and index.
Identifiers: LCCN 2024040477 (print) | LCCN 2024040478 (ebook) | ISBN 9780691254661 (hardback) | ISBN 9780691254678 (paperback) | ISBN 9780691254722 (ebook)
Subjects: LCSH: English poetry—History and criticism. | English language—Versification. | Versification—Databases. | Prosodic analysis (Linguistics)—Databases. | Digital humanities. | BISAC: LITERARY CRITICISM / Poetry | LANGUAGE ARTS & DISCIPLINES / Library & Information Science / Digital & Online Resources | LCGFT: Literary criticism.
Classification: LCC PR508.V45 M37 2025 (print) | LCC PR508.V45 (ebook) | DDC 821.001/4—dc23/eng/20241031
LC record available at https://lccn.loc.gov/2024040477
LC ebook record available at https://lccn.loc.gov/2024040478

British Library Cataloging-in-Publication Data is available

Editorial: Anne Savarese and James Collier
Production Editorial: Theresa Liu
Jacket/Cover Design: Karl Spurzem
Production: Lauren Reese
Publicity: William Pagdatoon
Copyeditor: Kathleen Kageff

This book has been composed in Arno

10 9 8 7 6 5 4 3 2 1

For Ada and for Joe

CONTENTS

List of Illustrations ix

Introduction [Read Me] 1
Exhibit A: Grammar 21

1 How We Count [Literary] 28
Exhibit B: Art 50

2 How We Read [Word Lists and Dictionaries] 55
Exhibit C: Table 77

3 How We Classify [Linguistic] 80
Exhibit D: Music 92

4 How We Express [Typographically Unique] 96
Exhibit E: Illustration 129

5 How We Argue [Original Bibliography] 134

6 Coda [How to Cite] 168

Appendix: Full Citation Information for PPA Sources 175
Acknowledgments 179
Bibliography 183
Index 203

ILLUSTRATIONS

1. Title page, Goold Brown, *The Grammar of English Grammars*, 1851 — 21
2. Goold Brown, *The Grammar of English Grammars*, 1884, 827 — 26
3. Goold Brown, *The Grammar of English Grammars*, 1884, 828 — 27
4. Image of three-ring binder — 43
5. Excerpt from George Saintsbury, "The Danger of Phonetics," *Athenaeum*, 1919 — 47
6. Title page, Edward Bysshe, *The Art of English Poetry*, 1702 — 50
7. Thomas Rowlandson, "Dr. Syntax Loses His Money," 1812 — 70
8. Racing calendar, 1823 — 71
9. James Ward, portrait of Dr. Syntax, 1820 — 74
10. S. S. Hamill, "Tabular View of the Science of Elocution," 1872 — 77
11. Library of Congress subject headings (LCSH) list — 82
12. William Gardiner, *The Music of Nature*, 1832, 156 — 92
13. William Gardiner, *The Music of Nature*, 1832, 39 — 94
14. George Saintsbury, *A History of English Prosody*, vol. 2, 1908, 548 — 97
15. John Thelwall, *Illustrations of English Rhythmus*, 1812, xlix — 98
16. Alexander Ellis, *The Essentials of Phonetics*, 1848, 77 — 98
17. Raymond Alden, *English Verse*, 1903, 4 — 99
18. William Thomson, *The Basis of English Rhythm*, 1904, 54 — 99
19. Princeton Prosody Archive logo and background image — 101
20. J. C. Zachos, *Analytic Elocution*, 1868, in PPA interface — 116

21. Close-up of Zachos, *Analytic Elocution*, 127	117
22. Text-only view of page 127, *Analytic Elocution*	117
23. Adelaide Crapsey, *A Study in English Metrics*, 1918, 21	123
24. L. T. Weeks's sonnet table, *Modern Language Notes*, 1910, 179	124
25. Herbert Tucker, "For Better for Verse"	125
26. Charles Hartman, Scandroid	127
27. John Thelwall, *Selections for the Illustration of a Course of Instructions*, 1812, xlvii	129
28. Joshua Steele, *An Essay toward Establishing the Melody and Measure of Speech*, 1779, 28	132
29. T. V. F. Brogan, table of contents, *English Versification*, 1981	137
30. T. V. F. Brogan, "The Development of Modern English Metrical Theory," 1981, 142	139
31. Paul Fussell, table of contents, *Poetic Meter and Poetic Form*, 1965	143
32. T. V. F. Brogan, "Navigating through the Book," *EVRG Hypertext Version*, 1999	155
33. T. V. F. Brogan, table of contents, *EVRG Hypertext Version*, 1999	156
34. T. V. F. Brogan, Samuel Johnson, entry *EVRG Hypertext Version*, 1999	157
35. *The New Princeton Encyclopedia of Poetry and Poetics* and *The New Princeton Handbook of Poetic Terms* workflow	162

POETRY'S DATA

Introduction [Read Me]

I NEVER WANTED to be a digital humanist. I wanted to read poems. I wanted to read poems and reconstruct the history of how poetry was read and taught and thought about across several disciplines in formation in the eighteenth and nineteenth centuries. I was interested in how poems showed up in odd, noncanonical, nonliterary places—grammar books and poetry handbooks—and how several had macrons or breves, accent marks or invented symbols of some kind. I had learned from researching and writing my first book that there was a whole range of discourses around what poetry was and how it meant, and most of this had something to do with how the word "poetry" signified at any given moment, in any given text. There was no one answer to what a poem was, and there was no one measure for a poem's successful adherence—or miserable failure to adhere—to a standard.

This book is about the history of how scholars measured the shifting standards of what a poem is, how a poem works, and what to count as the data in poems. And it is also about what I had to learn so that I could find, collect, and recount the traces of that history. My process of learning how to find and organize this various, fascinating, and not easily mappable discourse about the history of poetry turned me into the kind of reader who started to think differently about the sources on which I had relied, the research practices I had learned, and the data that underpinned it all. To write a new history of old poems, I needed to build a database, and to build a database I had to figure out what poetry and data had to do with one another.

This book, then, records several moments of media shift over the past decade and a half in which I thought about this question nearly every day. This book recounts poetry's role (or lack of role) in that media shift, how it has fared in the digital humanities era, and is my attempt to account for poetry's role in that shift. I never thought that the history of prosody would be part of the history of digital humanities, but it turns out that it is, and if I don't tell this story here, you might not otherwise know how to find it.

The key terms in this book's title—*poetry's data, digital humanities, the history of prosody*—all coalesce around my decade of work on the Princeton Prosody Archive (PPA), a database built by the Center for Digital Humanities, a center that I built at Princeton University over roughly the same time during which I participated in the collaborative work of the historical poetics reading group.[1] To read and understand the complicated valences of poetry's data, I had to learn everything I could about digital humanities and its history in computational humanities, about knowledge infrastructures in library and archival science, and about their relationship to the twenty-first-century version of digital humanities we are constantly redefining. And there is no better way to learn how something works than to try to build it, preferably with help, so learning how to build and define digital humanities at Princeton taught me, in turn, how to build and then define the work of the PPA.

Until recently, I thought I was writing a book about the history of linguistics and English poetic forms. I was curious about T. V. F. Brogan's insistence in 1981 that "metrical structure is in essence an extremely simple pattern of extremely simple elements," but that "the full and adequate explanation of English verse-structure still remains to be written." "Indeed," he continued, "I judge it is still about half a century away." For Brogan, metrical structure rests on "linguistic material that continues to astound us by its intricacy, even for what little of it we understand."[2] Brogan hinted at the importance of historical phonology to the study of poetry and lamented throughout his detailed reference guide that we would need to wait for the "last word" on a "unified field theory" for metrics, a solution that would bring to bear the modern discipline of linguistics to solve, once and for all, the intractable problem of how to measure a poem.[3] It was never my intention to present a unified field theory for the study of English meter, though I follow closely the scholars who work in that domain. Rather, I am interested in why the disciplinary histories of English literary studies and linguistics had such trouble arriving at a theory,

1. Historical Poetics, updated 2023, http://www.historicalpoetics.org/.
2. T. V. F. Brogan, *English Versification* (1981) (*EVRG*), xii–xiii.
3. Brogan, 16. This desire was also clear when a reviewer of *The Rise and Fall of Meter* longed for me to "rewrite Saintsbury's chapters on the nineteenth-century poets, 1860–1930, using the best available twenty-first-century knowledge about versification, poetic rhythm, and linguistic prosody."

and I began to suspect that the historical interactions between those disciplines might teach us something about the divisions between aesthetics and empiricism, about what we think poetry can and should do and how we interpret or describe it. To understand the complicated history of how poetry had been measured, I needed a structure that was different from that of a book. Eventually I understood that the structure I needed was a database, and initially the PPA's function was to collect the materials I wanted to analyze. And yet in the process of collecting these materials—in struggling to figure out how to access the materials I wanted, how to read them computationally, how to understand what digital archival work really meant—I learned about the mediated nature of all research over the past fifteen to fifty years and how little our profession seemed to know or care about it, how easily it had been dismissed as not pertinent to our work as literary scholars. I began to see the reticence to address or acknowledge the mediation of our research practices as of a piece with the reticence to address the mediation of poems, of poetry.

My own odd trajectory from historian of prosody to digital humanist to historian of "digital humanities" serves as a through line to this book, but my aim is to show scholars of literary studies the urgency of theorizing the practices that the adjacent disciplines of critical archival and critical data studies have understood as vital to our enterprise for quite some time. The collaborative work of creating and maintaining our shaky knowledge infrastructures in the digital age has taught me new ways of interpreting poetry. *Poetry's Data* analyzes in parallel the material mediation of poetry in the present digital age with the often unseen and underexplored materiality of poetry in the past.

This book makes three general arguments. First, the way we write and think about poetry's sounds (its data), and how we mark or textually encode these sounds, is mediated by literary and linguistic history that the discipline of literary studies generally does not bring to bear on the way it teaches poetry and poetic form. Second, scholarly research is itself mediated by technological infrastructures that have become knowledge infrastructures (data models, databases). Whether corporate controlled or scholar created, these knowledge infrastructures have historical antecedents that we have been trained to theorize (the "archive"); and yet we have not been trained to identify and navigate, so as to critique, the current landscape of knowledge production. Third, because we live and research in this technologically mediated landscape, our old models of reading and researching—methods that presume an autonomous, single scholar gathering resources and making claims—no longer hold. We need to theorize both the embeddedness of our sources inside multiple layers of mediation and how we are situated inside an information ecosystem that demands our active participation.

Reading and researching in the digital age is fundamentally collaborative and interdisciplinary. Of course, we can read a poem circulating online and value our intimate, individual response to that poem. But our continued disciplinary focus on individual interpretations of literary texts has undermined our ability to read the technologically mediated ways that poems circulate and the knowledge infrastructures that make that circulation possible, both past and present. It is precisely that mediated circulation that allowed readers, and continues to allow readers, to interpret poetry's data as a synecdoche of literary and aesthetic value systems.

Poetry's Data

Poetry is full of data. We read poetry informed by principles that we accept based on how we have been trained to read, speak, and interpret. We read poetry in its digital forms through technological mediations we seldom name or theorize, just as we might render invisible the varieties of print formats and market pressures that mediate a poem's circulation in a particular cultural field. In this book, I examine the evolving concepts of data in English poetry, what scholars believe poetry is made of, and their obsession with the ways poems function. I show how (what we think of as) a poem's component parts and mechanisms have been mediated by the ways information about poetry has circulated in texts that do not fit neatly into the category of the "literary" but nonetheless have had tremendous influence on how we approach what we understand to be the relevant information in a poem today. This category, the "literary" as such, determines what counts as poetry worth reading. These stories are connected. Poetry's data includes what is in the poem, what would be recognizable to its historical readers as its component parts—its versification, its sounds or sonic field, its various genres or modes of recognition, and what is around the poem—and where the poem appears (in a collection by an author, in an anthology, as an example in a grammar book, in a column of a newspaper, in a periodical). To find and understand the history of how scholars have thought about the data in English poems, to reconstruct an archive of how English poems have been read, we require new ways of reading as well as a deep understanding of all the ways we have already been taught to read.

But what do I mean by poems? By poetry? For the purposes of this book, I am referring primarily to English poems written and published between the sixteenth century and the first quarter of the twentieth century. The historical and linguistic structures of meter and rhythm in which these poems participated have been called both versification and prosody, but the discourse about "prosody" in the twentieth and twenty-first centuries, the lens through which we cannot help but view verse structures in the past, takes place in two distinct fields: literary studies and linguistics. In literary studies, prosody refers primarily to versification; in linguistics, prosody refers primarily to pronunciation.

My interest lies in the historical uses of the word "prosody" broadly construed, and how the confusion over its meaning has contributed to conflicting and entangled definitions of poetry. I have chosen to focus on the data of versification and pronunciation (*prosody's* data, if you will) to get at how scholars have selectively relied on prosody in definitions of poetry, which, in turn, has led to both disciplinary norms and disciplinary confusion over what constitutes the *relevant* data when we interpret a poem. In giving an account of these broad disciplinary trends in interpretation, a prehistory of one kind of close reading, I argue that studying the messy history of prosody reveals one reason that scholars might prefer to approach poetry *as if it is* unmediated, *as if it might* return us to some prior, unmediated sense of language or experience.

In many ways, it doesn't matter that I have the proof—the data—to show that poetry has never been only a black box that generates a special kind of aesthetic experience. The belief in poetry's transcendence of mediation is more important than the facts. I am not suggesting that we disregard whatever cumulative power we might assign to a poem as an object, or try to undermine the choices we make about what data we use to anchor our interpretations of poems. Rather, I argue that our critical desire for poetry's immediacy requires that we look away from other poems and archives and requires a disavowal of the broader historical fields out of which our contemporary understandings and misunderstandings of poetry emerged. *Poetry's Data* asks for an expanded understanding of context, especially in an era when "poetry" is asked, even more than it has been in the past, to represent "the human" across our data-mediated information environment.[4]

---

4. As just one example, Anthropic's model Claude has three tiers: "haiku," "sonnet," and "opus." https://www.anthropic.com/news/claude-3-family, accessed June 24, 2024. "Poetry" as a representation of uniquely human nuance and complexity is a marketing tool for AI companies, which flaunt their models' abilities to write plausible-sounding verses. See Köbis and Mossink, "Artificial Intelligence versus Maya Angelou: Experimental Evidence That People Cannot Differentiate AI-Generated from Human-Written Poetry"; Singh, "ChatGPT Amazes

I make these claims based on the Princeton Prosody Archive, a digital archive, which, it is important to note, is not a database of poems. Arguably, we don't need another database of poems. Poetry is easy to find on websites like poets.org, poetryfoundation.org, the bartleby.com verse collection (bartleby.com/lit-hub/verse), poems.com, and a number of other sites. Rather than collecting poems, the PPA collects information about historical poems on historical pages. The discourse *about* poetry and about the ways scholars have measured how particular texts might or might not count *as* poetry enables readers to trace how poems circulate beyond their original print contexts, reprinted in poetry handbooks, versification guides, grammar books, pronunciation guides, anthologies, and schoolbooks, and even on websites like poetry.org. *Poetry's Data* proposes that we confront not only the conditions of a poem's circulation in these less traditional texts, but the historical and contemporary conditions that mean we are less likely to see poems as extracted examples of versification or pronunciation. And just as we often read poems with a disregard for the way their prosody and sound are mediated by layers of history, so too do we often read digitized sources with a disregard for the technological infrastructures (the images generated from page scans and the accompanying text files, generated by optical character recognition, or OCR) that mediate our access to the past.

Our scholarly choices about how we read poems signal our participation in different literary histories and prosodic discourses. The PPA and this book urge us to consider why and how we read a poem a certain way; I aim to prove that our choices as readers signal our participation in one or another version of literary history and several possible theories of reading. Scholars take part in one kind of poetic reading practice when they pay attention only to poems that have been published in books, canonized, and anthologized; they read another way when they focus on the poetry that circulated widely in the periodical press and in reviews and journals (only sometimes making it into books), a relatively newer approach to literary history made vastly more accessible by digitization. And yet another kind of reconstructed literary history relies on perceived relationships between individual poems, taken out of their historical contexts and read via different theories, sometimes connected to their authors and sometimes not at all, but often as exemplars of historical,

---

Twitter Users with Shakespearean-Style Poem on Climate Change"; and Flood, "Robot Artist to Perform AI Generated Poetry in Response to Dante." The AI or computationally generated poem as a test for whether there is a uniquely human aesthetic sensibility has become an even more popular trope in recent years.

philosophical, or formal literary arguments. For those and other reasons I'll explore in the following pages, the PPA assembles historical materials about the ways that scholars in the past have read poetry; it is a collection of possible reading practices. And yet *this book* also thinks through how we have come to value our arguments in monograph form because we have not yet been trained to read the arguments that databases might make—or we have decided not to value those arguments, for reasons that have everything to do with the way that databases expose several kinds of mediation we would rather not acknowledge. In its collections, ongoing curation, history, and design, the PPA forwards several arguments that (it is my hope) this book will teach you how to read.

The kind of data I consider in the PPA is not comprehensive—no archive is—nor does it aim to represent every possible historical account of reading poetry, but it does attempt to gather, as far as is legally possible, the commingled literary and linguistic histories of how scholars approach English poetry's prosody, the primarily sonic data of a poem. A full-text searchable digital collection of materials related to the study of prosody, both versification and pronunciation, in English between 1532 and 1928, the PPA has at the time of this writing about seven thousand items (over two million pages, and 540 million words).[5] Some of the discourses in the PPA are hard to read because of historical provenance and semantic change; some of them are hard to read because they posit new ways of reading poetry that rely on squiggles and numbers and waves and triangles and dots and all sorts of odd-looking marks that do not resemble any of the diacritical marks to which our modern pronunciation guides might adhere. The database marks these typographically unique pages so that you can view them since there are no Unicode equivalents to their invented signs. This is not to say that you can't trace a concept of poetry's data in the shifting (and increasing) ways that interpretations of poetry moved from sonic data to examples of figurative language—that, too, is in the PPA—but my focus in this book is the historical use of prosody as versification and pronunciation. I trace an underexamined path through the history of poetic interpretation and English disciplinary history, a history that presents challenges to the modern poetry classroom. Without a collection of materials in a

5. By "words" I refer to word instances or tokens after running Optical Character Recognition correction. The count is 770 million nonalphabetic "tokens," which, because of OCR correction, are removed. This word count is talking about words as content *only*. For text analysis we performed OCR correction to (necessarily) remove suprasegmental marks like prosodic notation. I'll discuss this in more detail in chapter 4, "How We Express [Typographically Unique]."

clearly marked database, this underexamined path through the history of poetry's sonic data is likely to remain underexamined. The untranslatability between the image of the marked text and its underlying codes is one part of poetry's data that this book explores.

If the primary sense of *Poetry's Data* calls attention to the written inscription of sonic patterns in poetry as guides to versification, the title also refers to the difficult work of navigating and maintaining access to materials of the past in the digital age. At the time of this writing, scholars might still use Google Books to check a reference, though the ability to trust what Google Books is indexing might have already eroded.[6] The PPA collaborates with the HathiTrust Digital Library, which currently maintains the largest set of digitized books managed by academic and research libraries, as well as with Eighteenth Century Collections Online (ECCO), owned by Gale-Cengage, and Early English Books Online (EEBO), owned by ProQuest. I name these collections and their owners because this is an important part of the story of poetry's data and of the PPA. One argument of the PPA, and this book, is that we must theorize and understand the shaping mechanisms of the constraints on which we rely when we search full-text data and metadata for information. Search is not the same as research, as I'll explain in these chapters. The power of the PPA derives from the discoveries it enables within carefully constructed limits—or organizing principles—against the backdrop of a constantly shifting landscape of available digitized source material.

And so, unlike putting the words "versification" or "prosody" into larger databases and skimming the results for relevance, the PPA represents a careful and ongoing process of data curation and classification so that it can present the most complete collection of existing writing about prosody in English. The database contains books and articles, but also a great deal of paratextual material—prefaces, appendixes and front matter—which is where some of the most compelling prosodic discourse is nestled. These paratextual materials have been carefully excerpted from longer works when necessary. I pause over the words "collected" and "excerpted" in the pages that follow, since what the PPA provides on the whole is a focused distillation of the much larger digital resources I name above, as well as navigational pathways through them.

Just as the multiple valences of the word "prosody" are important to understand as part of the complicated history of poetry's data, so, too, is the word

---

6. David, "Google Books Reportedly Indexing Bad AI-Written Works"; Pechenick et al., "Characterizing the Google Books Corpus."

"archive." The collection's first impetus was to archive—as in to preserve—images of textual materials from the past that might otherwise be difficult to see or access. The poems that appear throughout the PPA are used as examples—for versification, for pronunciation, for criticism, for teaching. These examples highlight how scholars have extracted parts of poems as data to make claims about poetry, but they also highlight what past writers have noticed about poems broadly and at which historical moments and for what purposes. But just as in any archive, what is in the historical record of English poetry that the PPA collects is as useful for what it contains as it is for what it leaves out. I consider poetry's data to be incomplete.

The "archive" in the name Princeton Prosody Archive gestures to the concept of "digital archive" as it was understood in a bygone era of digital humanities (DH), hearkening back to the early 1990s in which many dreamed that the digital archive could be a way to expand and develop, as Jerome McGann put it, a "webwork of relations."[7] Here, "archive" is a way of rethinking our collective practices of preserving and accessing information from the past, and critical archival studies frameworks help me think through the collective relationships inside prosodic texts (for instance, in citational structures) and across institutional and legal frameworks that reveal and conceal power structures of the past and present. Like "digital humanities," "digital archives" as a term means something different now than it did in the past, and I situate the PPA and its arguments in the histories and possible futures of these contested terms. I consider both "data" and "archive" to be forms of mediation impacted by new technologies and by networks of relationships among archivists, catalogers, metadata librarians, bibliographers, information scientists, application developers, and user experience designers. Our research methods depend on institutional structures and collaborative labor by people we may never meet and systems we might never acknowledge or know how to name.[8]

The curatorial aspect of the term "archive" lingers in the PPA, as its initial bibliographic source material reconstructs what would have been "the papers of" the literary scholar T. V. F. Brogan, whose several bins of books about versification have been reconstructed in the collection titled "Original Bibliography." The idea of the PPA began as I was assembling materials for *The Rise and Fall of Meter*, in the five or six years before that book's publication in 2012.

    7. McGann, "Rationale of Hypertext."
    8. Cf. Leung and López-McKnight, *Knowledge Justice*; Caswell, *Urgent Archives*; Gitelman, "Raw Data"; Stauffer's *Book Traces* (chapter 5, p. 154) is clear on this point. See also Berry, "House Archives Built."

This was the era of "digital archives" before the critical archival turn. Collecting, classifying, and organizing so as to preserve access to this odd material about the history of prosody allowed me to rethink and ultimately reshape my relationship to several senses of the word "archive" as a fundamentally cocreative enterprise.[9]

How and why we arrived at our methodology for organizing the PPA into distinct "collections" is part of the argument of this book. The names of the chapters that follow are taken from the PPA's six collections and appear in brackets to signify their connection to the rectangular spreadsheet boxes by which we sorted and re-sorted the materials. In deciding how to transform the literary history of prosody into new entities, I learned how to see canonical forms of poetic knowledge making in the traces of the older entities that had never quite worked. In each of the chapters, you'll learn how and why each collection came to be, as well as the disciplinary assumptions I had to unlearn about how we count, how we search, how we classify, how we express, and how we argue as literary scholars. In all this unlearning, I learned how to read and understand poetry's data and poetry as data.

By poetry's data, I do not mean to suggest close or distant reading per se, but rather a way of reading that emerges in the wake of digitization that requires a historical approach to genre, format, and mediation.[10] Poetry's data can refer to the complicated and contradictory units of measure in a description of versification. It can refer to linguistic data like phonemes, emphasis, stress—any concept of sound before those were stabilized into linguistic terms. It can also refer to definitions of poetry in texts that were, again and again, and in conversation with and in opposition to one another over centuries, trying to define what makes a poem, what we might think of as networked data. Poetry's data is also *metadata*—how we find information about poems—and it involves the transformations of a variety of formats into data so that we can find (or fail to find) poems in a digital environment. Data is in the archive; it is on your computer; it mediates nearly every action we undertake as scholars today; and poetry, despite its lofty reputation, is no exception. But unlike prose (and even though poems might be viewed as easier to quantify since

---

9. See Owens, "What Do You Mean by Archive?" Go to https://prosody.princeton.edu/collections/ to view the collections in the PPA interface.

10. Cf. Gitelman, on Xerox, in *Paper Knowledge*; Gitelman, on Pitman, in *Scripts, Grooves and Writing Machines*; Emerson, *Lab Book*; Emerson, *Reading Writing Interfaces*; Tenen, *Plain Text*; Kirschenbaum, *Mechanisms*; Kirschenbaum, *Track Changes*; Kirschenbaum, *Bitstreams*; Cordell and Smith, *Viral Texts*.

they contain structures that seem more easily tractable), historical poetry has largely been ignored in theorizations of digital humanities and new media, though this book will detail the very few exceptions as well as ask why this has been the case.

Digital Humanities

Just as I never thought that studying the history of prosody would turn me into a digital humanist, neither could I have ever imagined that the history of digital humanities, or computational humanities, would be so deeply concerned with prosody, or to put it a different way, that the history of poetry was also a history of how to think about the cultural record—particularly its language—as data. And yet the converse of this realization was that the discourses about the data of poetry—as themselves part of the unexplored cultural record—were not amenable to being transformed into data in the ways that DH and humanistic data science have developed. This book tells a prehistory of DH that addresses some of the alienation scholars might feel when they see the title of this book—how can poetry have data? How can those two terms coexist? But the truth is that they have always coexisted, and the three time frames of this book show both how they coexist and why we might not want them to.

The first and longest time span I consider is the history (1532 to the present day) of how critics have been attentive to, and have attempted to fix, the quantifiable elements of English poetry into systems of meter, with particular attention to books about the sound of verse and language. We can study this longer historical arc only because of the large-scale digitization projects that parallel the rise of computational humanities over the course of the twentieth century. This large-scale digitization provides the second historical arc, snapping into place over the 1980s and 1990s and culminating in the establishment, normalization, and corporatization of the technologies that underlie most of our digitized reading today. The final time frame I consider is my personal historical arc, which plays out in what I call the Google Books era (roughly 2008 until 2024). Thinking critically about this period allows me to situate these two other histories in relation to the recent past. Because of the availability of these digital copies, the past twenty years have seen increased scholarly attention to the concepts of canon and archive, and a reconsideration of what Ted Underwood called "the broad contours of literary history."[11]

---

11. Underwood, "We Don't Already Understand the Broad Outlines of Literary History."

These three overlapping histories are interwoven into the book's argument. If we take seriously digital media as *mediation*, the process through which textual forms are transformed into data and delivered to us via data structures, then our reading of historical texts in digital formats must reckon with these mediations. *Poetry's Data* is about the shifting grounds of knowledge production, and our responsibility as literary scholars to engage actively with these shifts. I use these shifts to explore questions about labor, authority, property, and prestige. I explore how we have been taught to be comfortable in and around certain norms of print that are not the same as the norms of digital knowledge production, and what happens when we confuse the two. I confused them—I still might—but the narrower personal arc of this book builds to what I hope is a more complex, and collaborative, understanding.

Many of the methodologies of digital humanities have helped me understand poetry's data, and they are the backdrop of this book. "Digital humanities" is not one field, and I have learned that each evocation of that term must be situated in its historical, disciplinary, or institutional context. Just as Christine Borgman urges us to ask not "what is data" but "when is data," this book spans the longer history of what we might consider a computational humanities framework from each of the timescales I outline above.[12] It is nothing new to argue, for example, that nineteenth-century writers were grappling with issues of information overload and that reading their navigation of new print formats might help to guide contemporary scholarship. The long history of counting and grappling with how to count poetry's data joins other *longue durée* histories of literary quantification, navigating information overload, and grappling with new media worlds (textual and imaginary) that span several traditional historical periods.[13] Here and in the PPA, I show the prehistory of the separation between the practical and the theoretical (formerly universal or metaphysical) modes of poetic reading. I think through how, and why, for "poetry" to become synonymous with one concept of the "literary," literary studies needed to disregard and disavow precisely the kind of scholarship that makes up the PPA and that this book explores.[14]

12. Borgman, *Big Data, Little Data, No Data*, 4–5.

13. Cf. A. Blair, *Too Much to Know*; Lee *Overwhelmed*; Alfano and Stauffer, *Virtual Victorians*; and most recently, and brilliantly, Fyfe *Digital Victorians*.

14. Here I refer not only to philology, a favorite comparison for one track of disciplinary history, and not only to "rhetoric" as another historical arc that is relevant to the story I tell in this book, but to the overlapping disciplines of language teaching in grammar books and pronunciation guides, elocution handbooks, poetry teaching manuals, guides to versification, and

I also explore computational humanities and digital literary studies through the lens of historical poetics, thinking through what hopes for versification my predecessor T. V. F. Brogan pinned not only on the science of linguistics but on the technological advances of the 1970s–1990s. Here, I join longer histories of DH with histories of information science and critical archival studies.[15] Rather than focusing only on computation methods and trends during the rise of the World Wide Web, I focus on the way that "poetry," as a stand-in for a particular kind of creative output and interpretive practice, played a role in the movement of scholarly resources from university libraries to external corporations. I situate the study of poetry within the rise of scholar-created archives and alongside exploratory computational tools that might aid in the study of poetry, neither of which, I argue, adequately engages with the longer history of poetry's data.[16] Recent scholarship in critical DH explores the extractive and colonial logics of both traditional and digital archival projects as well as their subsequent infrastructures (and infrastructural failures). Concurrent with the technopositivism of the 1980s and 1990s, the fifty-year history of computational humanities to DH is a story about failed attempts at sustained collaborative cross-institutional and cross-disciplinary infrastructures. We witness, over this middle-distance history of the last fifty years or so, a continued and pervasive attachment to humanistic methods as individual, taught and rewarded as such, rather than opening up the possibility of (and institutional support for) new collaborative practices and modes of knowledge production. The constraint on institutional resources for humanities goes hand in hand

---

a collection of works that are less philological and more phonological. Though phonology has been considered at times as a branch of philology, often scholars who study the history of philology are referring to historical phonology in classical languages. Here, I consider phonology not as a residue of nineteenth-century philology but as a part of the history of linguistics as it pertains to the study of sound *specifically* in poetry. Henry Sweet usefully distinguished between "living philology" and antiquarian philology, and it is the former concept of a "living" philology, as a precursor to Otto Jespersen and Ferdinand de Saussure's "linguistics," that concerns me here. Henry Sweet, "Presidential Address (1877)," in Sweet, *Collected Papers*, 91. See also Ku-ming Kevin Chang, "Philology or Linguistics," in Pollock et al., *World Philology*, 311–31.

15. For a useful guide to information in media theory, see Hayot, Detwyler, and Pao, *Information*. For a longer history of language as information, see Binder, *Language and the Rise of the Algorithm*. My concern here is primarily the history of information *science* as opposed to information *theory*.

16. Cf. Amy Earhart's crucial historicization of digital literary studies between 1990 and 2015: *Traces of the Old, Uses of the New*. See also Mandell, *Breaking the Book*; Rockwell and Sinclair, *Hermeneutica*; and Siemans and Schreibman, *Companion to Digital Literary Studies*.

with the idea that humanities scholars can and should work alone, though I argue that we never have, and never can. Our archives, our source material, our access to information about the past have always relied on other scholars. This is not to say that these cross-institutional and cross-disciplinary infrastructures didn't exist (and don't continue to exist, though haltingly), but the transformative potential of collaborative modes of knowledge production in the humanities were and continue to be undervalued and were (and therefore are) largely unsustainable.

I started to learn about the digital humanities just as I was preparing to go up for tenure, a process that, in the humanities at my institution in 2012, relied on the production of a single-author monograph. At the same time as I was putting together my materials for tenure, I was trying to figure out how to find—which I quickly learned meant how to build—the resources I needed for the PPA. I had avoided all training in DH as a graduate student, even though my research had relied on at least one digitized archive. How did I get the feeling that I needed to travel to the physical archive to justify my reliance on the digital copy? There was no orientation to digital research methods at that time, and for that reason I narrate my education in the field as an accidental witness who then became an engaged participant in the field's development. I also use "accidental" here since my account of DH and its relationship to poetry over the past twenty or so years is not something I set out to understand. In fact, I actively resisted thinking that my subject of study (poetry) or my preferred methodology (historically contextualized close reading) could ever be relevant to computational methods, and I refused—or did not know how—to see my research as part of that process.

I was as wary of quantitative methods in humanistic research as I was wary of the prosodists who obsessively argued for their new methods of measuring English verse. I purposefully observed the field of computational approaches to poetry in the context of what I saw as its much longer history and felt relief that this literary historical vantage point meant that I didn't have to learn how to use or build these tools myself. My ignorance—my belief that poetry was somehow special or apart from the debates and discussions about digital scholarship—was hardwired into my training and into the profession, and it kept my scholarship apart from the actual workings of the institution and the multiple mediations of my source materials. This book contends with the messy materiality of this new information environment and the systems that underpin it, and it asks, what happens if we don't hold poetry apart from that uncomfortable space?

We are long past the separation of "the digital" from "the humanities" and have been for quite some time, and yet, for just a moment, think of the "digital" as representing that complicated material of technical infrastructures and information management; as the attempt to undermine hierarchical labor practices across undergraduate and graduate researchers, software engineers, archivists, and librarians; and as the long history of collective scholarly discussion about how to understand cultural materials in, and as, and through data in the library sciences. Before I learned anything about statistics or vectors or the possibilities of what a center for collaborative humanistic research could look like at Princeton, I learned that by holding on to the perception that there was a rarefied space for poetry that could transcend this entangled information landscape, I also upheld the idea that there was a rarefied space for me, as the scholar of literature, to exist above and yet in complete reliance on the invisible labor of the people who made it possible for me to do my work. One concept of poetic reading—close reading of a poem in a historical context as the highest mark of achievement in my professional field—clashed with my growing sense that even my ability to close read could not remain an individual activity. Along with my education in digital humanities and as a digital humanist, I became a scholar who works almost always in collaboration with others, and with an acute awareness of the complex interdependencies that structure these collaborations. The values that DH promoted—of translation between disciplines, of a variety of different skill sets coming together, of undermining academic hierarchies—were supported by my collaborative work in historical poetics.

Historical Poetics and the History of Prosody

Digital humanities, as an evolving orientation toward the project of archiving, reading, and defining our methods as humanists, clarified my thinking about historical prosody. We don't close read alone. Close reading can and does often happen in the classroom, where initial interpretations might yield to a collective understanding of a text. Heffernan and Buurma's *Teaching Archive* gives several examples of collaborative classroom activities to upend the common—and wrongful—assumptions about lone critics arriving at their insights based on years of quiet, individual study rather than testing out these ideas with students and other collaborators.[17] Their research shows that when we expand

---

17. Heffernan and Buurma, *Teaching Archive*.

our understanding of literary criticism to include additional interpretive texts like syllabi, lecture notes, lesson plans, and the like, we are better able to understand the critical approaches and literary histories that shape our profession.

My attention to the textual materials about the teaching of poetry prior to the twentieth century is not as specific to pedagogy as Heffernan and Buurma's, but the historical poetics reading group I have been participating in over the past two decades has taught me much about the value of nontraditional materials such as the poetry handbook for studying the history of poetry. The collaborative reading practices I learned in conversation with the historical poetics reading group have taught me how to approach poetry and historical material about poetry at the same time. Just as I don't believe we can navigate the new information environment as literary critics and believe we are in any way alone, so too did I learn that I am able to come to understand the material mediations of nineteenth-century poetry only with a group of devoted colleagues. Reading historical poems, reading about how scholars and critics in the past positioned these poems and positioned their own criticism of poetry in worlds of print, is difficult work to do without being able to draw on multiple kinds of expertise at once. Participating in this group also helped me understand that the poetry reading that interests me most explores how poems make meaning in multiple contexts and in relation to multiple discourses, sometimes overlapping and sometimes distinct.

From our collaboratively written statement, we define the Historical Poetics project as one in which "we pursue intensive reading of poems in relation to multiple discourses around, about, and in poetry, including (but not limited to) histories of genre, form, format, medium, prosody, parody, performance, circulation, translation and transmission. We read both forward and backward in history through poetry, to discover the historical constitution of poetics and the poetics of historical thinking."[18] As I'll explore throughout this book, digi-

---

18. See Historical Poetics. I have often quipped that the kind of collective reading that we model is ideal, and without Meredith McGill's model of melding book history and media studies in her readings of poetry, and Yopie Prins and Virginia Jackson's approach to the mediating work of meter and genre, my own work on the PPA would not have been possible. All of them serve on the advisory board for the project, but I learn most from them when I am participating in the reading group, reading a multiply-mediated poem in conversation, as voices cross in conversation, disagreement, and layered understanding, with several other voices to riff off of one another and finally build into an interpretation of a poem on a page that none of us would have been able to arrive at on our own.

tal humanities and historical poetics have evolved for me in close contact with one another, though not always in explicit alliance, and the availability of newly digitized materials has allowed our group to focus on historical approaches to poetry that we might not have otherwise been able to access. Because part of my methodology is to consider how a work circulated and how it was situated in relationship to different reading audiences in the past, this book presents a historical poetics in miniature of quickly changing media formats for conducting research over the past twenty years or so.

Part of the story of poetry's data is how we were taught not to read for certain kinds of data, not to look for evidence of circulation, and not to think about digital mediation when encountering the image of a historical page on a screen. And yet historical formats nevertheless mediate our ability to read those page images (which we might conveniently forget are images). Reading through and along with the multiple mediations of print and technological formats, with what we know, or think we know, about historical genres as themselves forms of mediation—these are all operations that we perform seamlessly without slowing down to consider each stage of the operation, to think about the ways information makes its way to us. We ignore mediation all the time when we read, but we can be better readers, and it is my hope that this book might nudge us to think together about how.

How to read literary forms in a variety of print and media contexts is not just a project for those of us who work on historical cultural materials. In addition to bringing to bear what we know about literary forms and their rich contexts from having studied the history of their circulation, we also need to understand how these forms are crucial to the way we read. The language of the past is mediated by today's technology, and in order to know how to read what corporations redefine for us as language worth reading, we need to feel confident that we are able to bring our skills as humanists to provide both historical contexts to the operations of today's technology and cultural contexts for the ways that generative language models proliferate texts that will need interpreting. This book argues for a wider adoption of the kind of collaborative critical thinking that might help us better interpret digitized source materials and, increasingly, statistically generated outputs about the past. These source materials now underlie what a model might recombine or transform into new material for us to interpret—all words and images dissolved back into the data that made them up to begin with. To know how to interpret these new outputs, we need to know how to navigate them thoughtfully.

Database : Collection :: Monograph : Chapter

The book explores what my engagement with poetry's data (its various interfaces, expressions, and visual formats) helped me understand about how we read poems and the literary history of poetry reading. It also uses, as its source, a web application that relies on the ongoing collaborative labor of a large group of people, and so I cannot guarantee that someone will be able to see the application far into the future. There are features that will break, bugs that we will decide not to fix. We have thought and theorized about the impossibility of the PPA continuing as a scholarly resource, and instead we are focusing on what it has taught us, here and in the site's final years in active development. Part of why a book's technology outlasts a web application's technology is that web applications require ongoing maintenance. We are actively exploring the implications of when, why, and how to end the development of the PPA, but in anticipation of PPA's eventual decline, *Poetry's Data* shares several images from the site's content in "exhibits" that are interleaved with the book's chapters.[19] Almost all these exhibit pages come from texts that appear in several of the "collections" in the database, indicated in brackets. The exhibits act as a hinge between the chapters, providing transition and provocation, and showing examples of the odd textual materials the PPA contains that we, as its creators, have struggled to classify. The exhibits correspond with and signal the concerns of the chapters that follow them, but they are also evidence of the strangeness of the data itself. The data in the PPA is messy, and does not fit neatly into any one category or history, which is part of the argument of the database. The books featured in the exhibits have trouble classifying themselves—"grammar of," "art of," "science of," "music of"—and are themselves mini-exercises in compilation, navigation, and classification.

Like the exhibits, the chapters each draw attention to the database's argumentative work. The questions suggested in the chapter titles refer to the many issues of classification-as-interpretation that working on prosody and data have taught me. This twin understanding of prosody (as part of the contested data in poems) and prosodic discourse (as the multidisciplinary data

---

19. In May 2025 we will hold a conference called "The Ends of Prosody" at Princeton, at which we will explore the data in the PPA collectively. We will add works to the database for a few years yet but do not plan to develop additional features. As Elika Ortega has said, "there is nothing more ephemeral than a website." Quinn Dombrowski (Stanford) chose this quote to print on a broadside at Ryan Cordell's Skeuemorph Press at the University of Illinois, Urbana-Champaign, https://bsky.app/profile/quinnanya.me/post/3ksf7vbm7of22, accessed September 26, 2024.

about poems), scattered as it is among various odd texts, informs the titles of each collection and the questions of each chapter. Together, each chapter reflects on how "poetry's data" changes over centuries. When is something a poem, verse, or song? When is a work a grammar book, teaching text, or schoolbook? When is a line divided into syllables, phenomes, accents, or beats? When you have a lot of material, how can you organize it so the parts make arguments? How do you do this in a database? How do you do this in a book? No one agrees on the data in poems, so while the PPA's construction allows for keyword searching and author, date, title, and other usual suspects of faceted search, there is an interpretive structure to the heterogeneous collection of materials that this book will argue is relevant to the understanding of historical poems. The leading questions in the chapters are intended to be applicable to the other chapters in a sort of database logic of serendipitous discovery.

In chapter 1, "How We Count [Literary]," I consider the still contentious question of what counts as literary criticism when our objects of study have not been solely "literary" for some time. How and what we count as objects worth studying, I argue, has been mediated by how cultural materials have been classified in the past and how our institutions value our work as literary critics in the present. This chapter thinks through the long history of what has and has not counted as poetry to rethink how and when we began to use poetry as a stand-in for one concept of "the literary" and how that shapes our approach to poetry in the past. Chapter 2, "How We Read [Word Lists and Dictionaries]," presents the two collections that are both deselected—or made optional—for the researcher in the PPA so as to explore the contexts we have been trained to ignore when we read poems, from historical formats, to historical sound, to the ever-expanding contours of literary history. In chapter 3, "How We Classify [Linguistic]," I reflect on how metadata restricts our ability to read the histories of disciplines in conversation. This chapter describes the challenges of locating prosody in the digital archive and the challenges of curating collections that adequately reflected the arguments in the PPA. In chapter 4, "How We Express [Typographically Unique]," I show how many marks for poetry intended to teach expression are rendered "mute" without a corresponding symbol in Unicode, the character encoding system used for textual data. Conversely, "expressive use," the only way to *see* these typographically unique symbols, is precisely what corporations who own these digitized page images restrict us from reading. The final chapter, "How We Argue [Original Bibliography]," reveals a longer history of technological challenges and innovations regarding how we might present poetry's data. Sections within the chapters move between the book's three time scales. The chapters are not chronological but purposefully recursive. A reader may chart their own path through the sections (though each section is related to the larger chapter and the collection on which it is based) in the same way that they might find a variety of suggestive connections in the PPA. Both structures serve an argumentative purpose. I call the coda "How to Cite" both as a gesture toward the PPA, which is itself scholarship that deserves citation, and to signal that even though this is a monograph, it is a collaborative one that I could not—and would not—have written alone.

Poetry's Data provides a thick description of an evolving methodology of reading and researching that I urge other scholars to record for themselves as we navigate together the way our access to our research materials is changing. In our profession, the idea that digital humanities means preservation, digitization, discovery, and digital scholarship has evolved to a broader concept of thinking about data in the humanities, or data-driven humanities, which both is part of the former idea of DH and also exceeds it. That shift from digital to data forces us to describe, collectively and individually, how we classify and represent our interpretive choices and research processes as experts, especially at a moment when access to the cultural record is no longer limited to those of us who were trained to distinguish and define the various print formats, genres, and modes of cultural production. I do not describe in minute detail the technology behind the database,[20] but if we do not understand this technology and those mediating our access to information, just as we might not bother to understand the technology of a poem, we might be more easily mystified by or convinced of its perceived power.

---

20. Anna Shechtman, in a review of *Bitstreams* by Matthew Kirschenbaum, wrote, "At a conference in 2016, a colleague and I discussed, with some frustration, a rhetorical tic that we saw developing among digital humanities scholars. Presuming, and rightly so, that most humanists know little to nothing about the mechanics of computation, DH scholars were turning to narrative to demystify their methods. This often led to first-person descriptions of unremarkable activities—*I turned on my monitor and opened a .csv file*—leading the reader through the banalities of scholarship, which academics using nondigital tools usually repress or relegate to the acknowledgment pages of their work." Shechtman describes this narrative turn as banal and jokes that it would not be methodologically interesting to narrate how nondigital humanists work: "*first I created a library account and requested various papers; then I went to the reading room.*" It is precisely this level of awareness I am interested in as method. Why did libraries have those papers and not others? Part of the point of narrating my journey through digital humanities questions is to show that these are not questions that are either digital *or* humanist, but crucially both. See Shechtman, "Matthew Kirschenbaum, *Bitstreams*," 1086.

EXHIBIT A: GRAMMAR

Goold Brown. *The Grammar of English Grammars*. New York: Samuel S. and William Wood, 1851. Title page caption: Goold Brown. *The Grammar of English Grammars*. New York: Samuel S. and William Wood, 1851. Title page (figure 1).
[Literary] [Linguistic] [Typographically Unique]

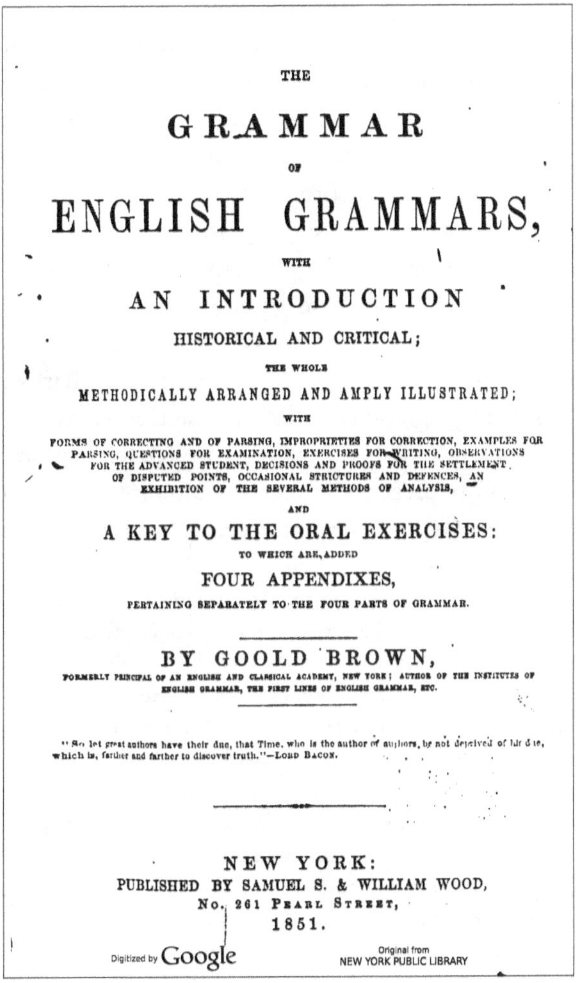

THE

GRAMMAR

OF

ENGLISH GRAMMARS,

WITH

AN INTRODUCTION

HISTORICAL AND CRITICAL;

THE WHOLE

METHODICALLY ARRANGED AND AMPLY ILLUSTRATED;

WITH

FORMS OF CORRECTING AND OF PARSING, IMPROPRIETIES FOR CORRECTION, EXAMPLES FOR PARSING, QUESTIONS FOR EXAMINATION, EXERCISES FOR WRITING, OBSERVATIONS FOR THE ADVANCED STUDENT, DECISIONS AND PROOFS FOR THE SETTLEMENT OF DISPUTED POINTS, OCCASIONAL STRICTURES AND DEFENCES, AN EXHIBITION OF THE SEVERAL METHODS OF ANALYSIS,

AND

A KEY TO THE ORAL EXERCISES:

TO WHICH ARE ADDED

FOUR APPENDIXES,

PERTAINING SEPARATELY TO THE FOUR PARTS OF GRAMMAR.

BY GOOLD BROWN,

FORMERLY PRINCIPAL OF AN ENGLISH AND CLASSICAL ACADEMY, NEW YORK; AUTHOR OF THE INSTITUTES OF ENGLISH GRAMMAR, THE FIRST LINES OF ENGLISH GRAMMAR, ETC.

"So let great authors have their due, that Time, who is the author of authors, be not deprived of his due, which is, farther and farther to discover truth."—LORD BACON.

NEW YORK:
PUBLISHED BY SAMUEL S. & WILLIAM WOOD,
No. 261 PEARL STREET,
1851.

FIGURE 1.

The Grammar of English Grammars tries to create order—invoking grammar as a structure—in the proliferation of published works in what had yet to become a formal field of study about the structure of language. Goold Brown's text is a monument to both the challenge and the long tradition of collecting information about the scholars who are, in turn, obsessed with presenting structured information about language. Brown's enormous editions of *The Grammar of English Grammars*, with more than one thousand pages of text, were accompanied by fifteen editions of a slimmer volume (only 325ish pages) titled *Institutes of English Grammar*, intended for use by schools, academies, and private learners, and an even more manageable *First Lines of English Grammar* (six editions between 1826 and 1880). Both *The Grammar of English Grammars* (around p. 820) and *Institutes of Grammar* (around p. 218) arrive at "Prosody" as the fourth and final section of the traditional divisions of the grammar book after "Orthography," "Etymology," and "Syntax." In each "prosody" section (after punctuation, utterance, and articulation) and therefore at the end of the book, we find versification. Brown's *Grammar of English Grammars* positions him as the ultimate counter of the counters, presenting a compendium of information not only about grammar but about that part of grammar—prosody—that contains versification, or how we measure language in "numbers" that might become poems. Brown's odd format allows him both to enumerate the various approaches to versification, and to chart a path through these approaches in typographically differentiated sections.

The Grammar of English Grammars went through ten editions between 1851 and 1884 and therefore presents an ongoing attempt to map discourse over time.[1] Or rather, Brown's reference book reveals the difficulty of mapping sev-

---

1. According to *The National Cyclopedia of American Biography* (8:265–66), Goold Brown "was born in Providence, R.I., March 7, 1791, a descendent of the earliest Quaker settlers in New England.... [He] was sent to the Friends' school.... At the age of nineteen he began teaching ... in the Friends' boarding-school in Duchess county, N.Y.... Two years later he opened an academy in New York City, which he conducted for twenty years, and which gained a large reputation for the thoroughness of its classical and literary training. His early studies made him alive to the imperfections in the then existing text-books in grammar, and his classwork developed new ideas and methods of teaching, which in 1823 he published under the title of 'Institutes of English Grammar.' The superiority of his method was at once recognized, and the book was widely adopted as a text-book in the schools. He also prepared an elementary grammar, called 'First Lines of English Grammar.' These two books have had an enormous circulation and are in very general use even to this day. In 1851 he finished his masterpiece, upon which his reputation in a large measure rests, 'Grammar of English Grammars.' It is the most exhaustive, most accurate, and most original treatise on the English language

eral discourses over time, but that difficulty is particularly pronounced in the section on versification. Despite robust approaches to discourse analysis in sociology, in literary studies we are often trained to think about cultural fields of production only as either literary or artistic—a paradigm that Brown's strange text resists.[2] The arrangement of accumulated materials in the fluctuating observations and notes sections of Brown's pages form an odd hierarchy; his larger font definitions appear at the top of the page ("definitions and principles") and derive from the authority he displays in the (often overwhelming) observations, which also serve as a kind of annotated bibliography. Even more personal annotations and pronouncements, exceptions, and qualifications,

---

ever written. The thoroughness with which he performed his task may be judged by the fact that his list of cited grammars and other works on the subject numbers 548, and its preparation occupied a period of twenty-three years. It is the court of last resort on matters grammatical, and will remain a lasting monument to the author's skill and labor.... He died in Lyon, March 31, 1857." Not all were as complimentary: a contributor to the *Saturday Review* wrote of *Grammar of English Grammars*, "A very ponderous work, with a title-page unusually elaborate in description, is the tenth edition of Mr. Goold Brown's *Grammar of English Grammar[s]* a treatise on the philosophy, principles, and practical use of grammar, occupying altogether 1,100 pages of large octavo size and rather small type, a sight from which all but the most omnivorous students must turn aghast, and which may well deter the most courageous critic from any attempt at a detailed analysis of its contents" ("Review of *The Grammar of English Grammars* by Goold Brown," 568); and another, in the *American*: "Goold Brown is to grammar what Worcester and Webster are to lexicography, and his 'Grammar of English Grammars' probably contains as much matter as either of the great unabridged dictionaries" ("Publications Received," 60).

2. Dotzler and Schmidgen, *Foucault, Digital*, solidifies the connection that many scholars of digital humanities have already noticed. Dotzler, Schmidgen, and Stein ("From the Archive to the Computer," 3) argue that "all practitioners in the digital humanities should read Foucault." Jussi Parikka has said, about the field of media archeology in relation to Foucault and Kittler in the 1990s, "Temporalities are conditioned by mediatic frameworks. This is where Ernst's particular take on media archeology stems from. The theoretical ideas from German and French theory were filtered into medium-specific ways to develop archaeologies of knowledge into archaeologies of knowledge as media—or media archeology.... This archeology starts to think through our mediatic world as the conditions for the way in which we know things and do them—knowledge and power." Parikka, "Introduction," in Ernst, *Digital Memory and the Archive*, 6. Though Brown's project might be read as a source text for a knowledge archeology of grammar within a media history of the reference book, we might just as easily see it as a snapshot of the midcentury linguistic power relations within which grammar itself is readable as a social field. The text signals a prehistory to the theories of discourse and communication for authors now squarely associated with literary sociology like Pierre Bourdieu, Max Weber, Jürgen Habermas, and Nicklas Luhman.

marked by asterisks or daggers, appear in minuscule font at the very bottom (figure 2 and figure 3).[3]

What kind of reference book is this? The observations and annotations, which are at times footnotes to footnotes, seem to prop up the authority Brown displays in the larger font "definitions and principles" section, but the more closely we read them the more his authority derives not from a masterful ability to present a consensus view, but from his understanding that prosodic discourse has no consensus view. What we learn from Brown, then, is that versification doesn't align with the prescriptive frameworks that he and others wanted to develop for grammar. Perhaps this is a reason why we haven't taken historical grammar books seriously as locations of cultural information: we might not expect a definition of poetry to appear in a book about the structure of language. And yet another reason is that the data we find about poetry is literally hard to see—it's printed in a teeny-tiny font that gets even tinier the further down the page we look. His observations, which proliferate quoted material about versification to the point that it is hard to keep track of which voice is his and which are his interlocutors, are often nearly impossible to read since they are so full of confusing constructions and lists of definitions from a variety of sources, some that we might consider literary (Edgar Allan Poe) and some we might not consider literary at all (*Comstock's Elocution* or *Webster's Dictionary*). But these appear together, in parallel, as Brown works through what versification is and how it works.

Brown's definition of "verses" and his concept of when verses might become "poetry" rely on the modulation of what he will call "*its least parts*," which are often syllables. Brown's prescription for poetry differentiates it from the rest of language; it is a special kind of "literary" composition that allows us to see the difference between the mere combination of words according to a rule and what will count as a poem. He wrote, "Versification is the forming of that species of literary composition which is called *verse*; that is, *poetry*, or *poetic numbers*." Verse, he continues, "is language arranged into metrical lines of some determinate length and rhythm—language so ordered as to produce harmony, by a due succession of poetic feet, or of syllables differing in quantity or stress." His first step is to define "rhythm," so that we can understand harmony: "The *rhythm* of verse is its relation to quantities; the modulation of its numbers; or, the kind of metre, measure, or movement, of

3. These three sections signal several intended audiences: those who would recognize his hard-earned authority as someone to be trusted in the newly crowded market for grammar books is its likely primary audience, since this massive tome supports his more popular (and shorter) *Institutes* and *First Lines*.

which it consists, or by which it is particularly distinguished." After Brown spends one short paragraph defining rhythm, he goes on to spend five trying to define quantity and comes around to defining it as the time it takes to pronounce syllables that have, or do not have, accent, emphasis, stress, energy, or loudness.

"In verse, the proportion which forms rhythm—that is, the chime of quantities—is applied to the *sounds* of syllables," but if we break rhythm down to "the reduction of its *least parts*," we "destroy the relation in which the thing consists." Rather than taking a rigid approach to poetry as a number by which we measure the propriety of a verse, he urges prosodists to think about rhythm as the proportion by which we might apprehend the modulation of sound.

He quotes Poe's "Notes upon English Verse" extensively in his third and fourth observation: "Versification is *not* the *art*, but the *act* of making verses." Brown corrects Poe's parallel of rhythm with meter to mean "the arrangement of words into two or more consecutive, equal, pulsations of time. These pulsations are *feet*. Two feet, at least, are requisite to constitute a *rhythm*; just as in mathematics, two units are necessary to form [a] number." Poe's math does not add up. Brown knows that a unit is a number, and that Poe's translation of the Greek "number" to "rhythm" is a mistranslation: number would be "arithm, as in *arithmetic*." Rhythm is *not* number, but "modulation, measured tune, or regular flow." So, what are poetic numbers, to Brown? They are the way we apprehend, via rhythm, the variety in the movement or proportion in the movements of the various parts of the line—neither time nor quantity, but the relation of the parts. This apprehension is both an act and an art. To measure only one part of poetry's data and not the other is to miss the relation that might make a line into poetry. It is the reader's apprehension of all the data in relation that makes a poem.

Of course, none of this solves the problem of how to talk about what the reader might be apprehending. Both poets and readers, Brown insists, need to know both how to count and what to count, but that is not all that they can or should know. They also need to see the conversations and debates, places where there has been concurrence and habits formed—likelihood that a definition will be familiar because it has been most taught in schools. Brown's *Grammar of English Grammars*, and commentaries like his, are shaping a concept of literary authority within prosodic discourse. It is both "literary" and "linguistic" (and we also include it in "Typographically Unique" since its many fonts present challenges to machine reading). But it also helps us to rethink the category of the literary as one that might depend entirely on how you have been trained to measure, or count, what that means.

FIGURE XVI.—ONOMATOPŒIA.

☞ [The following lines, from Swift's Poems, satirically mimick the imitative music of a violin.]

"Now slowly move your fiddle-stick;
Now, tantan, tantantivi, quick;
Now trembling, shivering, quivering, quaking,
Set hoping hearts of Lovers aching."

"Now sweep, sweep the deep.
See Celia, Celia dies,
While true Lovers' eyes
Weeping sleep, Sleeping weep,
Weeping sleep, Bo-peep, bo-peep."

CHAPTER IV.—VERSIFICATION.

Versification is the forming of that species of literary composition which is called *verse;* that is, *poetry,* or *poetic numbers.*

SECTION I.—OF VERSE.

Verse, in opposition to prose, is language arranged into metrical lines of some determinate length and rhythm—language so ordered as to produce harmony, by a due succession of poetic feet, or of syllables differing in quantity or stress.

DEFINITIONS AND PRINCIPLES.

The *rhythm* of verse is its relation of quantities; the modulation of its numbers; or, the kind of metre, measure, or movement, of which it consists, or by which it is particularly distinguished.

The *quantity* of a syllable, as commonly explained, is the relative portion of time occupied in uttering it. In poetry, every syllable is considered to be either long or short. A long syllable is usually reckoned to be equal to two short ones.

In the construction of English verse, long quantity coincides always with the primary accent, generally also with the secondary, as well as with emphasis; and short quantity, as reckoned by the poets, is found only in unaccented syllables, and unemphatical monosyllabic words.*

The quantity of a syllable, whether long or short, does not depend on what is called the long or the short sound of a vowel or diphthong, or on a supposed distinction of accent as affecting vowels in some cases and consonants in others, but principally on the degree of energy or loudness with which the syllable is uttered, whereby a greater or less portion of time is employed.

The open vowel sounds, which are commonly but not very accurately termed *long,* are those which are the most easily protracted, yet they often occur in the shortest and feeblest syllables; while, on the other hand, no vowel sound, that occurs under the usual stress of accent or of emphasis, is either so short in its own nature, or is so "quickly joined to the succeeding letter," that the syllable is not one of long quantity.

Most monosyllables, in English, are variable in quantity, and may be made either long or short, as strong or weak sounds suit the sense and rhythm; but words of greater length are, for the most part, fixed, their accented syllables being always long, and a syllable immediately before or after the accent almost always short.

One of the most obvious distinctions in poetry, is that of rhyme and blank verse. *Rhyme* is a similarity of sound, combined with a difference: occurring usually between the last syllables of different lines, but sometimes at other intervals; and so

---

* To this principle there seems to be now and then an exception, as when a weak disyllable begins a foot in an anapestic line, as in the following examples:—

"I think—let me see—yes, it is, I declare,
As long *ago now* as that Buckingham there."—*Leigh Hunt.*
"And Thomson, though best in his indolent fits,
Either slept himself weary, or blasted his wits."—*Id.*

Here, if we reckon the feet in question to be anapests, we have disyllables with both parts short. But some, accenting "*ago*" on the latter syllable, and "*Either*" on the former, will call "*ago now*" a bacchy, and "*Either slept*" an amphimac: because *they make them such* by their manner of reading.—G. B.

ordered that the rhyming syllables begin differently and end alike. *Blank verse* is verse without rhyme.

The principal rhyming syllables are almost always long. Double rhyme adds one short syllable; triple rhyme, two. Such syllables are redundant in iambic and anapestic verses; in lines of any other sort, they are generally, if not always, included in the measure.

A *Stanza* is a combination of several verses, or lines, which, taken together, make a regular division of a poem. It is the common practice of good versifiers, to form all stanzas of the same poem after one model. The possible variety of stanzas is infinite; and the actual variety met with in print is far too great for detail.

OBSERVATIONS.

OBS. 1.—*Verse*, in the broadest acceptation of the term, is poetry, or metrical language, in general. This, to the eye, is usually distinguished from prose by the manner in which it is written and printed. For, in very many instances, if this were not the case, the reader would be puzzled to discern the difference. The division of poetry into its peculiar lines, is therefore not a mere accident. The word *verse*, from the Latin *versus*, literally signifies a *turning*. Each full line of metre is accordingly called *a verse*; because, when its measure is complete, the writer *turns* to place an other under it. A *verse*, then, in the primary sense of the word with us, is, "A *line* consisting of a certain succession of sounds, and number of syllables."—*Johnson, Walker, Todd, Bolles*, and others. Or, according to *Webster*, it is, "A poetic *line*, consisting of a certain number of long and short syllables, disposed according to the rules of the species of poetry which the author intends to compose."—See *American Dict.*, 8vo.

OBS. 2.—If to settle the theory of English verse on true and consistent principles, is as difficult a matter, as the manifold contrarieties of doctrine among our prosodists would indicate, there can be no great hope of any scheme entirely satisfactory to the intelligent examiner. The very elements of the subject are much perplexed by the incompatible dogmas of authors deemed skilful to elucidate it. It will scarcely be thought a hard matter to distinguish true verse from prose, yet is it not well agreed, wherein the difference consists: what the generality regard as the most essential elements or characteristics of the former, some respectable authors dismiss entirely from their definitions of both verse and versification. The existence of quantity in our language; the dependence of our rhythms on the division of syllables into long and short; the concurrence of our accent, (except in some rare and questionable instances,) with long quantity only; the constant effect of emphasis to lengthen quantity; the limitation of quantity to mere duration of sound; the doctrine that quantity pertains to all *syllables* as such, and not merely to vowel sounds; the recognition of the same general principles of syllabication in poetry as in prose; the supposition that accent pertains not to certain *letters* in particular, but to certain *syllables* as such; the limitation of accent to stress, or percussion, only; the conversion of short syllables into long, and long into short, by a change of accent; our frequent formation of long syllables with what are called short vowels; our more frequent formation of short syllables with what are called long or open vowels; the necessity of some order in the succession of feet or syllables to form a rhythm; the need of framing each line to correspond with some other line or lines in length; the propriety of always making each line susceptible of scansion by itself: all these points, so essential to a true explanation of the nature of English verse, though, for the most part, well maintained by some prosodists, are nevertheless denied by some, so that opposite opinions may be cited concerning them all. I would not suggest that all or any of these points are thereby made *doubtful*; for there may be opposite judgements in a dozen cases, and yet concurrence enough (if concurrence can do it) to establish them every one.

OBS. 3.—An ingenious poet and prosodist now living,* Edgar Allan Poe, (to whom I owe a word or two of reply,) in his "Notes upon English Verse," with great self-complacency, represents, that, "While much has been written upon the structure of the Greek and Latin rhythms, comparatively *nothing* has been done as regards the English;" that, "It may be said, indeed, we are *without a treatise* upon our own versification;" that, "The very best" *definition* of versification† to be found in any of "*our ordinary treatises* on the topic," has "*not a single point* which does not involve an error;" that, "A *leading defect* in *each of these treatises* is the confining of the subject to mere *versification*, while metre, or rhythm, in general, is the real question at issue;" that, "Versification is *not* the *art*, but the *act*," of making verses; that, "A correspondence in the *length* of lines is by no means essential;" that, "*Harmony*," produced "by the regular alternation of syllables differing in quantity," does not include "*melody*;" that, "A *regular alternation*, as described, forms *no part* of the principle of metre;" that, "There is no necessity of *any regularity* in the succession of *feet*;" that, "By consequence," he ventures to "dispute the *essentiality* of any alternation, regular or irregular, of *syllables*-long and short;" that, "For *anything more intelligible* or *more satisfactory* than this definition [i. e., G. Brown's former definition of versification,] we shall look in vain in *any published treatise* upon the subject;" that, "So general and *so total a failure* can be

---

* "Edgar A. Poe, the author, died at Baltimore on Sunday" [the 7th].—*Daily Evening Traveller*, Boston Oct. 9, 1849. This was eight or ten months after the writing of these observations.—G. B.

† "Versification is the art of arranging words into lines of correspondent length, so as to produce harmony by the regular alternation of syllables differing in quantity."—*Brown's Institutes of E. Gram.*, p. 235.

FIGURE 3. Goold Brown, *The Grammar of English Grammars* (New York: Samuel S. and William Wood, 1884), 828.

1

How We Count [Literary]

> We need to better understand the interactions between methods and archives.
>
> ANDREW PIPER, *ENUMERATIONS:*
> *DATA AND LITERARY STUDY*, 2018, 10

THIS CHAPTER takes the largest curated collection in the Princeton Prosody Archive, "Literary," as a departure point for broader questions about how we might build a more inclusive and capacious profession. We purposefully reframed the collection "Literary" to signal how our concept of "the literary" relied, and still relies, on what we define it against. The kinds of material in the PPA are seldom considered part of literary history and, in fact, have been used to differentiate the development of twentieth-century "literary studies" in opposition to philology, rhetoric, linguistics, and elocution, to name a few. Shadows of all these prior and concurrent approaches to reading poetry haunt contemporary attempts to define what is distinct about a particularly "literary" approach to poems.[1] How can we rethink the evolution of our contemporary concepts of "literary criticism" and "literary scholarship" in the twenty-first century by looking at the historical texts that have been seen as marginal to those concepts? Not only does the collection bring these materials together, but it also compels scholars to consider why we have left these kinds of texts out of our disciplinary histories to begin with.

---

1. Momma, *From Philology to English Studies*, gives my favorite account of the prehistory of English studies and the lack of a clear account of a "history of linguistics and literature . . . as a kind of supra-disciplinary subject that operated on principles of 'grammar.'" Cf. Turner, *Philology*; Graff and Warner, *Origins of Literary Studies in America*; Graff, *Professing Literature*; Eagleton, *Function of Criticism*; Guillory, *Cultural Capital*.

As with marginal materials, contemporary disciplines that are seen adjacent to the literary, like critical archival studies, information science, critical data studies, bibliography, book history, media studies, and digital humanities, provide better frameworks for this reconsideration of "literary studies." My "literary" education took place during a time of mass digitization and the reorientation of archival science, but these shifts did not expand, question, or provide a cultural studies lens through which to rethink the discipline's research practices. I found then, as I do now, that the assumed procedures and methodologies of literary research were inadequate for understanding and tracing the stories of poetic forms.

What role does "poetry" play in the question of what does or does not count as literary? And how can the evolving methods of literary research that *have not* counted (as in, have not been valued) as literary help us recover and begin to answer this question? When I first began to collect and differentiate the textual materials that make up the prosody archive, I titled this collection "poetry" to distinguish it from the more grammatical, oratorical, and elocutionary material that I called "grammar" and then "speech" (and now "linguistics"). I was not trying to define "poetry," nor was I collecting poems, and I assumed (wrongly) that all poetry was literary. As I read through this material that had not been considered part of traditional literary history, I learned that these texts presented interesting and crucial challenges to the assumptions we make about poetic history. Is versification in poetry an exercise, an art, an action, a performance, a grammar? Is it poetic? Is it literary? Why or why not? The conservative and romanticized notion of a universalizing concept of "poetry" did not account for the history of versification, nor did it seem to acknowledge the historical conditions of poetry's materiality—its formats, its circulation, its sounds—either written or spoken. In fact, the more I looked at the history of poetry's data, the more outlandish one stable cultural concept of "poetry" became, to the point where I began to think that our discipline's desire for poetry's immediacy and intimacy *relied on* suppressing the history of poetry's highly mediated, structured, confusing, and conflicting data.

We might ask, for example, when, along the sliding scale of reading practices, does a song become known as, or begin to circulate as, a ballad, and when does it drift back into song? When is a Greek inscriptional verse considered a literary composition? How does mere versification overcome its perceived simplicity and become poetry, and who (take a wild guess) is more likely to produce poetry rather than mere versification?[2] All these questions emerge in the kinds of material that has not counted as "literary": texts about philology, treatises on the harmony of language, reviews of women's poetry in the public press. I am not concerned with one definition of poetry *as* literary language, but how considering approaches to poetry across texts that have seldom been considered part of the literary critical canon might teach us something new about what we still often hold out as a distinction between so-called literary and so-called linguistic approaches to reading poems.[3] Acknowledging our desire for, and our training in preparation for, creating cohesive narrative arguments about literary history and presenting evaluative close readings of poems, this chapter and this book seek to approach the formation of these methodologies with skepticism not only by presenting new evidence, but by asserting that our methods for assembling and viewing evidence about the literary past are inadequate. Locating the materials that provide a more nuanced understanding of the nonteleological history of English poetry requires new ways of reading and understanding the multiple mediations of the literary past. If we want to arrive at a truly capacious understanding of the conflicted and overlapping histories of literary language, we must acknowledge the exclusions at play when we read historical poems (historical sound; histories of format, circulation, and value; different reading practices in different communities) and the exclusions at play when we perform research about the history of poetry (what materials are digitized and why, archival silences, technologies that render language machine readable).[4]

And how we value and name this work is important. When we read the grammar book, the poetry handbook, and the elocution guide, for instance,

---

2. A random sample of these kind of questions can be found in Forsythe, "Modern Imitations of the Popular Ballad"; and Mitford, *Inquiry into the Principles of Harmony*; for poetry vs. versification and women's poetry in particular, see Martin, "Prosody."

3. Momma contextualizes this within the dissolution of philology, already diagnosed by Foucault in 1970. And yet Foucault did not have access to the same materials—the richer, more complicated history of texts pertaining to grammar, speech, elocution, and poetry that the PPA shows are fundamental to disciplinary development: "The New Criticism ... in particular is quintessentially a product of literary studies in a phase of grammar." Momma, *From Philology to English Studies*, 191.

4. Guillory, in *Cultural Capital*, wrote that "literary language ... cannot be characterized monolithically as the recurrent foregrounding of a particular linguistic feature (not even rhetoricity)" (68). I am not concerned with a definition of poetry *as* literary language, but how approaches to poetry across a variety of often disregarded texts might come to be judged as literary approaches.

as historical locations of the distinctions that created the conceptual categories "literary" and "poetry," we are not considered to be conducting traditional literary research. This book, and specifically this chapter, does not set out to perform a theoretical intervention that undermines the long-held assumptions of the distinctions between literary and linguistic approaches to poems; rather, it describes the material conditions that were necessary for me to gather the material allowing for such a critique, so as to demand that the material conditions of our scholarship in the digital age are brought to bear on the ways that we assert poetry's historical and present meaning-making capacities.

At the most basic level, gathering and reading textual materials about how poems are counted allows us to map the edges of a discourse about what counted as literary. The questions "when is a poem literary?" and "when is it not?" lurk beneath the value judgments of the materials in the history of versification just as they have reemerged, now, in discussions about whether the poetic output of large language models relying on versification "count" as poetry. The models get one thing right: there is no quantitative answer to the question of "what makes a poem" even though the history of poetic reading is full of attempts to enumerate, to provide a mathematical or scientific answer.[5] We don't—and can't—know what makes up the components and whole of poetry, and yet the history of prosody and its relationship to literary value and cultural studies have been left out of literary theory. We would be better readers of our mediated present if we could think with these histories rather than assume a stable, universal concept of "a poem." And beyond versification, prosody—as pronunciation, scansion systems and diacritical marks, national culture and class norms—revealed the layers of mediation through which I was already reading poetry (or what I understood as "poetry"). Prosodic discourse, across disciplines, hovered between the wavering commitments of subjective and objective approaches to patterned language itself, and assembling it as evidence—as data—meant coming to terms with the limitations of research and reading now.

To mark a historical moment: I began to research the history of prosody in graduate school. Where I could find, and how I could track, information about

---

5. Cf. Piper, *Enumerations*: "Humanism was in many ways founded upon the notion of studying linguistic and material differences, a practice of fostering the ability to understand the ways in which texts differ between times and places," and "quantity has been an essential component of literary meaning since its inception" and lists "a genre of poetry with exactly 14 lines that has lasted for over half a millennium (not to mention the entire field of prosody)" (4).

prosody was limited by the model of value that had emerged in the mid-twentieth century—the literary canon, literary histories, the anthology, the reference book, the reference librarian, work in a physical archive. None of these models accounted for or even seemed to reckon with the immensity of the media shift that was taking place during the time of my formation and training as a scholar. This media shift undermined the authority of those prior research methods by expanding the available resources (which allowed new questions about archival authority to emerge), but it also triggered a refusal, an almost performative helplessness, about the technologies that provided the mechanisms through which we accessed and compiled our research. I saw my task, as both a critic and a scholar, to "seek to illuminate" the literary work "from every conceivable angle, to make it as intelligible as possible by the uncovering and application of data residing outside itself."[6] And yet methodological approaches in literary criticism and scholarship did not keep pace with the media shift. When there is a seemingly limitless amount of information, how can older models of research remain valid or valuable? And what should our new models be?

Reading and understanding historical poetry required reading and understanding historical prosody, which, itself, was all about the challenges of representing nonprint formats (sound) on a printed page. The history of prosody,

---

6. Altick and Fenstermaker, *Art of Literary Research*, 1. For example, I wanted scholars to quickly see how Wordsworth's poem "A Slumber Did My Spirit Seal," which appeared in Thomas Ward's 1880 *The English Poets* (vol. 4), was then picked up for critical exegesis by Roden Noel (in 1886), whose *Essays on Poetry and Poets* describes them as "most sad, but wonderful verses" (6); by Frances Barton Gummere's widely adopted *Handbook of Poetics for Students of English Verse* (1886); and, as an example of "precision," by teacher Sarah Warner Brooks's 1890 *English Poetry and Poets* (305). It is included in several editions of *The Oxford Book of English Verse* (Couch) as well as *The Home Book of Verse: American and English* (Burton Egbert Stevenson). Rather than merely give my own account of Wordsworth's "A Slumber Did My Spirit Seal," I was interested thinking about *how* particular poems gained both cultural and linguistic capital and *why* that was the case. Otherwise, wasn't I providing a mere value judgment based on incomplete data? In the case of "A Slumber Did My Spirit Seal," we can ask how that now infamous poem (or is it a poem?) accrued this capital, and how we might think through those circuits and formats as carefully as we consider its authorial intention (or lack thereof), partially because of its treatment in Knapp and Michaels, "Against Theory," and its reconsideration in Kirschenbaum, "Again Theory." Though I am not suggesting supplanting the existing narratives of romanticism's relationship to modernism that this would entail, I am suggesting that how we accessed information about poetry in the past, as well as how we access information about poetry from the past, are questions we need to keep asking.

versification, and poetic forms was, and is, already mediated by rapidly shifting concepts of genre and print and media formats. And in this new digital research environment that I encountered as an early-career literary scholar, these materials took on additional layers of mediation, situated as they were within archives (both physical and digital) or within databases owned by corporations and sold back to the library. There was no ready or widely accepted model for the interpretive task of finding, collecting, organizing, and categorizing these newly available historical materials as a researcher, only an ambient anxiety that the digital posed a threat to literary scholarship or criticism.[7] Even talking about the mediation and remediation of historical materials felt as if I were admitting to some kind of disciplinary shortcut—the digital *as opposed to* the literary humanities, or the digital as a purely instrumental, noninterpretive method of accessing "the text." It was not that scholars hadn't been theorizing, thinking through, or demonstrating new digital research methods; it's that this work (along with critical bibliography, book history, and textual scholarship) was often characterized as adjacent to or not relevant enough to count as literary criticism.

Before Google Books (1999–2006)

I am part of the last generation of literary scholars to have witnessed the transition between analog and digital research practices, yet we are still living in an institutional landscape and a disciplinary structure that value most the expertise of humanities scholars deriving from physical books in physical archives. When I was in graduate school, the vast reckoning in archival studies, what came to be known as critical archival studies, was not yet a coherent field; the decade of debates about digital reading had not yet happened.[8] I was taught to think of physical books as superior to digital surrogates, of physical archives

---

7. McGann's *Radiant Textuality* argued against what he called "the revulsion many humanists express for the emergence of digital technology" (139); and it attempted to more critically examine and theorize the terms of debate that had become a simplified narrative analogous to *books equals good vs. undifferentiated digital media equals bad* following Sven Birkerts's 1994 *The Gutenberg Elegies*. Cf. the special issue of *Early Modern Literary Studies* 14, no. 2 (2008), on EEBO, especially Crowther et al., "New Scholarship, New Pedagogies."

8. See Schwartz and Cook, "Archives, Records and Power," an early moment. See also Caswell, Punzalan, and Sangwand's special issue of the *Journal of Library and Information Studies* in 2017, naming the field: Caswell, Punzalan, and Sangwand, "Critical Archival Studies: An Introduction"; and see Caswell, "'Archive' Is Not Archives."

as privileged spaces of discovery, of text as more important than context. If I couldn't define my "archive" I would not be able to produce "original" work in the humanities. But who could define "archive"? To the extent that I had one, my "archive" was already transgressive—nonliterary—because, instead of focusing on what T. S. Eliot or Ezra Pound had to say about meter, I was interested in the poetic production of thousands of anonymous World War I soldiers producing thousands of metrical verses.⁹ It was doubly transgressive because I was reading this poetry online. As the digital surrogates of the pages of *The Hydra: The Magazine of Craiglockhart War Hospital* loaded slowly in fits and jumps on my blue iMac G3, I felt guilty viewing these images on a screen instead of in a physical archive. I was also not equipped to theorize my own digital reading: for instance, I didn't associate the online copy of *The Hydra* with the people who put it there. Even if I had been trained in media studies instead of comparative literature, the history of media didn't yet seem to apply to old media that had been newly digitized. Searching among the many scholars of textual studies at the University of Michigan, the history of reading I needed had not yet arrived in the digital present that I found myself navigating at the turn of the twenty-first century.¹⁰

9. I only later made the connection between the glut of soldiers' mechanical verses and the popularization of the machine gun.

10. Even if I had bothered to read about the Joint Information Systems Committee's Technology Applications Program, or JTAP, which was the group I later learned was responsible for Oxford's digitization of much of the material about the First World War, I would not have mentioned it. I knew enough to know that, in that era, I could thank a library or an archive, and even a librarian or archivist by name, but I could not yet cite a digital archive in a literary dissertation. The address http://ww1lit.nsms.ox.ac.uk/ww1lit/collections/owen now leads directly to the Owen collection, which contains everything in the former First World War Poetry Digital Archive collection, but does not yet include the complete run of *The Hydra*; issues were missing until 2014, when they were discovered in an attic by a Tolkien scholar named John Garth, who wrote about it on his blog (Garth, *Secrets of "The Hydra"*). The digitized versions of the newly discovered issues are not available in the First World War Poetry collection at Oxford, but they are viewable via Napier University, at https://www.napier.ac.uk/about-us/our-location/our-campuses/special-collections/war-poets-collection/the-hydra. In general, the history of digitization projects, sustainability, and the labor of creating and maintaining access to digital materials has not been a central concern in media studies, whereas the concept of "the archive" or "languages of code," considered metaphorically, is central. Cf. Chun and Keenen, *New Media, Old Media*. Sayers, *Routledge Companion to Media Studies and Digital Humanities*, is an exception, with chapters "Searching, Mining, and Interpreting Media Histories Big Data," by Eric Hoyt, Tony Tran, Derek Long, Kit Hughes, and Kevin Ponto (413–21), on the digitization side; and "Relationships, Not Records: Digital Heritage and the Ethics of Sharing Indig-

And yet, in 1998, J. Hillis Miller could praise digitization and note how important it was to be able to see illustrations in Victorian novels. He could laud Jerome McGann's ambitions to curate an online resource called *British Poetry 1780–1910: A Hypertext Archive of Scholarly Editions* at the University of Virginia, ambitions that resulted in the now canonical Rossetti Archive online.[11] Scholar-created "archives" existed, and continue to exist, in a liminal authoritative space; as far as we count value by tenure and promotion standards, the impact of collaborative humanities research is, at the time of this writing and at most institutions, something most scholars and administrators have not bothered to learn how to value. The productions of highly specialized textual scholars often focused on one figure or one digital textual edition and relied on their own authority as scholars in the field but did not necessarily involve the expertise of scholars in archival science, information management, or information retrieval. If they had been more embedded in library science, it's possible that these digital publication projects might have tipped too squarely into the realm of "service" and not scholarship, a "resource" and not research. What we seem to have valued, in the early aughts of digital textual editions and DH projects, was the interpretive enterprise of these bespoke and ephemeral locations of knowledge; when these became long-term projects, they ceased to exist as interpretable sources of knowledge and transformed into seemingly neutral sources of information.[12]

But what if, at that moment, we had not abdicated our responsibility and had shouldered some of the labor for cocreating sustainable, long-term digital infrastructures in the research library? We now know, and many knew then, that there is no such thing as a neutral source of information. At the turn of the twenty-first century, University of Michigan's early policy documents aimed to "fit digitization into the context of traditional collection development." What if we had turned, as a discipline, toward collaborating with libraries to cocreate the collections that would impact new knowledge? I had no sense of what Abby Smith, director of programs at the Council on Library and Information Resources (CLIR), had presciently called in 2001 "the magic of critical mass." I would learn only later about what she called

---

enous Knowledge Online," by Kimberly Chastain (403–12) on the archives side. Miriam Posner, Lauren Tilton, and Lauren Klein are the three scholars who live most comfortably in the intersection of media studies and digital humanities.

11. Miller, "Graphic or Verbal."
12. Compare, for instance, *Walt Whitman Archive*, and S. Brown et al., *Orlando Project*.

"the transformative power" of technology to "not only re-create a collection online but also give it new functionality, allow for new purposes, and ultimately create new audiences that make it available for novel queries."[13] Imagine if we had focused less on the threat of digitization to reading in the abstract and more on the material challenges our research libraries were (and are) facing?[14] Or what if we had more urgently partnered with information scientists to think about how our access to scholarly information in the wake of the World Wide Web would be forever altered? As a young scholar, I accessed online archives mainly to find out whether it would be worth my time to travel to a physical location. Instead of working with my library to understand the labor involved in building and maintaining scholarly resources, I naively desired period-specific replicas of corporate-controlled resources like EEBO and ECCO. I was thrilled to find and use resources like George Landow's *Victorian Web*, which seemed to anticipate the dream of the 1990s. And it was clear that increased access to nonliterary sources recontextualized, reframed, and expanded the notion of the literary field.[15] What periodical scholars had long realized about the fortuitous connections available in nontraditional textual sources was about to reshape several fields at once. What if more scholars had been able to imagine themselves as cocreators of these field-changing databases and therefore were encouraged to adequately theorize their use? What if their creation had been integrated into the academy rather than sold back to us as products?

It is now, as it was then, undertheorized as a pivotal moment in our access to, and therefore relationship to, the literary past. Technology, in the pre–Google Books era, promised access, completeness, and new forms of knowledge, but it was both expensive and difficult to scale at the level of the individual library. It is no wonder that libraries, whose partnerships and relationships with faculty varied from institution to institution, felt pressure to partner with corporate-owned database vendors and could only do their

13. All quotations in this paragraph are from A. Smith, *Strategies for Building Digitized Collections*, 5, 7, 17. See also Guthrie, "JSTOR and the University of Michigan."

14. Between the publication of Moretti's *Graphs, Maps, Trees* in 2005 and his *Distant Reading* in 2013, there was, I think, an apex of anxiety. Whatever digital humanities meant before 2010, when there were a series of articles about it in the *New York Times* (I'll discuss these in chapter 4), thereafter digital humanities was more closely associated with what we now call text and data mining than to digital textual scholarship. While McGann's *Radiant Textuality* posited a new approach to textual criticism, I needed a new guide to literary research.

15. Stauffer, *Book Traces*; Fyfe, "Access, Computational Analysis, and Fair Use"; Noviskie, "Speculative Collections and the Emancipatory Library"; Noble, "Future for Intersectional Black Feminist Technology Studies"; Ernst, "Radically De-historicising the Archive," 10.

best to support scholar-built digital archives. It was by sheer luck that I found a digital edition of what would become my main bibliographic resource for the Princeton Prosody Archive—a (then) hypertext version of T. V. F. Brogan's *English Versification, 1570–1980: A Reference Guide with a Global Appendix* (*EVRG*), published in an online scholarly journal called *Versification: An Electronic Journal of Literary Prosody*.[16] Neither is now available, by which I mean maintained, in the online formats through which I accessed them in 2003. These scholar-built digital projects, both very much of their digital moment, but neither valued as literary scholarship, were foundational in my formation as a literary scholar and to my creation of the Princeton Prosody Archive.

Counting the Counters

A large black book printed in what looked like a dot matrix printer typeface, *English Versification, 1570–1980: A Reference Guide with a Global Appendix*, had been published by Johns Hopkins University Press in 1981; its computerized font initially made me doubt whether it was a legitimate source.[17] And yet T. V. F. Brogan's reference guide, which I used to map the late nineteenth-century and early twentieth-century discourse about versification for my first book, showed me that there was no one literary history that could account for the breadth of discourse about English prosody. I didn't know how to read this book; it didn't function like Saintsbury's three-volume *History of English Prosody from the Twelfth Century to the Present Day*, with English meter emerging as a triumphant national ideology. Brogan's guide was not teleological, like so many of the other stories of English meter I had encountered in English literary histories. In fact, there were more ways to measure English verse and more stories about English versification and how to measure it than I could count. I didn't realize at the time that my tabulations, made by hand in a notebook, put me in a long line of historians of prosody who wanted to understand what it was about this subject that attracted such obsessive collecting, counting, disagreement, and one-upmanship. Prosodists had listed their predecessors in introductions only to build on or negate their theories. Bibliographers, like Brogan, tried to quantify the field so that others could chart the right path through the history of reading poetry. Brogan was the ultimate bibliographer,

16. *Versification: An Electronic Journal of Literary Prosody*, https://arsversificandi.info/, accessed September 26, 2024.

17. A developer has re-created this IBM3270 font, which looks closer to me than IBM Plex Mono. Figure 29 displays the font.

charting approaches and metanarratives, and annotating all of these in his cantankerous tone. I couldn't possibly fit this history (the evidence of the disagreement about English meter that proved my argument in *The Rise and Fall of Meter*) into an annotated bibliography, but I wanted to know whether he had left anything out, and what. I wanted to count the counters—to keep track of who was also obsessively counting the errors of the past, but not so that I could correct the errors, rather so that I could study how versification and prosody, more broadly, helped poetry "count" or "not count" as literary.

Brogan built his bibliography in the late 1970s by relying on interlibrary services at the University of Texas and consulting with experts across the country as well as with librarians at the British Museum and the Library of Congress. He says nothing more about his research in the acknowledgments in his guide other than that his methods were "unusual." Brogan himself did not intend for his bibliography to serve as a "keen new blade to cut our thickened thinking into ever-finer distinctions."[18] And yet his hope was to provide what he called "conspectus and contour."[19] If a table of contents for any historical periodical was available to him and he felt it was relevant, he surveyed its entire print run for any evidence of any article pertaining to English versification (and not just those written in English for English speakers). To give only a small sense of the scope of the project, he provides abbreviations for and highlights seven periodicals in German and also includes abbreviations for an additional fourteen more catalogs and periodicals: *British Museum General Catalogue of Printed Books, Comprehensive Dissertation Index, International Dissertation Abstracts, Essays and Studies by Members of the English Association, Journal of Aesthetics and Art Criticism, Journal of English and Germanic Philology, Modern Language Notes, Modern Language Quarterly, Modern Language Review, Modern Philology, The National Union Catalogue, Philological Quarterly, Studies in Philology,* and *Times Literary Supplement*. Because those that study prosody and versification tend to write a great deal about their predecessors, Brogan had several remarkable historical bibliographies at his disposal.

Despite his extensive work, even in 2006 I thought I had access to more resources than he did—I could expand and build on his work because of digitally mediated research. I wanted to supplement his bibliography, but I also wanted to search across all the materials he had found by collecting full-text

18. T. V. F. Brogan, *EVRG*, xi.
19. Brogan, xii.

version of the books named in his bibliography. Though it is difficult to reconstruct what the research landscape looked like at that time, Google Books began in 2004 as "Project Ocean" and was not yet in widespread use; the HathiTrust Digital Library did not exist until 2008. If I had the full texts of the works he listed in his bibliography, I could see who quoted whom at length, who stole without attribution from whom, and about which topics and why. Prosodists famously borrowed from and built on one another's theories, and being able to search inside these texts in one place would add to my ability to see, at a middle distance, how the stories of poetic forms took shape and cohered over time. For instance, why were there so many contradictory definitions of a ballad, and at what point did the ballad stanza (as a metrical form) start to replace the earlier, more culturally specific definition of the genre apart from its meter? The collection of materials, once assembled, might help other researchers who were asking similar questions of poetry in English. I was also interested in how the role of reprinting and circulation influenced how we now define those terms. Brogan had noted some reprints in his guide, but I thought that I could ascertain exactly how often these works were reprinted using OCLC (then the Ohio College Library Center, now the Online Computer Library Center), which I mistakenly thought was comprehensive. Could I track a concept's popularity as it stayed in, or was dropped from, multiple editions?[20] Rather than stating that one theory was correct or not correct as a literary critic might conclude after surveying failed attempts at a particular model of scansion, my questions were about how particular models of scansion as interpretation gained or lost popularity, and why. These were literary historical questions and also distant reading questions, though I did not know enough to know that term in 2006.[21] I had no concept of how to begin to think of my materials as data, or the difference between a database and a data set, even though I understood how seriously the prosodists Brogan collected took poetry's data.

Between the years 2007 and 2011, I worked steadily through various approaches to gathering all the material that I knew pertained to the study of versification in English from Brogan's research guide. I had been lucky enough to track Brogan down (no small task) and conducted two interviews with him in 2010. In the first, he narrated to me the story of how he began working on the project as a graduate student at UT Austin in the late 1970s. He approached

---

20. See Underwood *Distant Horizons*, "Appendix A Data," 173–84, and chapter 3 for discussion about the challenges of tracking reprints as measures of popularity.

21. See Underwood, "Genealogy of Distant Reading."

his professor, eminent medievalist Tom Cable, asking whether there was a book he could read about the history of versification. When Tom answered with T. S. Omond's 1903 *A Study of Metre*, Brogan realized he needed to write the contemporary version of the book himself. He first started piling books on the floor but soon ran out of room. He then moved to tracking books and articles on 4 × 6 notecards, every book or article getting its own notecard. He did not initially know how he would structure the book, nor did he know, at the start, how he would distinguish English versification from prosody; that came to him later.

> For the longest time I had this enormous card file—a plywood box with five thousand cards in it, about two feet wide by three feet deep, 4 × 6 notecards. Every book got a card, every article. All done by cards, all the cross-references, cross-linking was done after I had the indexing strategy, A–Z, L–M, whatnot. Once I had that I could cross-link cards and do cross references. Grew steadily year after year. My friends worked on their dissertations; they thought I was nuts. I probably was; it had no guarantee of a job after that—the dissertation took about a month. I just sat down and wrote it. My dissertation adviser had changed about three times. Eventually I got this guy who just said, "You've worked so hard and you've done so much, just write something down."[22]

This was one way to map a discourse about English versification, and within his guide (which I'll detail in chapter 5) there were several systems that showed networks of thought and theoretical schools, pathways and approaches to ver-

---

22. Notecards are a familiar origin story for what is now known as digital humanities, and they are also the origin of fifteen million records in Paul Otlet's Universal Bibliography, another genealogy for the networked web. Otlet wrote, "These cards, minutely subdivided, each one annotated as to the genus and species of information they contain . . . could then be accurately placed in a general alphabetical catalogue and updated each day." Quoted in Wright, *Cataloging the World*, 81. Father Roberto Busa's attempt to use handwritten index cards to make a concordance; his meeting with Thomas Watson Sr., IBM's president and founder in 1949; and his eventual translation of Aquinas's poetry (ideal because punch cards at that time could fit only eighty characters) for a proof of concept for the *Index Thomasticus* published finally in 1967: all started with notecards. *English Versification*, Brogan's main contribution, was under contract while Brogan was still in graduate school; he recounts asking the professor in his department who had published the most how to go about pitching it, and his advice was "start at the top, all they can do is say no." The top was Johns Hopkins, and they accepted it, he says, within a week of receiving the proposal. It took him three years to complete. See Wright, *Cataloging the World*. See also Day, *Indexing It All*, especially chapters 2 and 3; and Day, *Documentarity*, chapter 2.

sification in English, some more literary, some more linguistic, some more folkloric. I was fascinated and intimidated by its structure of internal citation. The book's brief availability online in a hypertext version meant I could use control F to search (the hypertext links were broken), and Brogan sent me additional bibliographies of medieval versification he'd been working on. I dutifully downloaded all I could.

From those downloads, a technology specialist at Princeton, Ben Johnston, created a spreadsheet of author and book data. Ben's conversion of Brogan's bibliography into a spreadsheet was the first time I was able to see, in a more manageable form than his published book, the breadth of records he had gathered and categorized. That original spreadsheet became the only way I could distinguish whether my own research in periodicals databases could truly supplement what Brogan had already found. All of this felt like an acceptable expansion of what I had been trained to do, and in Ben's view (and my own, at the time) it was not my responsibility to know how Ben converted those bibliographic records into a spreadsheet. My interest was in the materials themselves and what they could teach me about versification in the nineteenth century, using the expanded cultural record of digitized periodicals to augment Brogan's original work. The twofold project—of supplementing Brogan's bibliography, on the one hand, and trying to get access to the new texts I was finding in addition to the original texts Brogan had found, on the other hand, so that I could both read them *and* search across them—stalled when I realized that my project exceeded the methods of literary research. Now, there are resources to prevent scholars from going down the wrong paths, as I did, yet those resources and guides, and the tools and methods they describe, are still not widely understood, taught, adopted, or discussed.[23] This is a failure of our collective imagination, and I present the following cautionary tale to show

---

Krajewski, *Paper Machines*, provides a fascinating account of the era leading up to Otlet and Busa.

23. Like the materials that I could find between 2007 and 2011, much of the methodology described or cited here might be out of date by the time you read this, though I have tried to choose sources with broad overviews and research questions in addition to technical details. Online sources include *Programming Historian* and *Data-Sitters Club*. Books for beginners include Lemercier and Zalc, *Quantitative Methods in the Humanities*; Blaney et al., *Doing Digital History*; Drucker, *Digital Humanities Coursebook*; the book I truly wish I had had about scholarship on the importance of understanding data in our scholarship today is Borgman's *Big Data, Little Data, No Data*. Several books in the Routledge Digital Research in the Arts and Humanities series might be useful to beginners.

how desperately our discipline needs reorientation within the new information infrastructures of today's digital information environment.

A Brief Cautionary Tale (2007–11)

Would that I had simply constructed a plywood box and bought some notecards. A scholar looking at this binder today would likely know what they are looking at: hundreds of pages downloaded from a database of historical materials—in this case page images from the *Athenaeum*—in portable document format (PDF) that were then printed out, using a ridiculous amount of toner, and organized in a three-ring binder. These pages are the analog version of the earliest supplemental material I added to Brogan's *EVRG*. I knew enough to know that I should keep track of them in some sort of bibliography, so at first a librarian suggested I use Endnote, and then eventually someone familiar enough with Zotero, which had been released in 2006, suggested I track the new materials there. But why did I print these pages? First, I did not know how long I would have access to the materials, which, in the case of this binder, were all from the ProQuest collection British Periodicals II (our subject specialist asked us in the department to review it as part of a trial subscription). Second, I did not know how to organize them by topic in a way that would allow me to easily find them. They were too large, at that time, for me to store easily on my computer, and in fact having that volume of PDF files even on an external hard drive proved difficult. Cross-referenced notecards and three-ring binders were analog data structures like the file cabinets in my office where I had alphabetized records of printed PDFs and photocopies in subject-specific drawers. I knew how to read and organize my sources with a three-hole punch and tab, how to move my eyes up and down printed periodical pages and spy what a poem looked like. There was no equivalent in the new world of bibliographic software.

When I was confronted with the new periodical databases, I didn't scope my research question to something manageable like "how was the so-called hexameter mania portrayed in periodicals between 1850 and 1870?" because I had not been trained to manage thousands of results. Instead, I trained myself by trying to come up with organizational tactics that would allow me to find what I knew was supplemental to Brogan's research on versification. Some of these questions included those I stated above, about the ways that concepts shifted over time, and it was by collecting those materials, even in the early days, that I could begin to shape my sense that, in addition to periodicals, the

HOW WE COUNT [LITERARY] 43

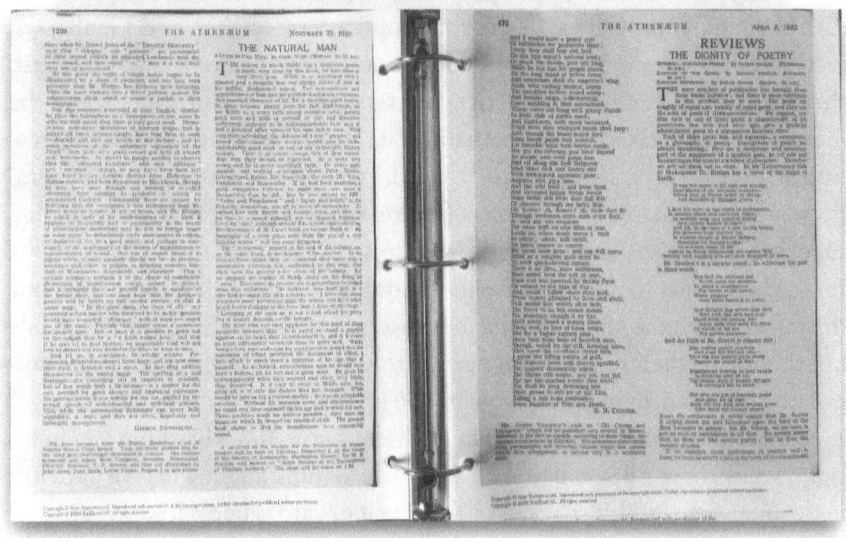

FIGURE 4. Three-ring binder from the side, and then open to pages downloaded and printed out from ProQuest British Periodicals– owned scans of the *Athenaeum*. Photo credit: Meagan Wilson.

variety of grammar books and pamphlets expanded the vernacular audience and mobilized even more distinct approaches to versification. I tried organizing by key figure: what uncollected material had George Saintsbury and Robert Bridges published, and could it tell me anything new about English meter? I used the search bar, trusting that it was reading the documents just as I would read them, and then I downloaded the articles. I hoarded them because it was 2009 and I didn't know what resources I was going to have access to going forward.[24]

24. There is now a "digital hoarding" disorder. See Neave et al., "Digital Hoarding Behaviours"; Sweeten et al., "Digital Hoarding Behaviours."

Mapping a discourse across several kinds of formats meant that I was working across several different databases, printing and downloading materials, thinking that I could somehow reassemble them in another format (after all, if I could search across them in this online collection, why couldn't I create a similar collection for myself?). Had I wanted to collect the controversies about pronunciation, I would need access to the Society for Pure English pamphlets, digitized only by Project Gutenberg, and I would want to track the mention of these pamphlets across their appearance in periodicals owned by ProQuest. This is a regular procedure of the contemporary researcher, and I embarked on the collection process thinking about how to map prosodic discourse first, the formats in which I found that work second, and the provenance of the information (which I did not understand at the time was part of its paratextual information) a very distant third.[25] What I am trying to mark here is the in-between moment in which scholars (historians, literary scholars, information theorists) could not keep up with the resources that were available in digital form, did not yet have a cohesive methodology for accessing and organizing the information they found in the new research landscape, and were certainly not theorizing their research practices in the context of technological and corporate mediation. In many ways we still do not have a cohesive methodology.[26] It is uncomfortable to narrate what I did not know and what I now, in hindsight, would have done differently, as well as to think about what we have lost in the once manageable space of a file cabinet or card catalog. It is also uncomfortable to note that I eagerly turned toward digital humanities to provide a practical, rather than theoretical, solution. The issues that those of us working in digital humanities grappled with in our research were profoundly mediated by the institutional landscapes in which we found ourselves and how those institutions valued, or did not value, the new and (still seemingly) controversial computational approaches to historical and literary study in all its valences. By this I mean that some institutions were ahead of others when it came to

25. By provenance here I mean the library the digitized text was from, the database I found it in, and how it was OCR'd and made available. Ryan Cordell had not yet published his work on critical bibliography, and OCR was also far from my mind; this was before I even understood what OCR was or how it worked. Nadine Desrochers and Patricia Tomaszek explore paratextual apparatus in electronic literature (i.e., comments hidden in source code) in "Bridging the Unknown." But here I am following Alice Wickenden, who argues, in "Things to Know before Beginning, or: Why Provenance Matters in the Library," that "expanding the question of provenance . . . opens up theoretical questions regarding cataloguing, materiality and taxonomy."

26. Underwood's article title "Theorizing Research Practices We Forgot to Theorize Twenty Years Ago" is evergreen, though he focuses more on keyword search.

recognizing the immense media shift in the research library, and what that meant for scholarship.

I reached out to other scholars, trying to figure out whether this was a project that they could advise and shape, both in the history of poetry and in digital humanities. Had I met more regularly with colleagues in the library instead of scholars in the field, I might have learned that the question I was asking—"How to I search across this already digitized material?"—was not the right question at that historical moment. The question I should have been asking: "How should I go about this research given the technological limitations of this current landscape?" The cautionary tale, then, is not that I asked the wrong questions, but that I didn't realize soon enough that my research questions exceeded the technological capacities of my institution. To build my institution's capacity for supporting humanities research in this new way, I had to put many of my research questions on the back burner to build a Center for Digital Humanities.

I knew nothing about what Lev Manovich has called the database logic of new media because I was convinced that my materials were *old*, and I did not know to think of them as media—as data—at all; in fact the work on hypertext, new media, and even DH at the time had very little guidance for me about what to do with material that had been converted from historical print formats; I did not want to learn about the text-encoding initiative, or TEI, and I was not interested in transcriptions. I was learning that preserving the formats of the book and periodical pages was important, especially for the material that contained metrical marks.[27] I didn't have a project that mapped onto Franco Moretti's *Distant Reading* or the work coming out of Stanford, nor could I see how my strangely formatted paratextual materials could be searchable even as more and more scholars began to build databases. My archive was not (yet) a

27. Manovich, *Language of New Media*, 218–43, focuses on databases as antinarrative. A 2007 special issue of *PMLA* (122, no. 5) debates the polemical position of Ed Folsom that databases are themselves a new genre also opposed to narrative. Cf. Folsom, "Database as Genre," 1576: "Database is a new genre, the genre of the twenty-first century. Its development may turn out to be the most significant effect computer culture will have on the literary world, because literary genres have always been tools, families of technologies for exploring the realms of verbal representation as it moves from the lyrical to the narrative to the referential, from vision to action, from romance to comedy to satire to tragedy, from story to play to poem to essay, with all the subgroups and various meldings that genre theory has spawned over the centuries." I take issue with the teleology in Folsom's "moves from" here, as it undermines the recursive generic and prosodic conversations that do not always adhere to a comprehensive story of development. And databases, I will argue, do have arguments; we just do not always know how to read them.

data set and it was not (yet) a corpus. When I looked for models circa 2012 in digital and computational humanities, none of them seemed to be using these proprietary databases and their text files, digital images, and metadata (of course, I had no idea then, that text files, image data, and metadata would become, for me, poetry's data over the next decade).

Document Unavailable

Many of the discourses I wanted to map and represent—work that Brogan had perhaps hinted at but not followed all the way through on—had to do with the history of sound as a virtually unexplored topic for English literary study. Looking at the binder in figure 4, from that original trial subscription to ProQuest's British Periodicals, there are page images of an article by George Saintsbury called "The Danger of Phonetics" from issue 4674 of the *Athenaeum* (figure 5).[28] The article is a review of Robert Bridges's second tract for the Society for Pure English (or SPE), *On English Homophones* (Oxford: Clarendon).

The content of the review shows Saintsbury's antagonism toward pronunciation guides and phonetics (he is against the phonetician Daniel Jones) and reveals his ever stronger dedication to upper-class speech ("the shape of insufficient distinction of vowel-sounds ... certainly does not prevail largely in speakers of the better class"), and it was Saintsbury's hope to do away with pronouncing dictionaries altogether (a delusion and a snare), never mind their promise to upward mobility:

> The spelling of a real language—one consisting not of counters or symbols, but of live words with a life-history—is a matter for the eye, assisted by good literary and historical education. Its pronunciation is one wholly for the ear, guided by the actual speech of well-educated and well-bred persons.[29]

In Saintsbury's dismissal of the phonetician Jones, we can read a consolidation of correct spelling and pronunciation as a natural result of "literary and historical education" primarily intended for "well-educated and well-bred persons," as well as a dismissal of phonetics *tout court*. This microcosm of the narratives of our discipline in formation that have been left out—from philology to pho-

---

28. Saintsbury, "Danger of Phonetics."
29. Saintsbury, 1258.

> ## THE DANGER OF PHONETICS
> On English Homophones. By Robert Bridges. "S.P.E."·
> Tract II. (Oxford, Clarendon Press. 2s. 6d. net.)
>
> IF anybody, after reading the second publication of the Society for Pure English (the first contained only a manifesto and a list of members), were to venture on the couplet
>> Who is't that dangers do environ ? He
>> Who wields that two-edged weapon, irony,
>
> he might be in danger of expulsion from, or blackballing at, the Society itself. But he might also plead, not merely a Hudibrastic justification, but a double inducement in Mr. Bridges's tract. In the first place, the parody suggests, though it does not completely exemplify, the signification of "homophone." This is not an instrument of any kind, but a word which is pronounced in exactly the same fashion as another word, though it has an entirely different meaning and origin. Thus "bell" and "ball" in their various senses are not homophones, because these various senses are all connected ; but "arc" and "ark"

FIGURE 5. Excerpt from George Saintsbury, "The Danger of Phonetics," *Athenaeum*, November 28, 1919, 1257–58.

netics—is one of the many histories that the prosody archive brings to light. These grammarians, prosodists, rhetoricians, and linguists in the PPA are pro-toliterary, in the sense that the establishment of "literary criticism" in the twentieth century largely believes the story handed to them by George Saintsbury: that meter is an abstraction. If we read prosody's archive for what it holds stable and what it still finds unstable about poetry's data, we reveal the ways that objective literary judgment that relies on the component parts of poems is always already situated in a subjective understanding of the operation of language. The cultural value ascribed to a particular kind of poetic interpretation in the humanities must necessarily erase the ideological underpinnings of this subjective understanding, which believes poetry's data to be somehow objective. Poetry's data is situated data, on several intersecting scales.

Could I consolidate access to this historical material so as to make it central to our understanding of the development of poetry's position within literary studies? Could it change, or at least complicate, our concept of the poem beyond the "literary"?[30] Though the archive's aim was not to try to

---

30. See Dworkin, *Consequences of Innovation*, 6–7: "Because we have a single term, we imagine that all of the things designated by that term share a family resemblance. The category of

comprehensively gather poems themselves, the twin project of historical poetics (learning how to read poems that were not canonical, or read canonical poems anew) and the new availability of digital archives meant that I *was* keenly interested in how poems of the past had been classified—how some were able to survive as poems—via the critical discourse that had also been dismissed (pronunciation, grammar) but had nevertheless influenced the generation of early twentieth-century critics with whom we associate the establishment of the discipline of English. The most influential of these—Sidney Lanier and Frances Barton Gummere in the United States and Coventry Patmore and George Saintsbury in England—were all concerned with the best way to count in poems and to ensure that poems counted as the symbol of the nation.

With prosody, there is no distance between judgment and interpretation. The history of prosody and prosodic criticism shows that interpretation relies squarely on a critic's judgment of what counts as poetry and how the internal features of poems—their sounds—will be counted.[31] The elision of this history in favor of abstractions about metrical form haunts both literary and lin-

---

'poetry' inclines us to forget that one 'poem' may have much more to do with a film, or a musical composition, or something else entirely than with another text that also happens to be called a poem. More troubling, a further implication of these figures is that that models we have for literary knowledge and expertise, as well as the kinds of activities that we imagine to constitute scholarship, need to be radically revised or entirely replaced. Surveys, broad synoptic claims, arguments based on norms, strong accounts of large-scale historical change, and other modes of inquiry by individual readers based on comprehensive knowledge can no longer be maintained.... On the one hand ... rather than a series of evaluative close readings, critics might assemble data about work that could be analyzed—either collectively or mechanically—at some remove. Instead of attempting to account for individual books, the task would be to graph and model the complex poetic ecosystem itself, or to map data in ways that their composite assembly would reveal new information. Rather than look at discrete texts, criticism would turn to charting the relations among texts and visualizing those networks themselves.... The focus is not on the production of new data, but on new ways of accessing, ordering, and displaying large quantities of already accumulated data." The PPA did not begin with this in mind at all, but I am hoping that this is what it has now become.

31. Guillory, *Professing Criticism*, 56n26: "We tend to forget that the postwar settlement also entailed a rewriting of the history of literary criticism itself. Although the term 'literary criticism' began to appear with some frequency in the later nineteenth century, it meant just what 'criticism' had always meant—judgment. The critics of the time possessed the freedom to range over multiple domains of social and cultural life, while retaining a kind of anchor in the literary field." Guillory's concern is the melding of criticism and scholarship or "the displacement of judgment by interpretation" (58).

guistic disciplinary formations. How our research infrastructures allowed and allow that abstraction to hold is one of the subjects of this book. Another subject is the disregard for the praxis of prosodic criticism as at once "amateur" (i.e., not theoretical enough) and too specialized (i.e., so complicated a system that we must take the scholar's authoritative word on the subject); this disregard has erased it from the history of criticism as an object of criticism's history. I see the same abstraction and dismissal (too simple or too complex) happening with the technological labors that underpin our access to digital material and to the creation of online scholarly research projects.

I needed to understand who owned the material and how to negotiate for access to it, what "search" meant in the digital environment, and how information about a work, the page image of a work, and its underlying text are entirely different materials with different provenances and different histories; and I needed to understand that I could not reassemble the texts I wanted to read in one place in a new database without letting go of my reluctance to learn an entirely new field (digital humanities). Digital infrastructures had made manifest Saintsbury's polemic that "the spelling of a real language—one consisting not of counters or symbols, but of live words with a life-history—is a matter for the eye."[32] I was realizing that the counters and symbols of the history of prosody would remain invisible to researchers unless I could keep their words in view. But first, I had to learn how to find them again.

32. Saintsbury, "Danger of Phonetics," 1258.

EXHIBIT B: ART

Edward Bysshe. *The Art of English Poetry Containing, I. Rules for Making Verses. II A Dictionary of Rhymes. III. A Collection of the Most Natural, Agreeable, and Notable Thoughts, Viz. Allusions, Similes, Descriptions, and Characters, of Persons and Things, That Are to Be Found in the Best English Poets.* London: R. Knaplock at the Angel in St. Paul's Church-Yard; E. Castle next Scotland-Yard-Gate by White-Hall; and B. Tooke at the Middle-Temple-Gate in Fleet Street, 1702 (figure 6).

[Typographically Unique] [Literary] [Linguistic] [Original Bibliography]

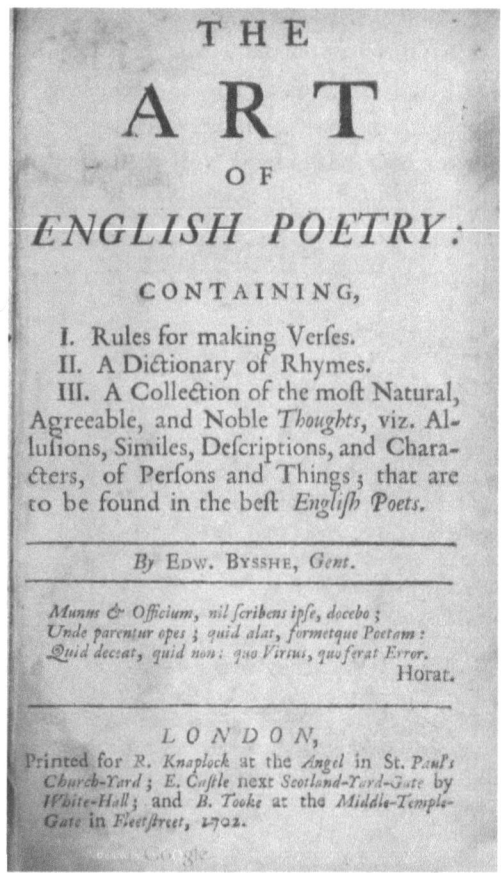

FIGURE 6.

EDWARD BYSSHE HAS BEEN described as both a hack writer and an intellectual. He lived in London around the same time as Percy Bysshe Shelley's grandfather. George Saintsbury centers Bysshe's importance in his *History of English Criticism* (for which he says he was "taken to task") and again in his *History of English Prosody*, where "this importance cannot be exaggerated."[1] If Saintsbury situated Bysshe as a critic, then Dwight Culler characterizes him as a kind of craftsman's helper. In 1948, Culler wrote that "behind the poem often lie the 'unsightly' dictionary of rhymes, the thesaurus, the dictionary of synonyms—all the helps which collectively we call the poet's handbook."[2] But both can be right. For Saintsbury, Bysshe's importance was in establishing a kind of orthodoxy, a critical maneuver that allowed other handbooks to flourish in disagreement. He wrote that what Bysshe, "in his downright way, codified and mummified was the actual creed of almost everybody from a time pretty well before Bysshe's probable birth to a time many years after his probable death."[3] By bringing out what might have been an orthodox *practice*, Saintsbury argues, he "formulated and crystallised it" even if he was "utterly wrong."[4]

Poetry handbooks are one way to measure the shifting standards of practice in verse writing. Culler showed that Bysshe relied heavily on Joshua Poole's *English Parnassus: Or, a Helpe to English Poesie* (1657), which, in turn, relied on all manner of guides to help English schoolboys compose Latin verses. Poole's *English Parnassus* was modeled on the "Institutio Poetica," which accompanied the Latin phrasebook.[5] Culler tracks the competition against each of the nine volumes of Bysshe's work, especially the 1718 *Complete Art of Poetry* by Charles Gildon, which moved beyond versification to address the larger "art" of poetry. Gildon wrote, "How came you by this worthy Author, who writing the *Art of Poetry*, would perswade us, that there is no *Art* at all in it, and aims chiefly at the Knack of *Versifying*; and yet, even in that, is full of *gross Absurdities*, and *visible Contradictions*?" If poetry was being measured by Bysshe's corrupt standards, then the idea that "the chief excellence of poetry lies in *number* and *rhime*" put all of England's "young readers and

---

1. Saintsbury, *History of English Criticism*; Saintsbury, *History of English Prosody from the Twelfth Century to the Present Day*, 2:537.
2. D. Culler, "Edward Bysshe and the Poet's Handbook." 858.
3. Saintsbury, *History of English Prosody*, 541.
4. Saintsbury, 542.
5. D. Culler, "Edward Bysshe and the Poet's Handbook," 859–60. Culler mentions that both Dryden and Watts owned a copy.

lovers of poetry" at risk.[6] Gildon distinguishes between Bysshe's "Art" and true poetry, asserting that Bysshe's more rigid syllabic system (translated from the French) would not allow the genius of English verse to flourish. Though Culler wrote that the book is "misconceived as a work of criticism instead of reference," Gildon felt its influence as a potential application of the wrong kind of critical judgment: if English verses were judged according to Bysshe's mistaken syllabic scheme, England's future readers and writers of poetry would not know how to distinguish poetry from mere mechanic verses.[7]

But what is at stake in this exhibit is not so much the particulars of Bysshe's rules, and whether they were right or wrong, as the debate over how to characterize Bysshe's book in the first place. While the archive of prosodic material contains recognizable genres of discourse, such as scholarly articles, poetic treatises, and literary histories, it also contains works that straddle or combine several genres and evade easy categorization. All the books in the exhibits are such nonstandard, hybrid texts, and to read them requires attending to the bespoke structures they create and announce for themselves in title pages and tables of contents. And when we read such a book digitally, these structures might be rendered more or less visible depending on the structures of the database in which it resides: whether the database has a hyperlinked e–table of contents with semantically meaningful headings, like Gale-Cengage's Eighteenth Century Collections Online does, or encourages keyword searching over structural navigation, like the HathiTrust Digital Library.

For instance, Bysshe's handbook, in its long eighteenth-century title, is divided into three parts: "I. Rules for Making Verses, II. A Dictionary of Rhymes, and III. A Collection" (of quotations). A poem in the "Rules" section is an example of versification (even if that versification system is widely seen as flawed). Both Bysshe's rival Gildon and future literary historians noted that the main source for Bysshe's rules was *Quatre traitez de poësies, latine, françoise, italienne, et espagnole* (1663) by Claude Lancelot, of Port Royal. He took the rules of the caesura from Italian and his entire prosodic system from the French, down to the repeated chapter instructions.[8] Other, more technical prosodists (Samuel Say, John Mason, Edward Manwaring, Joshua Steele) were frustrated by the popularity of the imported syllabic system, but it was teach-

---

6. Gildon, *Complete Art of Poetry*, 91; Gildon, *Laws of Poetry*, 72.
7. D. Culler, "Edward Bysshe and the Poet's Handbook," 867.
8. Culler, 877–78.

able, and so it was taught (most prominently in Isaac Watts's *Art of Reading and Writing English*). As Culler notes, it was found "in the school grammars and dictionaries, in popular literary essays, and in other handbooks for poets" throughout the eighteenth century.[9] That is to say, Bysshe's handbook was part of the poetic discourse about versification and influenced what has been called an overemphasis on the heroic line of ten syllables (particularly in couplets) throughout the eighteenth century; yet his prosodic system was not one that other critics who concerned themselves with the technicalities of how English poetry *should* be measured felt was worth their time.

A poem in the "Collection" or commonplace section is an exemplar of the "Genius" that the aspiring poet might achieve if he follows the rules. Jacqueline Labbe compares the mechanical rules of part 1 to what Bysshe calls, in the preface to the collections section (in the second corrected and enlarged edition in 1705), the "true Genius of Poetry."[10] She tracks how eighteenth-century handbooks emphasize mastery of the rules first; "Genius" is "a close second, but Genius without an adherence to rules remains in a rude and unformed state."[11] Ostensibly, the anthological specimens (or collection or commonplace book) served as proof that poets could get that balance right, and there is a much wider field of study that traces the paths of Bysshe's imagined library through poetry and novels (most famously Samuel Richardson and William Blake).[12] But even if the "Rules" were, as Culler asserts, "the beginning of modern English prosody" and the "Collections" became a signal of possible genius, as in other accounts, it is the "unsightly" rhyme words in the middle section that gain authority, by proximity to those oft-reprinted rules, and by virtue of the fact that they were likely circulated more broadly than the rules (part 1) and collection (part 3).

The word lists in the rhyming dictionary all teach pronunciation in a way that both relies on but also exists (and circulates) separately from the poems. Culler notes that from 1702 to 1775 the "Dictionary" "was the standard rhyming dictionary for the English poet" until John Walker's *Rhyming Dictionary*

---

9. Culler, 879.

10. Edward Bysshe, "The Preface," in Bysshe *Art of English Poetry: The Second Edition Corrected and Improved*, Eighteenth Century Collections Online, accessed September 24, 2024, via *Princeton Prosody Archive*, edited by Meredith Martin et al., Center for Digital Humanities, Princeton University, https://prosody.princeton.edu/archive/CW0110721087/.

11. Labbe, "Poetics," 146.

12. Price, *Anthology and the Rise of the Novel*; Bernard, "Edward Bysshe and 'The Art of English Poetry'"; Labbe, "Poetics."

superseded it.[13] The rhyming dictionary *and* rules portion of Bysshe's handbook had a long afterlife in Thomas Hood's *Practical Guide for English Versification*.[14] Rudyard Kipling admits to having read Hood's early version of his *Rules for Rhyme* "again and again" in a letter to his friend Brander Matthews, who was himself inspired to write his own *Study of Versification* (1911) to improve on Hood's "little book."[15] Bysshe's title is the "Art" of poetry, but that "Art" means not only the rules and the examples, but also what Bysshe himself calls the "the Mechanick Tools of a Poet"—the unsightly data that go into making a poem.[16] The poetic handbook presents us with a snapshot of the various ways that these hybrid historical texts have several uses for several different reading audiences and afterlives far longer than we may easily track. The historical structures of nonstandard texts like Bysshe's are as unsightly as the concept of rhyming dictionaries to the historical poet or critic. Yet both are crucial to understanding historical poetry in our mediated present.

13. D. Culler, "Edward Bysshe and the Poet's Handbook," 872 and 866.
14. Hood, *Practical Guide for English Versification*. See also Swidzinski, "Uncouth Rhymes."
15. Pinney, *Letters of Rudyard Kipling*, 4:33–34.
16. Bysshe, *Art of English Poetry* (1702), 4.

2

How We Read
[Word Lists and Dictionaries]

Prosody before Linguistics

This chapter ties some of the information structures about versification and pronunciation to today's largely text-based search environment. As two linked but distinct types of collections, both "word lists" and "dictionaries" argue for a different way of understanding historical language in the cultural contexts of historical sound. I parallel the ways that individual readers might extract a poetic text from its historical soundscape to the ways that we might miss the argumentative structures of historical print materials—as well as the implicit arguments of the databases and corporations that own the digital surrogates of these materials—when we rely primarily on keyword searching in our database-assisted research.

Most modern readings of historical poetry render the history of sound both immaterial and irrelevant. For historical poetry, rhyming dictionaries provide one example of the ways that prelinguistic scholarship on pronunciation and phonetics produced templates that could, in turn, shape a metrical line, its syntax and meaning. Horatio Winslow's 1914 *Rhymes and Meters: A Practical Manual for Versifiers* warns that "above all one must avoid the rhyming dictionary," stating that even when used to "ascertain whether a word belongs" to the class of words that have no rhyme, "the dictionary is useful, though still a trifle dangerous."[1] For Winslow, too much reliance on the rhyming dictionary threatens to turn a poet into "an amateur popular song writer" rather than a true poet. For literary critics and historians, rhyming dictionaries and their

---

1. Winslow, *Rhymes and Meters*, 30.

critics help us track controversies about how and when certain rhyme words were "allowable" in English and shed light on how accent, alliteration, and emphasis participated in the discourse about the history of poetry.[2] "Word lists" for rhyme and pronunciation acted as one data point among many against which to measure a poet's success or failure at any given moment.

Though rhyme served a dual purpose as an aid to verse construction and as an aid to pronunciation, the data that these rhyming dictionaries present does not add up to any stable history of English meter or phonetic change over time. As George Marsh records in 1860, Walker's *Rhyming Dictionary* contains "five or six thousand words" that are "without rhymes" and calculates that "there remain about nine thousand rhymed endings to twenty-five thousand words, so that the average number of words to an ending or, what comes to the same thing, the number of rhymes to the words capable of rhyming would be less than three." The history of rhyming dictionaries records more than a history of sound; it records a history of when and how particular "un-English" words become "authorized" as English, and how these words make their way into poetic usage over time. Rhyming dictionaries were used as examples to show how difficult English rhymes could be (by counting the number of words with "no rhymes") and these dictionaries were also largely accused of presenting only "false" rhymes. Critic Alphonso Newcomer wrote in the *Nation* in 1899 that "system-makers, carried away by their passion for reducing everything to uniformity ... have tried to dictate to the poets, whose verses, to be sure, would have inestimable value as a criterion of old pronunciation to philologists a thousand years hence."[3] For Newcomer, rhyme is a literary (and therefore aesthetic) phenomenon, not a linguistic (and therefore dogmatic) one.

Newcomer references Sir William Jones, George Puttenham, Dr. Edwin Guest, and Professor Brander Matthews among the prosodists who dared criticize the poets, but a mere thirty years earlier Alexander John Ellis had been using Walker's rhyming dictionary to track early English pronunciation,[4] and

2. Cf. "Elizabeth Barrett Browning's Pathways through the PPA," *Princeton Prosody Archive*, version 3.12.1 (Princeton, NJ: Center for Digital Humanities at Princeton March 17, 2019), https://prosody.princeton.edu/editorial/2019/03/elizabeth-barrett-brownings-pathways-through-ppa/, accessed May 26, 2024.

3. Marsh, *Lectures on the English Language*, 500–501; Mead, *Versification of Pope*, 48; Newcomer, "License in English Rhyme," 83.

4. See Ellis, *On Early English Pronunciation*. Ellis references Walker in two volumes of his magisterial study, and this work forms an important part of his "systematic notation of all spoken sounds" (4:1035, 3:955).

Arvid Gabrielson, ten years later, titled his study *Rime as a Criterion of the Pronunciation of Spenser, Pope, Byron, and Swinburne: A Contribution to the History of the Present English Stressed Vowels*. Whether poets liked it or not, rhyming lists were part of both the history of poetic composition ("a great saving of time and labor")[5] and the unstable history of pronunciation, built on available records of historical sound that were, themselves, contested. All these records coexist in the collection "Word Lists," where the spelling dictionary (orthography) spins out of the grammar book from the earliest example. Anne Fisher's 1773 *An Accurate New Spelling Dictionary, and Expositor of the English Language* was a compendium of grammar, works of ancient poets, a dictionary of heathen gods and goddesses, and a "much larger collection of modern words than any book of the kind and price extant."[6] Lyman Cobb's 1842 *Cobb's New Spelling Book* itself contains fifty-nine examples from John Walker's textbooks: his ubiquitous *Rhyming Dictionary* as well as *A Critical Pronouncing Dictionary and Expositor of the English Language*. Orthography's relationship to spelling reform and the phonetic movement is also relevant to the debates about diacritical marks. (And the standardization of those marks for pronunciation is visible in the collection "Dictionaries.")

Reading Walker's *Rhyming Dictionary* without the context of his *Critical Pronouncing Dictionary* detaches his aims in the former from his aims in the latter, which was to help foreigners gain the ability to pronounce English properly without a teacher. Walker's sense that poetry was the best teacher of English is clear in his instructions to foreigners:

> Scarcely any method will be so useful for gaining the English accent as the reading of verse. This will naturally lead the ear to a right accentuation; and though a different position of the accent is frequently to be met with in the beginning of a verse, there is a sufficient regularity to render the pronouncing of a verse a powerful means of obtaining such a distinction of force and feebleness as is commonly called the accent.[7]

Walker starts out by suggesting that, for a foreigner, accent in verse and accent in pronunciation are mutually beneficial. The phonological mastery of English is important for assimilation both for foreigners and for English speakers whose pronunciation might be deemed too vulgar to represent English in its more "natural" form. We know well how pronunciation was and is used to

---

5. Boyd, *Elements of English Composition*, 380.
6. Fisher, *Accurate New Spelling Dictionary*.
7. Walker, *Critical Pronouncing Dictionary*, 14.

mark certain speech communities—beyond idiomatic speech, the concept of "native" speaker here is meant to denote those who are "native" *and* correct speakers, and poetry's symbol of this normative and prescriptive model of Englishness should be familiar:

> for it may be observed, that a foreigner is no less distinguishable by placing an accent upon certain words to which the English gives no stress, than by placing the stress upon a wrong syllable. Thus, if a foreigner, when he calls for bread at table, by saying *give me some bread,* lays an equal stress upon every word, though every word should be pronounced with its exact sound, we immediately perceive he is not a native. An Englishman would pronounce these four words like two, with the accent on the first syllable of the first, and on the last syllable of the last, as if written *g'iveme somebréd;* or rather *gívme sumbréd;* or more commonly, though vulgarly, *gímme sombréd.*[8]

Walker uses his own version of phonetic speech, a hotbed of debate and discussion among lexicographers and phonologists (and something rendered invisible by OCR, as I'll discuss in chapter 4). Though he wrote above that poems have some regulatory structure that is helpful, he cannot help but notice that it is not *always* helpful. "Injudicious" natives, those whose ears have not been trained toward the ease of pronunciation by enough context and literary historical knowledge—who take the poem's sounds at face value, that is—run into a problem of interpretation: What if the flaw in pronunciation was one that the poet set up as part of the poem's meaning? A pronunciation error might create false equivalence but also reveal that the foreigner needs to read a lot of Pope—and to understand Pope not only as a guide to pronunciation but as a poet—to become equivalent to a native (trained) reader of poems:

> Verse may sometimes induce a foreigner, as it does sometimes injudicious natives, to lay the accent on a syllable in long words which ought to have none, as in a couplet of Pope's Essay on Criticism:
>
>> "False eloquence, like the prismatick glass
>> Its gaudy colours spreads on every place."
>
> Here a foreigner would be apt to place an accent on the last syllable of *eloquence* as well as the first, which would be certainly wrong; but this fault

---

8. Walker, 14.

is so trifling when compared with that of laying the accent on the second syllable, that it almost vanishes from observation; and this misaccentuation, the verse will generally guard him from. The reading of verse, therefore, will, if I am not mistaken, be found a powerful regulator both of accents and emphasis.[9]

Walker tries to guide readers toward the awareness that poets themselves send up poor pronunciation in recitation as "false eloquence," echoing its wrongness (though a stress on the second syllable would be even less eloquent). What pronunciation would be certainly "right" here? Walker leaves that to us, potentially injudicious natives and future readers, always already foreigners to the sonic worlds of the poem.

Though Walker is one of the most common characters in the "Word List" collection, Isaac Watts, father of modern hymnody and a largely underexamined influence on our understanding of rhythm in language, is a close second. Watts rivals Walker in the attempt to stabilize pronunciation for all English speakers. Isaac Watts wrote *The Art of Reading and Writing English: Or, the Chief Principles and Rules of Pronouncing the Mother-Tongue* as well as *Watts's Compleat Spelling-Book*. In the first, Watts includes "A Table of Words accented on different syllables, according to the Custom of the Speaker, even when they are used to signify the same thing."[10] Here we learn that the accent might move position but retain the same meaning. Watts notes,

> I do not suppose both the Ways of Pronounciation to be equally proper; but both are used, and that among Persons of Education and Learning in different Parts of the Nation; and Custom is the great Rule of Pronouncing; as well as of Spelling, so that every one should usually speak according to Custom.[11]

His next table—"A Table of Words which are accented on the first Syllable when they signify the Name of a Thing; but on the latter Syllable, when they signify an Action. The first is a Noun, the second a Verb"—chooses as its example "An A'ccent To accént."[12] There are ten such tables, which have lists of words for various pedagogical purposes. These arts of reading are not the same as ours—unlike Watts and Walker, we have not worried over the mediating

---

9. Walker, 14.
10. Watts, *Art of Reading*, 101.
11. Watts, 102.
12. Watts, 102.

layers of historical sound nor the cultural and national systems and standards that have rendered certain words translatable and immediately transmissible to our ears. But by removing the cultural history of this level of encoding language, we remove another possible trace—another historical, prosodic trace—of the way that poems, that language, might have made meaning.[13]

My focus on historical sound, here, is to draw attention our discomfort with the evidence of mediation beyond circulation, book history, and print culture. Though new work in sound and media studies is finally addressing the long-ignored media of historical sound, the history of prosody displays that the evidence of disagreement about sound's function in language and how it should be rendered in print is everywhere and yet still seldom seen as central to the history of poetic reading. Collecting and understanding textual representation of historical sound alongside reading historical poetry means moving slightly away from what has been rewarded and valued most in literary close reading, which is an easy sense of intimacy and immediacy as well as individual interpretation (to a subjective yet still normative and civilized ear). Reading through these layers of mediation helpfully defamiliarizes even the most recognizable features of historical poems. The existence of so many rhyming lists as data for the historical study of both poetry and pronunciation is itself an untold history of poetic criticism, and it is precisely what the collections "word lists" and "dictionaries" try to foreground in the PPA. We aimed to show how these features served a historical pedagogical function, and we aimed for them to serve a pedagogical function for the user so that they could understand the choices we made in constructing the collection.

The reading approach I describe here and in the rest of this book reads English poems across and within several layers of hierarchies: social hierarchies of native/national versus foreign/other; class hierarchies such as upper class (educated, perhaps with classical-language knowledge to build on) and lower class (educated in the vernacular, or with self-directed learning); and print hierarchies (variegated genres from the treatise or tract to the parody or review). And it thinks about how all these layers not only were mediated by print technologies then but also are mediated by digital technology now. By proposing this way of reading (which many of us already take part in, even if we do not explicitly acknowledge it), I want to make explicit the study of po-

13. Our comfort with erasing historical sounds might be read in the context of our discomfort with the uncanny immediacy of ever better voicing technologies. Cf. Faber, *Computer's Voice*; and review of Faber and Simone Natale in Grobe, "Can the Computer Speak?" Also see chapter 4, "How We Express [Typographically Unique]."

etry as historical prosody—poetry in conversation about how poetry should mean in a culture. The way we read poems now, as single scholars, is not the way poems were read, and is not the way poems (historical and contemporary) are now read, performed, spoken, and written. The project of historical prosody is to show the tension between the high-culture concept of "right reading" (which comes out of trying and failing to generate objective knowledge out of the science of prosody) and the more popular reading practices, or the social lives of poems. Poems are structured data and exist within historical and contemporary data structures. My project over the last decade or more has been to think about these structures together. Poems are part of a large network of conversations and relations, education systems, pronunciation decisions, and constructed social worlds of family, class, and nation. When we erase, eliminate, or make invisible all this data—the too-muchness of it—for our own convenience of reading and to construct our own authority as readers, we are rendering all these relations invisible.

How to Find a Word List

"Word Lists" and "Dictionaries" have been left out of the history of how we think about versification and poetry. In the Princeton Prosody Archive, "Word Lists" and "Dictionaries" as collections function like the stop words of any full-text search because they are by default deselected from the PPA's full-text search interface. Had we left both "dictionaries" and "word lists" in the larger set of searchable materials, the first search results would be crowded with either definitions of words, or pronouncing dictionaries, spelling dictionaries, etymological guides, and rhyming dictionaries. For instance, a search for the use of the word "accent" might return several reprints of a pronunciation guide trying to distinguish between a noun and a verb. And, in fact, this is how we figured out that we needed to argue something more with these collections. Their absence from the main search interface (you need to opt in) is a structural argument about the implicit and explicit absences in all archives. If we had left rhyming dictionaries inside the regular search functionality of the PPA, the experience of anyone using our database would have been to first see all the ways the searched-for word was defined or rhymed across a few centuries. Rather than have a results page full of rhymes (an inefficient replica of the rhyming dictionary) or definitions, we deselected these collections so that researchers particularly interested in rhyme or in historical dictionaries (both of which also contained information about versification) would have to choose whether to search inside them. These collections, therefore, can teach us how dangerous it is to generate meaning from search results without a fully contextualized understanding of the data in which we are searching. "Word Lists," and its sister collection "Dictionaries" are therefore marginal to the PPA, and yet what they teach us about the limitations and interpretive choices of digital research are central to this book. Put another way, the marginal material history of prosody is what our reading practices and our current technological mediations—our page ranks and character recognitions, our programmatic outputs and agreed-on standards—have discarded.

The digitized book makes our historical navigational systems (table of contents or index) within a book just that much more horizontal text to search, and often much of this additional navigational information (and whatever corresponding headers might go with it) is also deliberately left out of full-text searching.[14] We trade a book's structure and format, or the magazine's or the journal's structure and format, for a list of words. By replacing our human interaction with a book's codex technology with a series of targeted searches, we have traded the arguments that books (a poetic handbook) might make in their structures with the arguments that databases make in their structures. But unlike the attempt to replicate the book's structure, even with a page image of the table of contents or a slightly helpful "go to" section page, the argument of the database behind what you are searching is invisible. That is one reason why I am taking such pains to describe the arguments built into the PPA; they, too, are there to preserve the already marginal history of English poetry.

Poetry after Punch Cards

In the early days of DH, when scholarship in computational literary studies galvanized around distant reading the novel, poetry was nowhere to be found. If large-scale text analysis relied on transforming historical texts into machine-readable lists of words, novels had a lot more words, and poetry had fewer words *and* presented unique challenges in its forms and formats.

14. Elaine Freedgood ("Divination," 224) wrote that "interpreting "with digital assistance adds another layer of uncertain data, of complicated information that may or may not constitute new knowledge. It is a matter of reading again, of scrutinizing all the kinds of lines that one can read and thinking about the lines that underlie reading now." This "uncertain data" and "complicated information" does, I argue, constitute new knowledge but only if we take an active role in understanding and crediting that knowledge-creating work.

Jerome McGann and other scholars of the early web's textual environment theorized the ways that markdown and text encoding were necessary to preserve poetry's distinct visuality—its line breaks and spacing—in a nonprint interface.[15] Data-rich textual editing for poetry on the web included transcriptions and TEI XML markup with negotiated relationships with partner institutions to provide manuscript images for poets like Walt Whitman, Emily Dickinson, William Blake, Claude McKay, and Dante Gabriel Rossetti. The ability to see and compare revisions and look at poems online in searchable formats allowed (and allows) scholars to see and compare the digital transcriptions of poems with handwritten versions and images of print editions.[16] (Other early scholarship about new, transformative ways of reading were also deeply interested in contextual reading practices that put poems amid other materials like letters, fragments, manuscripts, paintings, and other versions.) Core tags for poetry transcriptions in TEI include modules focused on the structures of verse lines, stanzas, alignment, caesura, even metrical structure and rhyme schemes. All this additional data was necessary to preserve poetry's distinctive structures so that poems weren't rendered as mere lists of words in this new information environment.

By necessity, then, the technological transformation of poetry has had to focus more on preserving this internal structure rather than on keeping poems within their historical formats or contexts. When they are not construed as page images of printed texts, poems are visible on the web as poems only because of these (underlying, invisible-to-readers) markup languages; or, to put it another way, the TEI encoder has already performed at least one close reading of the poem on the digital page, slowing down to mark each end of line, stanza break, rhyme pattern, metrical pattern (more on this in chapter 4), and instance of a nonrhyming line before the lay reader can apprehend the poem on the digital page. Both close and distant reading of poetry in the digital age has eschewed historical print formats to preserve access to the poem as object.

The (very few) scholars who wanted to analyze poetry's data at scale therefore had to rely on poems taken out of their historical formats.[17] Twelve years

15. McGann, "Database, Interface, and Archival Fever"; McGann, "Dialogue and Interpretation"; Samuels and McGann, "Deformance and Interpretation."

16. The archives are whitmanarchive.org, dickinson.org, blakearchive.org, scalar.lehigh.edu/mckay/index, rossettiarchive.org.

17. The Plotting Poetry research group has been investigating "mechanically-enhanced reading tools" for poetry for quite some time; see plottingpoetry.org. See also Bories, Purnelle, and

ago, Glenn Layne-Worthey, then Stanford librarian; Ryan Heuser, then Stanford graduate student, now faculty at Cambridge University; and Mark Algee-Hewitt, now director of the Stanford Literary Lab and faculty at Stanford University, worked together to create a corpus of poems from the Chadwyck-Healey poetry collection.[18] Chadwyck-Healey was, for quite some time, one of the only reliable data sets on which scholars could base computational approaches to historical English poems.[19] It was "reliable" because it was a data-

---

Marchal, *Plotting Poetry*; Plecháč et al., *Tackling the Toolkit*; Bories, Plecháč, and Ruiz, *Computational Stylistics*. See also McCurdy et al., "Poemage." By "historical poetry" I mean poetry that circulated first in print formats before it could be composed on a modern form or circulated in electronic form.

18. Chadwyck-Healey was founded by Sir Charles Chadwyck-Healey, fifth baronet, who had links through his grandfather to Herman Hollerith (creator of the punch card) and Thomas Watson, founder of IBM. He started his business in 1973 and recounted how librarians fronted him the funding for microfiche editions of the Parliamentary Papers (a liability because of the acid paper) during an era of university budget cuts in the 1980s: "Partly due to the cut in university budgets, the librarians who had signed up to this legally binding contract [to purchase the microfiche editions of the Parliamentary Papers] decided they needed to get the money out of their budget and into my hands up front.... From that time onwards we never looked back because we had discovered that if you published something that was expensive enough—over £5000—and you announced it before you published it, usually with a pre-publication offer, libraries all over the world would not only order it, but also pay for it.... In theory those libraries could have asked for their money back, but fortunately they never did." Chadwyck-Healey said, "The great thing about microfilm as a publishing medium was that you just made a negative, just photographing the manuscripts or books once, and then you made copies to order so you did not have the publisher's problem of having to invest in a stock of copies which might take years to sell." For Chadwyck-Healey, he felt that his success came because, as he states, "I have often found the attitude of other publishers toward things like microfilm, CD-ROM, extremely precious because what you want to do is to have ways of distributing information ... I don't care what format people read things in; I think the new formats are even better for images; our own photographs often look better on computer monitors than in print form." Chadwyck-Healey, "Personal Interview." He sold the company in 1999, at which time it was acquired by ProQuest, which now boasts several collections of historical poetry for libraries to purchase and make available. See also Chadwyck-Healey, *Publishing for Libraries at the Dawn of the Digital Age*, for a fascinating firsthand account of the development of microfilm. For the relationship between Hollerith and the development of the punch-card machine, see Campbell-Kelly *I.C.L.*

19. *Poetry Magazine* began publishing its website around 2003, and now you can find data sets scraped from the Poetry Foundation website as well as from Project Gutenberg. Alexander Huber's "Eighteenth-Century Poetry Archive" began in 2015 (eighteenthcenturypoetry.org), and he has also created a "Romantic Period Poetry Archive," currently in "alpha," which maps "global Romantic poetry" with a sense of the limitations of both the word "global" and the word "Romantic" in that title (romanticperiodpoetry.org). Poetry of the eighteenth century is avail-

base that libraries paid to access, as opposed to the ethically dubious process of creating data sets by web scraping Poetry Foundation, or even jankier sites like poets.org or PoemHunter.[20]

But where do the poems in Chadwyck-Healey come from? In 1992, Chadwyck-Healey's *English Poetry* electronic archive was launched on CD ROM, described as "a Shelleyan universal anthology waiting to be dipped into by random hands."[21] This first edition of the database contained 160,000 poems drawn from *The New Cambridge Bibliography*, which was first published between 1969 and 1972. Given this provenance, it unsurprisingly contained serious omissions: for instance, it contained English poetry *written from the British Isles* only, so any conclusions drawn about "English poetry" from large-scale text analysis of this first edition tacitly excluded American poetry, African American poetry, and poetry from the broader Anglophone world. The only Victorian women poets it included were Amy Levy and Augusta Webster, and it included them only after 2000, after Daniel Karlin wrote up a case study about using the English Full-Text Poetry Database as a source for the 1997 *Penguin Book of Victorian Verse*.[22] The second (2000) edition included poetry from "Ireland, Australia, and New Zealand, and other parts of the world." But does that include the Indian subcontinent, or Africa? What if your university subscribes only to the first, and not the second (expanded), edition of the database? For a database that markets itself as "the most comprehensive electronic archive of English poetry available" and that has the authority of the university library behind it, this problem of representation is a pressing one, as is the issue of gaining the critical literacy needed to evaluate such claims made by digital databases. Foundational work in critical archival studies by Ann Laura Stoler, Michel-Rolph Trouillot, Carolyn Steedman, Roopika

---

able in database form through various projects like Monluzin, "Poetry of the *Gentleman's Magazine*," and Williams, "Digital Miscellanies Index," which allow scholars to search for poetry in collections of eighteenth-century verse miscellanies.

20. There are few or no authorship attributions to the critical essays that contextualize the poets and movements on poets.org, the Academy of American Poets site that rivals the Poetry Foundation's website in online poetry education as the time of this writing.

21. "About English Poetry," Chadwyck-Healey Literature Collections, http://collections.chadwyck.co.uk/marketing/products/about_ilc.jsp?collection=e_poetry, June 24, 2024.

22. Karlin, "Victorian Poetry and the English Poetry Full-Text Database." For comparison, Bartelby.com has "tens of thousands of poems by thousands of authors." https://www.bartleby.com/lit-hub/verse/, accessed June 24, 2024. Interestingly, Bartleby's founder Steven H. van Leeuwen began the site in 1993 with Whitman's *Leaves of Grass* (though the link to that original page is broken).

Risam, and others has trained us to ask such questions as where these poems came from and who they represent.[23] Doing so reveals Chadwyck-Healey to be a classic example of an imperial archive: a collection that displays the ongoing power of the past empire in shaping future work because it has already decided whose history and traditions are worth preserving, and it presents this work as if it is a comprehensive and near-exhaustive approach to the past.[24] We need to bring the lessons of critical archival studies to bear more on literary and computational literary studies, rather than settling for the data sets that are available to us and taking their claims at face value.

In addition to privileging certain voices, Chadwyck-Healey privileged the textual form of the whole poem over the historical formats that interested nineteenth-century periodical scholars like Alison Chapman and Natalie Houston. These scholars have, separately, been working for years to transcribe poetry that appears in a large swath of nineteenth-century newspapers, but this work is time-consuming and takes large teams and years of effort.[25] Much like the flagship projects of Susan Brown (Orlando) and Julia Flanders ("Women Writers Project"), these resources bring poetry to wide audiences by promoting their accessibility in digital formats with transcriptions and also serve as a training ground in digital tools and methods for scholarship, archival research, document analysis, and markup.[26] Though many of these scholars are attuned to historical formats and have been trying to preserve access to, and metadata about, historical pages in the web environment, their primary method of interacting with these historical pages has been through transcribing what is found there.[27] As an abstraction from the historical page, transcription reproduces the sense of immediacy we rehearse when we close read and, ironically, makes it easier to forget the labor and mediations of archives and databases.[28] We know, implicitly, that there is interpretation all the way

23. Stoler, *Along the Archival Grain*; Trouillot, *Silencing the Past*; Steedman, *Dust*.

24. Risam, "Revising History" (an earlier version of chapter 2 of Risam, *New Digital Worlds*).

25. Chapman, "Digital Victorian Periodical Poetry"; Houston, "Periodical Poetry Index."

26. Flanders, "Women Writers Project"; Susan Brown, "The Orlando Project: Feminist Literary History and Digital Humanities," in S. Brown, *Orlando Project*.

27. Chapman, "Transatlantic Mediations"; Chapman, "Digital Studies"; Chapman, "Virtual Victorian Poetry"; Chapman, "Digital Victorian Periodical Poetry"; Cordell and Mullen, "Fugitive Verses"; Cordell, Smith, and Mullen, "Reprinting"; Cordell, Smith, and Mullen, "Computational Methods" (accompanying methods piece posted May 22, 2015); Cordell, "Viral Textuality."

28. Cf. Putnam, "Transnational and the Text-Searchable."

down—from the choice of what gets digitized to the way that digital copy is or is not available at an institution, to the way credit for the interpretive collaborative labor of creating and maintaining digital scholarly resources is withheld at tenure and promotion. Ignoring the mediation of digital source materials is an active way to sustain the fantasy of the lone scholar at the expense of the labor of the archivist, the librarian, the research software engineer; their labor must be invisible in order for the individual scholar to continue to succeed in an academy that still values single-author monographs and articles as the highest forms of knowledge creation.[29]

As a "poetry corpus" that isn't really a poetry corpus, the PPA intervenes in this history of digital poetry reading to preserve the various ways that poetry has been read—not only the (thumbnail) page itself (more on this in chapter 5), but also the ways poems have been cut up and used as examples over time to illustrate a particular prosodic concept or to record an instance of historical sound or "right" reading. Our project team reflects on, and explicitly communicates whenever possible, the choices we make about the data we are privileging or deemphasizing, such as when we suppress word lists, which are an important part of many of these books' structures, so that we can get more varied—and what we've determined to be more "meaningful"—search results in the PPA.

Prosody, Syntax, and the Limits of Search

The deselected collections of dictionaries and word lists bring to light, on the micro level of the PPA, a macro issue throughout our digital research environment that we seldom discuss or critique: the ways databases, search engines, and digital platforms are designed to facilitate and circumscribe certain kinds of discovery.[30] On one level, what we discover is limited by what gets digitized; much of the early work in digital humanities participated in attempts to rebalance and supplement the archival record from inside and outside of the library.[31] At present, there is a patchwork collection of scholarly generated

29. Bode, "What's the Matter with Computational Literary Studies?"
30. Gitelman, "Searching and Thinking"; and Robson, "How We Search Now," who calls these (then) new methodologies of search a mix of "newfangled and oldfangled ways" (13).
31. Thiemer, "Archives in Context and as Context"; Hering et al., "Digital Historiography and the Archives." See especially Risam and Josephs, *Digital Black Atlantic*; Sneha, "Alternative Histories of Digital Humanities." See also Gallon, "Making a Case for the Black Digital Humanities"; McPherson, "Why Are the Digital Humanities So White?"

digital editions, projects, and largely undercredited data work, such as the Colored Conventions Project, crucial to the broader conversations about "undisciplining" English and underpinning the necessary expansion of our digital source material.[32] The complicated institutional relationships between research libraries and faculty-driven digital archival projects are too fraught to explore in all their complexity here, but my point is that scholars need to consider what they're searching *in*, as much as what they're searching *for*.

And what they're searching *for* is circumscribed, as well. In 2014, Ted Underwood wrote that "full-text search is not a finding aid analogous to a card catalog," but rather, it is "a name for a large family of algorithms that humanists have been using for several decades to test hypotheses and sort documents by relevance to their hypothesis.[33] His article "Theorizing Research Practices We Forgot to Theorize Twenty Years Ago" (in a volume of *Representations* dedicated to what we mean by "search") is ten years old at the time of this writing, and yet most scholars still don't theorize their research practices adequately, if at all, nor do we approach our digital source material with the requisite understanding of how those materials came to appear in our library's collection of databases, or how those databases were built. We don't think about how the

---

32. Cf. Chatterjee, Christoff, and Wong, "Undisciplining Victorian Studies"; and the Commission to Fostering and Sustaining Diverse Digital Scholarship, https://www.acls.org/digital-commission-sustaining-diverse-scholarship/: "Employing an ecosystem approach that considers both systems and institutional change, the Commission will engage the expertise of various stakeholder communities—e.g. digital project leaders, university leadership, scholarly publishers, public-facing scholars, financial consultants—in order to move beyond improvised and patchwork solutions to these pressing questions. The problem at hand is not a straightforward matter of library practices or software choices; it is more akin to a public health issue where the solutions for supporting the work of marginalized communities involve entities from different sectors and different modes of thinking. To that end, this effort needs to be supported (1) at the institutional level where most digital projects originate and are initially designed and supported, (2) within a trans-institutional infrastructure, wherein inter-institutional and field-wide bases of support are enlisted, and (3) emerging and often under-institutionalized or institutionally marginalized communities and voices, where voices and perspectives that challenge institutional norms might design and value projects that do not fit within current institutional algorithms. The Commission will thus recommend the necessary areas of research and action." It will be interesting to see whether university libraries are able to follow the commission's recommendations. The Collections as Data reports moved libraries a bit more toward a broader concept of data stewardship, but libraries are slow ships to turn, and despite a wealth of enthusiasm and projects by archivists and librarians, it is difficult to assess what the next decade will hold for this work and how it might intersect with corollary efforts in research computing.

33. Underwood, "Theorizing Research Practices," 65.

various digital resources we use were made and are maintained, or how or why digital materials appear in, or remain buried by, our search results in those platforms or in Google or in Google Books.

A prime example of how being "good at searching" is not the same thing as being "good at researching" is my own early experiments with the Google Ngram Viewer.[34] In 2010, I excitedly tested the distributional hypothesis by looking for words that I knew appeared in grammar books near the word "prosody"—"syntax" and "orthography." But when I first entered "prosody" into the Ngram Viewer, I noticed spikes in the graph that I did not expect. What had happened in 1823 to cause such a large spike in the words "prosody" and "syntax"? I felt that excitement of discovery—had I found a new debate about prosody like the 1860s "hexameter mania," which grew from conflicts about how to translate Homer? I was excited to dig into the (Google Books) data and figure out what all the bibliographers had missed, though I worried that this spike in the graph would undermine the argument I was making in my book, that discussions of prosody in particular rose steadily around the passage of the 1870 Education Act (this was part of the "rise" in my book's title *The Rise and Fall of Meter*). I narrowed the results by decade (1820–40), and what I saw was a delightful surprise. No grammar books, no guides to prosody, but racing calendars and sporting magazines showing that "Prosody" and "Dr. Syntax" were two horses who were performing well at the track. This unexpected discovery led me to search more widely for Dr. Syntax, which, I learned, was the name of the main character in a popular comic poem begun in 1809. William Combe's *The Tour of Doctor Syntax in Search of the Picturesque* was published in 1812 and was inspired by Thomas Rowlandson's aquatints. Dr. Syntax was so successful that Combe published two sequels: *The Second Tour of Dr. Syntax in Search of Consolation* (1820) and *The Third Tour of Dr. Syntax*

---

34. This general question is impossible to answer as, of course, it does not consider the research in Information Seeking Systems (ISS) or Human Computer Interaction (HCI), nor the relation between search interfaces, filters, and a variety of use cases. I am interested in the development of search interfaces that are increasingly simplified—Google's empty box, like a mail slot but instead of putting in a personal letter (though we are putting in *all* our personal data) we receive, instead, information that is no longer mediated by a human (as it would be if we were to speak to an expert or walk into a library). This information is mediated by algorithms we are not able to alter. But for the purposes of this chapter, I'll just note that search interfaces would do well to show *less* simplicity and give *more* information about how they are designed, such as from what sources they are gathering their information. Chirag Shah and Emily Bender give a good overview of the evolution of search technology and interfaces and argue for more interaction rather than less in "Situating Search."

FIGURE 7. *Regency Gentleman Watching a Horse Race at York Racecourse.* Photographer: Florilegius via Getty Images. Image is taken from William Combe, *The Tour of Doctor Syntax: In Search of the Picturesque, a Poem* (London: Rudolph Ackerman, 1812), 112, and was drawn by Thomas Rowlandson, originally titled "Dr. Syntax Loses His Money on the Race-Ground at York," May 1, 1812. Plate 12.

in Search of a Wife (1821). These were hugely popular: you can still buy figurines, prints, teacups, saucers, plates, custard cups, and fabric patterns based on the aquatints, and the books were translated into French, German, and Dutch (figure 7).

Dr. Syntax appears on, or with, horses in several of Rowlandson's aquatints, but this new knowledge of Dr. Syntax and Prosody as racehorses would not have normally risen to my attention had it not been for the accident of the n-gram at the historical moment when Google Books happened to have scanned many racing newspapers from somewhere. This early serendipity was possible only because the majority of books with the word "prosody" in them (hundreds of Greek and Latin prosody textbooks) had not yet been scanned. My initial n-gram misreading led me to an unexpected but nevertheless literary example: a comic poem by William Combe that was illustrated and widely popular had led (I assume) to the naming of racehorses, which then, in turn, led me to think that the names of these racehorses showing up in my search results were evidence of some cultural debate about prosody (proof of my tacit hypothesis that we hadn't found all the ways people talked about prosody despite the bibliographies). In 1821 Combe wrote a second comic poem, also

> THE RACING CALENDAR, 1823.   71
>
> The GOLD CUP, free for any horse, &c.: three-year-olds, 6st.; four, 7st. 7lb.; five, 8st. 3lb.; six, 8st. 11lb.: and aged, 9st.—The winner of any subscription purse at York this year, to carry 4lb. extra; or two subscription purses at York this year, 7lb.—Four miles.
>
> Mr. T. O. Powlett's b. c. *Figaro*, by Haphazard (Lye) 1
> Mr. Watt's b. f. Muta, 4 yrs old 2
> Lord Kelburne's br. c. May Day, 4 yrs old 3
> Mr. Riddell's br. h. Doctor Syntax, aged 4
> The following also started, but were not placed:
> Mr. Lambton's ch. m. Fortuna, 5 yrs old 0
> Lord Exeter's b. c. Holbein, 4 yrs old ... 0
> Mr. Peirse's ch. c. Crab, 3 yrs old 0
> Sir W. Milner's bl. c. Angler, by Walton, 4 yrs old 0
> Mr. Peirse's gr. f. by Walton, 4 yrs old 0
> Mr. Winn's br. g. Little Driver, by Ardrossan, 4 yrs old 0
> Six to 4 agst Figaro, 7 to 2 agst May Day, 4 to 1 agst Doctor Syntax, and 7 to 1 agst Crab. A most beautiful race, and won by half a neck. Run in 7 min. 40 sec.
>
> MATCH for 50gs.—Two miles.
> Lord Queensberry's br. c. *Prosody*, 8st. 3lb. (Smith) 1
> Mr. Wilson's ch. c. Fearnought, by Comus, 8st. 3lb. 2
> Five to 2 on Prosody. Won very easy.
>
> MATCH for 100 sovs.—St. Leger Course.
> Lord Queensberry's br. c. *Prosody*, 8st. 3lb. (B. Smith)............................ 1
> Lord Kelburne's b. f. Sister to May Day, 8st. 2
> Two to 1 on Prosody. Won easy.

FIGURE 8. "The Racing Calendar, 1823," *Sporting Magazine or Monthly Calendar of the Transactions of The Turf and the Chase and Every Other Diversion Interesting to the Man of Pleasure, Enterprise, and Spirit*, n.s. 12; o.s. 1, no. 62 (London: Printed for J. Pittman, Warwick Square, 1823): 71.

accompanied by aquatints by Rowlandson, titled *The Tour of Doctor Prosody in Search of the Antique and Picturesque, through Scotland, the Hebrides, the Orkney, and Shetland Isles*. The existence of both the Dr. Syntax and the Dr. Prosody poems supported one part of what I was searching for—that prosody and syntax as concepts were associated with fussy professors who were ripe for satire and were part of a culture that ridiculed certain ideas about education and where upper-class students were trained in pursuits such as Greek, Latin, and racing horses. But both characters were, of course, named for the actual concepts of "syntax" and "prosody" and were likely associated with the tremendous number of Greek and Latin grammar books circulating at the beginning of the 1800s—not to debates about prosody in English. Was this research? Or search? Where did one start and the other stop (figure 8 and figure 9)?

When I told David Mimno, computer scientist at Cornell who was at that time a postdoctoral scholar at Princeton, about my discovery, he used the "racehorse problem" to popularize and justify a different kind of navigational tool that he had been working on with David Blei called topic modeling. David and I agreed that those racehorses turning up instead of some discovery about prosody at that historical moment was both depressing and encouraging. In

David's mind, the words "syntax" and "prosody" should be the best case—the limit case for a tool as exciting as the Ngram Viewer. These words, to him and really to most people, are about the most specific, concrete, single-meaning words you're going to get—how can you get more specific than a word that most people don't even use every day? Yet even a word we seldom use except in extremely specific contexts will likely have multiple unknown historical contexts that must be surfaced for us to interpret it correctly. Prosody is not prosody is not prosody is not prosody. In other words, it is not enough to search for "prosody," the word, within a million books; I needed to look for "prosody" within contexts, "poetry" within contexts.[35]

The larger point that this case study demonstrates, however, is that this discovery—the spike in the n-gram, the view I could see based on what Google Books had digitized in 2012—is no longer visible because the amount of material that has now been scanned into Google Books is so immense that I now need to know to put "prosody" next to "horse" in my full-text search in order to even find the racing calendars again (see figure 8).[36] In 2012, Google

---

35. I note this for the historical moment of topic modeling; several kinds of contextual embeddings with user feedback are now possible with LLMs.

36. On topic models in the humanities (or, what DH cared about a lot in 2012), see the special issue of *Digital Humanities Quarterly* 2, no. 1 (Winter 2012), and especially Schmidt, "Words Alone." Schmidt does excellent work comparing topic modeling to other kinds of modeling and argues for simplicity and transparency. Of the work of Matthew Jockers, whose book *Macroanalysis* (2013) discusses latent Dirichlet allocation (LDA) in detail, Schmidt wrote, "even those as deep into the plumbing as Jockers will have a hard time bringing other humanistic readers along on the interpretive choices they make in tuning their topic models, and instead will have to rely on protestations of authority. And most humanists who do what I have just done—blindly throw data into MALLET [the topic modeling application] will not be able to give the results the pushback they deserve." Schmidt is referring Jockers's blog post "The LDA Buffet Is Now Open," from 2011 https://www.matthewjockers.net/2011/09/29/the-lda-buffet-is-now-open-or-latent-dirichlet-allocation-for-english-majors/.

I excerpt here a short description of our attempts to use topic modeling on the PPA, written by Meagan Wilson, Travis Brown, and myself for a 2014 NEH application (which we did not receive). Rebecca Koeser is now technical lead for the PPA. "Topic modeling, specifically Latent Dirichlet Allocation (LDA), received a lot of attention in the digital humanities community partially because of its unsupervised method—it does not require expensive training methods or elaborate encodings—but also because it's relatively robust against textual errors. Given a collection of plain text documents, LDA will return a set of clusters of words (called topics but not really topics) that often characterize the semantic and thematic composition of the corpus in ways that can sometimes be surprising. For example, one 'topic' learned from the contents of the PPA begins with the following words: "poetry poem epic sublime subject poet great

Books had scanned about twenty million volumes. Mimno recalls that he couldn't recreate the 1823 spike in the Google Ngram Viewer as early as 2013; now, in 2024, it's impossible. In 2019, Google estimated that the number of scanned books was more than forty million titles, roughly a third of Google's 2010 estimate of 130 million distinct titles in the world. Prosody and Dr. Syntax the racehorses appear throughout the nineteenth century, but you must know how to look for them. It is telling that the Google Books blog, which used to report updates on the project, was merged into the larger blog for Google Search as early as 2012. Returning "Books" to "Search" was returning the project to its beginnings, in inverse.[37] Google, as we know, painted a utopian vision

---

homer descriptions figure virgil figures metaphor objects milton imagination sublimity poetical book kind" and another "sounds voice sounds music tone ear speech musical tones harmony words note notes pitch melody tongue mouth effect heard breath." The method does not assign labels to these lists of words, but frequently the topics do seem to correspond closely to categories that a human reader might identify with a single term, in these cases possibly "Epic Poetry" and "Music and Song." The model also assigns a distribution over topics to each document in the corpus, so that we can list the five hundred documents most strongly associated with the "Epic Poetry" topic. The distributions (both the topics and the assignments we give them, or the clusters and how we name them) are learned from the corpus without any external input about what the words mean; the model simply captures patterns of co-occurrence in a way that often aligns with human judgments about the contents of the corpus. One interesting "side effect" of this lack of external input about the meaning of words is that the model attempts to explain digitization artifacts in the same way that it attempts to explains thematic content: these artifacts are just another kind of pattern of co-occurrence. For example, the PPA model also includes this topic:

> fo fame fome fuch thofe thefe firft muft language moft found fenfe faid fay alfo ii art reafon ufe part

The model has clearly identified mistranscribed instances of the tall nonterminal "s" (ſ)—a common feature in eighteenth-century typefaces—as a significant pattern in the corpus, and we can, for example, identify all the documents that have a strong association with this topic and target them for either manual or automated correction (this is also referred to as the long s).

This identification can also be used for different kinds of prosodic or musical notation, and pages that contain such notation—not because the notation has been transcribed or encoded correctly, but specifically because it has been incorrectly transcribed more or less consistently. Performing useful diacritic-aware OCR or other forms of image analysis on the several million facsimile page images in the archive is not currently feasible either methodologically or computationally, but using topic modeling to identify patterns of OCR errors in the transcriptions can help us to focus both our correction efforts and our analysis."

37. "Google Books History," which also states that "in 1996, Google cofounders Sergey Brin and Lawrence Page were computer science graduate students working on a research project

FIGURE 9. *Dr. Syntax, a Bay Racehorse, Standing in a Coastal Landscape, an Estuary Beyond*, James Ward, 1769–1859, British, 1920, oil on canvas. Photographer: Sepia Times via Getty Images.

of the "democratization of knowledge," and we live in the damaging aftereffects of that successful ad campaign, as Cathy O'Neil, Safiya Noble, Meredith Broussard, and others have shown.[38] Citational practice has always been historically variable and serves to skew the historical record toward the texts that are already circulating, that have already been digitized, that are already part of the dominant narrative. If research is about learning both broadly and

---

supported by the Stanford Digital Library Technologies Project. Their goal was to make digital libraries work, and their big idea was as follows: in a future world in which vast collections of books are digitized, people would use a web crawler to index the books' content and analyze the connections between them, determining any given book's relevance and usefulness by tracking the number and quality of citations from other books. The crawler they wound up building was called BackRub, and it was this modern twist on traditional citation analysis that inspired Google's PageRank algorithms—the core search technology that makes Google, well, Google." See also Brin and Page, "Anatomy."

38. See O'Neil, *Weapons of Math Destruction*; Noble, *Algorithms of Oppression*; Broussard, *Artificial Unintelligence*; and Broussard, *More Than a Glitch*.

deeply about a particular topic, then modern search is not about finding what you are looking for but about both narrowing your results and eliminating what the algorithm thinks is less relevant to you based on the terms you use.[39] Rethinking how and in what contexts we search the historical record is crucial in a research environment in which both history and algorithms continue to reward the only those who are ranked the winners.

Modern search is the dream of decontextualized individual reading: you don't have to cite; you don't have to know where it came from; you just have an unmediated aesthetic experience of the object. It is (bizarrely) new critical in the sense of I. A. Richards's sense of practical (the interface has rendered invisible the impracticalities, the need for theory or history), and so close reading (but not closer reading) a poem without thinking about the broader context of prosody is choosing to dematerialize it. To a search engine, everything is a word list. Topic models are one way to assign structure to patterns, but these models do not detect the actual structures that were important in the books themselves—the data structures that allow us to understand how to navigate a text to begin with. We have already rendered a great deal of literary history invisible in the study of poetry; the PPA is my attempt to rescue the historical study of poetry from what Matthew Kirschenbaum rightly

---

39. "On the web, choices we make—and links we click—have far-reaching consequences for what others find, see and click. We are not neutral bystanders to an unfolding natural process on which we exert no influence. What we choose to look at and link to is what we reward and recommend to others. What we ignore, we eventually obscure—if others concur. This process entails a form of political power exercised through sociability, where networks, protocols and ranking mechanisms supplant the exercise of direct force, and algorithms become wholesale distributors of visibility and obsolescence. Results displayed at the top of a ranked list are 'naturally' considered more relevant than ones at the bottom." And "currently the hierarchy of relevance applied by ranking algorithms propels a hierarchy of influence: the initial relevance of results topping the list is reaffirmed by the public's browsing behavior. The more relevant a result, the easier it is found and clicked on, and the more it eventually will get seen, read and linked to. Such a ranking process risks constituting a self-fulfilling prophecy of relevance." Metahaven, "Peripheral Forces"; see also Rosenberg, "Search"; and Warner, *Human Information Retrieval*: "In relation to classic information-retrieval research, relevance has not been identified with a similarity in meaning or even seen as a simple function of meaning. The assumption of the value of delivering all (and possibly, *only* all) the relevant records is not resurrected" (112). Tee also Edmond et al., *Trouble with Big Data*, 65–66. Two chapters in Daston, *Science in the Archives*, are particularly helpful: Rosenberg, "Archive of Words"; M. Jones, "Querying the Archive." For a technical and theoretical approach to the concept of "Search," see Arafat and Ashoori, *Search Foundations*.

predicts will be a "textpocalypse."[40] Especially in the age of large language models (LLMs) we need to think about how to save historical sources from becoming mere content. How can we keep historical poems from blending into the rest of the decontextualized—mere lists and lists and lists of words?

40. Kirschenbaum, "Prepare for the Textpocalypse."

EXHIBIT C: TABLE

S. S. Hamill. *The Science of Elocution*. New York: Nelson and Philips, 1872 (figure 10).
[Linguistic] [Literary] [Typographically Unique] [Word Lists]

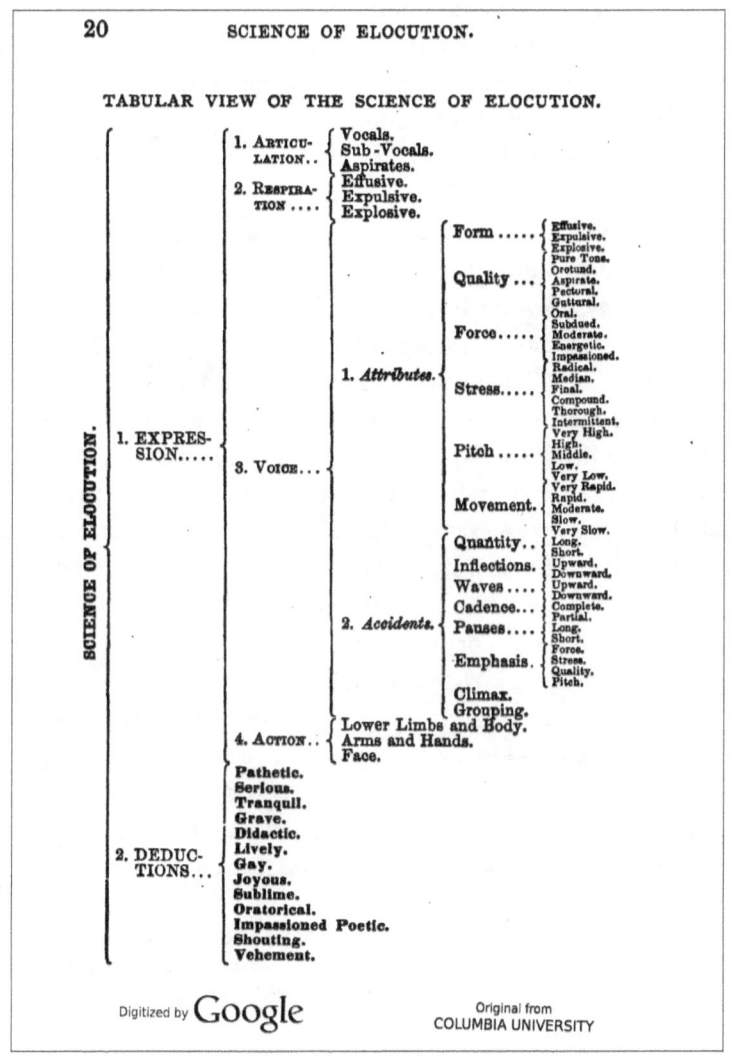

FIGURE 10.

HAMILL'S WORK IS ONE of around five hundred in the Princeton Prosody Archive that refer to elocution in relation to pronunciation. Like grammar books and rhyming dictionaries, guides to speaking, voicing, rhetoric, speech, and elocution were sites of prosodic discourse. The elocution movement was an early and clear break from the classical and philological approaches to poetry, but one that doesn't enjoy much if any prestige, likely because of its devotion to performance and gesture rather than textuality. In the middle of the 1750s, "rhetoric" broke away from the "classical doctrines of invention, arrangement, and style" and toward the "study of oratorical delivery and its twin aspects of voice and gesture."[1] "Orthoepy," or proper pronunciation, was an important part of skilled oratory, and how we pronounce syllables, and decide how to emphasize them with intonation and aided by rhythm, was a question that crossed the contested fields of how to define "meter," "rhythm," and even "expression."[2] Newer work on elocution focuses on its role in the training of speech to overcome impediments. Today, linguists study prosody to treat issues with rhythm and intonation in speech, to treat stammering, aphasia, and other forms of dysprosody. In children, demonstrating adequate prosodic variation and expression is the sign of an advancing reader. The history of prosody to treat impediments includes writers as diverse as William Enfield, John Thelwall, Ebenezer Porter, James Rush, and Andrew Comstock.[3]

There are too many overlapping branches of the elocution movement to account for, and Hamill's tabular view does little to clarify even his own method, but it presents an example, in difficult-to-read graphical form, of the difficult-to-read nontextual history of poetry in performance that does not fit neatly into traditional histories of reading poetry. What if all reading is a performance? Where is this history of poetry in performance in our consideration of poetic interpretation and right reading? The art—or science—of elocution moves steadily from "rhetoric" to "speech" over the nineteenth century. Versification, for the various elocution movements, was an aid to proper vocal modulation and performance, and each book had competing methods for how to employ it. From the more famous phoneticians (and proponents of phonetic speech) like Isaac Pitman, Alexander Melville Bell, and Henry Sweet,

1. Howell, "Sources of the Elocutionary Movement in England," 1.

2. Coventry Patmore's *English Metrical Critics* was a review of Edwin Guest's *A History of English Rhythms*, William O'Brian's *The Ancient Rhythmical Art Recovered*, and George Vandenoff's *The Art of Elocution*.

3. Duchan, "History of Speech-Language Pathology." See also E. Jones, *Turn of Rhythm*, 25–33.

whose early phonetic guides made it into the first version of the *New English Dictionary*, to the more dramatic style of vocal exercises meant for actors in both musical and theatrical contexts, to the necessity for improved public speaking for rhetorical purposes (with the line leading back to Hugh Blair) for clergymen or businessmen, elocution was almost always a means toward improvement, and memorizing poems and reciting them in moments of leisure was one of the best ways to improve. And yet these texts—with their graphs and charts, new modes of spelling and universal alphabets, images of larynxes and respiratory systems—are also rendered invisible by traditional search methods.

In 1908, Henry Sweet wrote that language was, itself, a "vague and floating entity."[4] This vagueness, floating above and hovering around the way we approach literary texts, is why I include Hamill's chart here: we might think of it as an attempt at categorization among many, a trajectory of poetry in performance told through the development not of poetry's data but of poetry's metadata. Hamill's attempts to classify, organize, and present a history for the development of elocution in a tabular view tips it into the history of information visualization. The table also shows a rich and complicated discourse about performance, including physical gestures and the hope that the vocal transmission of affect might develop into a science and not only an interpretive art (Tennyson's "Break! Break! Break!" is given as an example on which to practice "pathos and sublimity").[5] To look at Hamill's chart is to witness how the contours of poetry's uses in performance, rather than print, might be visible only in the vague and floating entities that constitute poetry's metadata.

4. Sweet, *Sounds of English*, 8.
5. Hamill, *New Science of Elocution*, 162, 163, and 165.

3

How We Classify [Linguistic]

Locating Prosody

This chapter, and this collection, are not about the history of linguistics. This chapter concerns what I cannot account for within the disciplinary histories of literary studies and linguistics I have on hand. In this collection, and in this chapter, I describe how those disciplines have, or have not, situated poetic form as pronunciation and versification in the historical record. In chapter 2, I described how without intense mediation poetry online might exist merely as lists of words and that, in such an environment, it is even more important to know what we are searching in than what we are searching for. This chapter argues the information we use to describe our data is another important interpretive choice that guarantees that some cultural objects are preserved while others are not. This chapter is not so much about poetry's data as it is about poetry's metadata.

I knew that I wanted to supplement the texts in T. V. F. Brogan's *English Versification* with additional material that I had found using database-assisted, mostly keyword-based research in periodicals databases that were, at that time, owned by ProQuest (see "A Brief Cautionary Tale [2007–11]" in chapter 1). In 2012, we had the bibliographic metadata for everything that Brogan had collected, and we had all the bibliographic metadata for the additional materials I had found—fifteen hundred bibliographic records in total. With the help of Grant Wythoff, and after having tried, and failed, to convince ProQuest to let us have access to their records, we finally negotiated a memorandum of agreement with the HathiTrust Digital Library for images, full-text data, and bibliographic metadata.[1] It seemed to us like an opportunity to see what else

---

1. There is a much longer story here of how Grant Wythoff and I had already been trying to classify the material we had collected in bibliographies and folders of PDFs, but once we were

HathiTrust might have that could be useful, especially after realizing how undependable relying on Google Books alone could be. Even though over 97 percent of the material in HathiTrust had been scanned by Google, HathiTrust made it its mission to work directly with research libraries to try to provide better metadata. And even though Library of Congress (LOC) subject headings were used consistently on only about 60 percent of HathiTrust, we still felt that using the LOC subject headings as a guide might help us find information about poetry that might have been left out of other bibliographies. We had already consulted every known bibliography to see if Brogan had left anything out (he hardly missed anything) and knew that there were works that were not yet in HathiTrust, but that was okay; we had let go of any concept of completeness. HathiTrust and LOC subject headings were still going to help us see the grammar books and elocutionary manuals Brogan had left out.[2]

---

able to facilitate an agreement with HathiTrust, we started this process anew and took the opportunity to see what additional materials we might put into play, as well as how that additional material might complicate the categories we had already been considering.

2. For about a year, Grant, Ben Johnston, and I worked with an external programmer who was in way over his head to try to get the 1,574 PDF files we had into some sort of searchable format that would simultaneously allow us to display page images alongside the text we were searching; we were interested in locating *where* the information was, not only *what* it was (so using grep after pdftotext was not an option we explored, though no one suggested it, either). In June 2011, Grant and I were tearing our hair out over having sunk precious grant money into a developer who wasn't able to deliver anything he had promised. Johnston had several other projects and was volunteering extra time on nights and weekends to try to guide us, though he was always interested in the project and gave us crucial advice about how to store information on Princeton's servers. It was also in 2011 that Ben, Grant, David Mimno, Cliff Wulfman, and I started to meet with a broader group on campus to form a Digital Humanities Initiative. Grant and I had met Bethany Noviskie, Andrew Stauffer, and Laura Mandell in 2012 at a conference that helped to generate the first report on how to evaluate digital scholarship for promotion and tenure in 2012. Via a conversation with Bethany, in which I naively asked if she knew of anyone or any service that could help us with transcription (since that was what everyone else seemed to be doing), I learned about Cliff Wulfman who had been hired as a Digital Scholarship Specialist at Princeton. I met Cliff only because I met Bethany in Virginia. By studying other successful projects, we assembled an advisory board and a technological advisory board and began to look for funding to start over using the HathiTrust Digital Library as our main source for data and metadata via their two APIs. I became a digital humanist in 2011. I think, honestly, once you learn how an API works, there is no going back (and of course there are longer stories here about navigating library administration and Princeton's long history with humanities computing).

```
English language rhythm                              poetry 12
    e.l. grammar 1151                                versification 10
    e.l. rhetoric 616                                english poetry 8
    e.l. composition and exercises 453               comp lit 6
    e.l. etymology 241                               comp lit classical and modern 6
    e.l. orthography and spelling 241                comp lit modern and classical 6
    english literature 210                           american poetry 5
    e.l. study and teaching 209                      english lang terms and phrases 5
    e.l. history 160                                 eng lang versification 5
    e.l. Rhetoric 156                                poetry history and criticism 5
    e.l. pronunciation 134                           rhetoric 5
    e.l. pronunciation 113                           aesthetics 4
    e.l. versification 113                           american poetry history and criticism 4
English language versification                       english poetry history and criticism 4
English language phonology                           literature modern 4
English language rhyme                           Versification
    rhyme                                            versification 376
        english language                         English poetry history and criticism
        english language etymology                   english poetry 1112
        el terms and phrases                         english language 218
        el rhyme                                     english poetry history and criticism 204
        el versification                             english poetry history and criticism 202
    rhetoric 106                                     english poetry early modern 1500-1700 187
English language pronunciation                       poetry 182
    pronunciation 425                                poetry 128
English language phonetics                           english poetry 18th c history and criticism 119
    phonetics 376                                    english poetry 19th c history and criticism 114
    phonology 125                                American poetry history and criticism
English language grammar                             american poetry 151
English language early modern                        poetry history and criticism 99
    english poetry early modern 1500-1700 history and criticism 301    criticism 63
    english drama early modern and elizabethan history and crit 226  Singing diction
    english literature early modern bibliography 178     singing diction 16
    english literature early modern history and criticism 150    Elocution
    english poetry 18th century history and criticism 88     elocution 694
    romances, english history and criticism 56       Voice culture
Poetics                                                  voice culture 89
    poetics 35                                   Rhetoric
    English language 25                              rhetoric 1036
    english language versification 13
```

FIGURE 11. Screenshot of Library of Congress headings, by Grant Wythoff.

After a great deal of back-and-forth, the subject headings from the Library of Congress that we sent to HathiTrust are shown in figure 11.

Notice that prosody does not exist as a subject, and so by asking HathiTrust to deliver these works to us from these selected LOC headings, we were acting on our own authority and that of our advisory board to cast a wide enough net to catch any additional texts that Brogan's bibliography and our own additional research had missed.[3] Why did we decide to use LCSH? Expediency. We had

3. Library of Congress is famously not the most progressive or forward-looking standard of classification, as scholars—from Loukissas, to Geoffrey Bowker and Susan Leigh Star in *Sorting Things Out*, to countless others in information science—have noted. Cf. Adler and Nightingale, "Books and Imaginary Being(s)"; Adler, *Cruising the Library*; and Day, *Documentarity*. For historical sources of the hegemony of LOC's "dominant role" in developing standards of automated bibliographic systems, particularly the MARC system, see Michael Malinconico and Paul J. Fasana, "Machine-Readable Cataloging Data," in Malinconico and Fasana, *Future of*

exhausted bibliographies and reference materials on grammar, elocution, and rhetoric, and needed to steer clear of non-English materials to search across them, which meant navigating the addition of any new material cautiously. But when we received the records, books, and images and began the process of sifting through the material, the real work of classification—and classification as interpretation—began. Rethinking how "prosody" had evolved in English literary study and linguistics meant that we had to learn more about metadata than we ever imagined.

For many theorists in critical data studies, the question of *what* is data is less useful than the questions *where* and *when* is data.[4] All data is situated, in data settings both local and collected from heterogenous sources, each with their own local attachments, as Yanni Loukissas has argued. Narrative implications about our objects of study exist already at the moment of data collection—of research—even if we don't yet know how to see our research as shaped by these invisible infrastructures.[5] We received over eight thousand book records from HathiTrust and began the difficult task of deciding what pathways through the history of poetry we might make visible with our own interpretive classifications. While the LOC subject headings fell away, we gained provenance information (which library owned the scanned books), a richer sense of what we might learn from the metadata, and a way we might create our own to guide researchers through the materials.

Though we considered foregrounding metadata like author gender and publication location, we learned that for our materials, the resource from which we were drawing was already heavily skewed toward items digitized by libraries located in North America. It was also immediately clear that, though date of publication was important, we couldn't draw from it any conclusions about representativeness since, again, we knew that HathiTrust, like most digitized collections at that time, overrepresented the nineteenth century.[6] Type of book was also a problematic category: the books themselves self-declared inconsistently across guide, handbook, poetic treatise, art of poetry, and so on.

---

the Catalog, 22, or just spend ten minutes looking at titles in the incredible *Cataloguing and Classification Quarterly* journal.

4. Cf. Borgman, *Big Data, Little Data, No Data*.

5. Loukissas, *All Data Are Local*; Lisa Gitelman and Virginia Jackson, introduction to Gitelman, "Raw Data," 1–14.

6. Underwood, "Distant Reading and Representativeness"; Benjamin Schmidt, "A Guided Tour of the Digital Library," in Schmidt, *Creating Data*; and "What's in the HathiTrust?," February 3, 2022, Sapping Attention, http://sappingattention.blogspot.com/.

And though we could get some sense of intended audience by markers like "for use in schools," particularly in grammar books, other books that were titled "grammars" were for making arguments aimed at new ways of conceiving of English grammar altogether. Titles were not a consistent marker of genre, and even within a single work, subsections could signal a variety of discourses. For instance, an 1832 *Abridgment of Lectures on Rhetoric* by Hugh Blair, in a new edition by "A Teacher of Philadelphia," covered the structures of sentences and several types of poetry in one volume (there are three copies of this version in the PPA, including copies published in 1837 and 1854).[7] Keeping Blair's rules about poetry and versification near his rules about oratory informed both discourses, but Blair's version of rhetoric was different from William Tanner's, in his 1922 *Composition and Rhetoric*, in which composition is defined as "the expression of what we have to say in accordance with the rules of grammar and the principles of rhetoric."[8] In Tanner's book, versification is a mere appendix, and composition as expression takes place principally in prose. These texts *felt like* prosodic discourse to me, but not the part that concentrated squarely on versification. Just as a poem's theme might have a thematic rather than formal relationship to its genre, so, too, was I seeing how the structural relationships of books overdetermined their future consideration as relevant to the (later) norms of scholarship. Historical poetics helped me see ways to navigate poetry's metadata so that I could assemble different structural relationships to the past in the database.

In practice, because versification was not the main subject of these kinds of texts, they did not belong to the collection I had first named "Poetry" and which later became "Literary"; however, because versification still formed some component part of them, we moved through a range of subcategories to try to capture that contiguity. We had entire sections on music, musical theory, and dramatic speech, which we eventually suppressed; a graduate student spent a year researching what texts we should add to this collection before we realized that it was too far afield of versification and pronunciation to merit inclusion. After long discussions with members of the advisory board who worked on the eighteenth century in 2013, I settled on naming the collection "Speech." This collection title was broad enough to contain Blair's definition of rhetoric, as performed and expressive forms of oratory; the diffusion of these ideas into elocution and recitation in its various forms and also recitation in the classroom; guides to proper speech and pronunciation that were part of

---

7. H. Blair, *Abridgment*.
8. Tanner, *Composition and Rhetoric*, 2.

evolving grammar pedagogy; and phonetics-in-development in the form of experimental symbols for sound in writing in the period leading up to (and even sometime after) the development of the International Phonetic Alphabet. Part of why "speech" worked as a collection title and as an argument, at that moment, was because as a contemporary reader I understood it as an approach to a history of debate and argument that was visible in some of the earlier rhetorical manuals, but also aligned with the emergence of composition in the later nineteenth century as a parallel to, and then a replacement for, recitation in the classroom. None of this iterative renaming will come as a surprise to library scientists, whose subtle work to reflect cultural change in library catalogs happens daily. For me, these tensions helped me understand how the ways we think about poetry had been conscripted by narrower concepts of the literary in the metadata itself.

How could we make these otherwise invisible structures visible? All this work necessarily took place in spreadsheets. Title, author, publication information, and what collection the work might belong to existed across columns and rows. We could see that we had multiple editions of texts—reprints like Blair's abridged grammar mentioned above. As part of our task was to track discourse across time, we kept these. We also had works of multiple volumes, like Samuel Johnson's *Works of the Poets*, in which his prefaces contained critical commentary about the poems. However, not every work with more than one copy (and by copy I mean digital surrogate) signaled a reprinted edition or multivolume work; sometimes it signaled instead that we had received from HathiTrust two (or more) digital surrogates of the identical edition—just scanned at different libraries. Meagan Wilson, who undertook this painstaking labor of deduplication, cleaned and deduplicated the material so that when we launched the third version of the PPA in 2019, each digital surrogate corresponded to the holdings of only one library.[9]

That provenance information HathiTrust had included turned out to be some of the most valuable metadata we received, since it showed where the physical books the digital surrogates were based on were located. Meagan's work eliminated about 40 percent of the original material from HathiTrust.

---

9. Wilson and Naydan, "Deduplicating the Archive." We began with four main collections in 2012: "Brogan's English Versification" (578 works), "Prosody Archive" (1,308 works not listed in Brogan that I added to his guide via my own research); "Subject Search" (6,873 works: the result of the subject headings cataloged by HathiTrust partner libraries [see figure 10] from which we attempted to filter out works that were not in English). The final of the first four initial collections we called "Graphically/Typographically Unique" because we knew, by looking at the pages, that these texts had interesting marks that were likely not machine readable.

The traces of Meagan's deduplicating work are visible on the item detail pages on the website, where you can see the location of the original books that were scanned by the heterogeneous libraries who participated in the Google Books project via their unique volume IDs ("nyp.33433074840152," for instance, identifies a book originating in host institution the New York Public Library). We could prioritize books in Princeton and then books from libraries in the Research Collection and Preservation consortium, or ReCAP. As Meagan verified that our metadata corresponded to only the records we wanted and no additional copies, we marked places where we noticed incorrect metadata and wanted to rethink our own metadata categories.

As a result of this process, I realized that "Speech" as a collection wasn't going to work after all. What we found in the spreadsheets was the more capacious and yet still nebulous category "Linguistic." What could we learn about "Linguistics" beyond "Philology"? The result is the five collections, "Literary," "Dictionaries and Word Lists," "Linguistic," "Typographically Unique," and "Original Bibliography," that currently organize the materials in the PPA and that now make up the titles of the chapters for this book. From the time we got the HathiTrust data in 2012, it took another seven years, and another project manager, the inimitable Mary Naydan (who is more likely than not the other part of the plural "we" throughout the majority of this book), before we could follow through on redesigning the project's interface and completely rebuilding the site architecture, work that happened in fits and starts after 2014 and mapped roughly on to the first decade of the Center for Digital Humanities at Princeton.[10] But the data work—ongoing, iterative, and something we

10. By 2014, I was a full-time director of the new Center for Digital Humanities (though still also a full-time professor teaching and researching and doing other university administration), which had officially launched. In addition to the management and hiring, we oversaw the construction of a new space in the library and wrote internal and external grants. The intense data work we undertook between 2015 and 2017 was in some ways a relief because it meant focused tasks that we could do at odd hours. I was building the center and making sure it succeeded; I also had a child and, in 2018, had to reorganize the leadership structure of the center entirely. Having a personal research project as the flagship of a very public research center that was often asked, by a revolving door of deans and provosts, to justify its existence also meant that my research was the sandbox for all manner of procedures, from project management to UX/UI design and testing to back-end architecture to long-term service agreements. It was incredibly delicate for me to manage avoiding a center focused on my own research project, which is why I prioritized projects by my colleagues over my own, for both center time and my time. The data work of the PPA was not an afterthought, and it helped to change the trajectory of the center toward one that offered data fellowships and critical data studies and critical archival studies as part of its fellowship structure for researchers *before* we would collaboratively agree to build any software application with them that required data. But it also meant, necessarily and often

revisit every time we add a new work to the collection—has taught us that the interpretive labor of close reading spreadsheets is a skill that all humanists should practice, and that the work of classification is always incomplete.

The materials in the PPA, in this newer, reclassified collection "Linguistic," are a placeholder for a range of materials that intersect with the history of versification but now stand in for prosody that is "not directly about poetry." The other materials about the development of phonetics and its relationship to linguistics in the nineteenth century are now a story for another book, which this research has clarified. That discourse is now "suppressed" in the archive, just like "music."

We are always rethinking whether the collections will hold when we add new material. We were particularly nervous that we were going to have to rethink our collections when we finally came up with an agreement with Gale-Cengage to work with its Eighteenth Century Collections Online; what would integrating materials from the eighteenth century do? Would "Linguistic" still make sense for a collection that could now help us track the ways versification and pronunciation did and did not show up in the early history of lexicography? Thankfully, it didn't, nor does it seem to be the case that we'll need to rethink everything with the integration of the few remaining early modern materials we need from Early English Books Online. And because we have provenance information already built into our metadata in each item record, the material from these differently located data sources is marked by a different record ID.

Part of the reason to create metadata—to classify in this way—is to keep the argument of the database in mind. The collected materials in the PPA argue that reading the scholars who mostly fall outside the boundaries of literary history can give new ways of thinking about the contours of that history. The metadata can show that the contested history of meter did not resolve but recurred in different historical moments for different reasons, and it argues that reading the history of how poetry was taught helps us to track the pedagogical changes that moved poetry from being considered something that was primarily heard to its being considered something that was primarily read. The metadata also reveals how these two approaches did not change one to the next but continued to exist in tension in scholarly and pedagogical materials

---

frustratingly, that my project was the one we put aside when someone else's was running over time or needed new features or fixes. We are often lauded in the larger DH world for our successful attention to process *and* product, our attention to design and sustainability, and our training in data work. The challenges (particularly invisible, particularly gendered) of balancing research with my leadership of the center is another story for yet another kind of book.

(as they do to this day). But each individual collection, as this book shows, also makes discrete arguments. We eliminated "music" because we did not have the capacity, or the relevant material, to make an argument about its relationship to prosody. And when we add additional data from T. V. F. Brogan's versification guide, as we will every copyright year for a few years yet, this additional material won't change the project's overall argument. Categories and data work help us make interpretive curatorial decisions that also allow arguments to take shape. Metadata is a way to trace a path through complicated, overlapping discourses so that we can tell stories. And we are responsible for learning how metadata works in our field so that we can see how all literary histories are underpinned by these often invisible structures, layered onto contingent categories and forming another network in the social and institutional life of literature.

It's often the case that we are already choosing to look at one kind of data as a focal point for close reading or one kind of historical or social context toward which to relate that close reading. Learning to see social and historical contexts at the metadata level is crucial. The nexus of critical archival studies and critical data studies allows us to dispense with the mystique of serendipity and share the responsibility of stewardship. But we can also close read our contextual choices, and, as the PPA and this book argues, we *must* close read them, because those contexts, traceable by metadata, carry authorial and institutional power. And finally, like in the case of "Prosody," when we see classificatory systems that don't work for our interpretation of the past, then we are able to speculate, explore, and build the story that we think is missing. The performative approaches to poems that overlap in oratory and elocution, parlor recitation and school performance, phonetics laboratories and physiologists' offices, are a story that scholars are only now beginning to tell in the history of poetry. Classification is and should be seen as iterative. The collections in the PPA are suggested pathways that might help researchers navigate its materials. But we also intend for the collections to serve as meta-arguments about how you might find or lose your way in the larger archive of materials, an incomplete archive that is understood to be changing along with our understanding of the past.

Poetry's Classification

How to classify poetry *inside* the texts in the PPA is one of the questions we are now posing. The information in prosodic treatises and poetic handbooks is not structured like a traditional cause-and-effect narrative, and through what

Alison Booth and Grant Wythoff call "mid-range" reading, I learned to see "prosody" as the subject of the last section of the grammar book. That is, using tables of contents and book metadata, I could see whether a grammar book discussed versification, and that is how one version of the data set that is now called "Linguistic" was first classified.[11] Within the more poetic, less grammatical treatises themselves, classification acts to bolster arguments: the type of poem had to match the type of meter; meters in Latin signified generic categories, and the question of whether meters in English should do the same was an ongoing topic of debate and experiment. What did it mean to write a ballad in blank verse, or an epic in ballad meter? Metrical choices signaled to constituencies of readers they might find moments of recognition if they had been trained in a certain kind of metrical reading. For prosodists who wanted to classify what was inside the verse lines that made up a poem, they ventured systems of measuring accent and syllable, with tables, proofs, and symbols aiming to teach the reader how to recognize these patterns within the wider system of metrical genres. Sometimes these systems were translated into the popular terms for Latin meters, but often they were not. And yet there were writers who were interested in some version of an objective model for prosody, in versification treatises and grammar books, that interacted with a more subjective model of performance and reading of a poem or text.

Within each broad classification I tried to define, as speech, grammar, or rhetoric, I found exceptions. All classifications are a constraint, and I knew that mine, in particular—even if I made them by consulting with my collaborators and with my advisory board, even if I wrote a book about them—would still eventually become invisible to people using the site. As Bowker and Star wrote, largely invisible classifications are at work in every built information environment. In the same way, the long history of confusion in terminology for poetic terms is everywhere evident in these texts, and these classificatory systems, too, become invisible infrastructures for poetic reading. We might also call these poetic forms.

Whether in poetic reading or in scholarly research, the encounter between scholar and scholarly object is mediated by these invisible infrastructures that determine what data we pay attention to and what metadata classifications allowed us to find it in the first place. As part of a broader reassessment of Library of Congress subject headings (LCSH), Laura Helton wrote how

---

11. "Mid-range Reading: Manifesto Edition" panel at Alliance of Digital Humanities Organizations conference, June 26–29, 2018. See especially Booth, "Mid-range Reading"; and Wythoff, "Tacit Computing and Method in the Humanities."

"card-tray tables" rarely command a central plotline in studies of reading. She continues,

> The history of information is of increasing interest to scholars of literacy, who have shown, for example, that there is no story of early modern knowledge production without its zeal for inventories, or of American public libraries without Melvil Dewey's decimals, or of contemporary textuality without algorithms. In such accounts, catalogs come into focus as analog databases that backfill the media history of our own "information age." And yet, the true scenes of literary practice are usually cast as encounters between readers and writings, not between readers and index cards. The search for evidence of reading moves past the catalog to artifacts like commonplaces, marginalia, and memoir—inscriptions that record the intimacies of what was read rather than how it was found.[12]

I tell this story to answer Helton's charge to "pause . . . at the catalog as a scene of reading" in order to "bring into focus the bibliographic experiences of readers, as well as the bibliographic labor, often performed by women." Helton's work on Black print culture tells the story of a long history of "literary workers" including Dorothy Porter who "authored infrastructure." The issues she raises, and her own bibliography, contextualize classification for modern literary workers who author their own bibliographies. In turn, we might turn these bibliographies into searchable online databases, authoring infrastructure within the larger landscapes of knowledge that are being assembled by corporations and dismantled and reassembled differently by individuals and collectives of scholars.

As one such dismantled and reassembled archive, the PPA is not a collection of materials that will generate broad agreement, and it isn't intended to. It is a collection of materials trying to upend stable classifications for all kinds of poetic terms to show, perhaps, where disagreement and agreement have been mobilized for institutional, national, or even aesthetic reasons. I did not think about the data classification we were doing a decade ago as a data set, though it would been tremendously helpful if I had. I did not know to think of it in that way because I did not consider my sources to be data—I had not yet learned to historicize that visceral reaction against thinking of poetry as

12. Helton, "On Decimals, Catalogs, and Racial Imaginaries of Reading," 102; Battles, *Library*; Berman, *Prejudices and Antipathies*; Bowker and Star, *Sorting Things Out*; and Bowker et al., "Toward Information Infrastructure Studies," 97–117. Cf. A. Blair, *Too Much to Know*; Foucault, *Order of Things*; Drabinksi, "Queering the Catalog."

data as a way to puncture its magical properties, its transcendental possibilities, nor to consider why that felt so threatening (why poetry needed to remain special—I also felt it!). I also, at that time, didn't really know what the term *data set* meant. This was before digital humanities had begun to theorize data as a broader concept. Even now, the work and methodologies of data collection and classification are still seen as secondary to analysis and interpretation; as I argue elsewhere, the labor of classifying and annotating data is seen as menial instead of meaningful. We do not have a place to talk about this work in the academy because it is seldom considered interpretive.

Deciding how to categorize poetry in a spreadsheet entity, so that I can later ask questions about the history of how poetry has been used as an example of classification at scale, is a compromise that doesn't threaten poetry's inherent value; rather, it increases it. This is because to ask, "In what ways have poems been classified poems in the past?," we first have to answer, "How can we best classify prosodic discourse in texts for future work?" If language is a "vague and floating entity," my story of the clear structural instabilities involved in determining poetry's metadata—of the inability, or at least hesitancy, to classify in a temporally stable way—should show that the local and situated reading practices of the catalog, of the poem, of how we might think about reading poems within and among a variety of reading cultures, might bring a more accessible kind of reading for those who wonder why some poems, or different ways of reading poems, have been left out of the cultural record.

EXHIBIT D: MUSIC

William Gardiner. *The Music of Nature; or, Attempt to Prove That What Is Passionate and Pleasing in the Art of Singing, Speaking, and Performing upon Musical Instruments, Is Derived from the Sounds of the Animated World; With Curious and Interesting Illustrations.* London: Rees, Orme, Brown, Green, and Longham, 1832 (figure 12).
[Linguistic] [Literary] [Original Bibliography] [Typographically Unique]

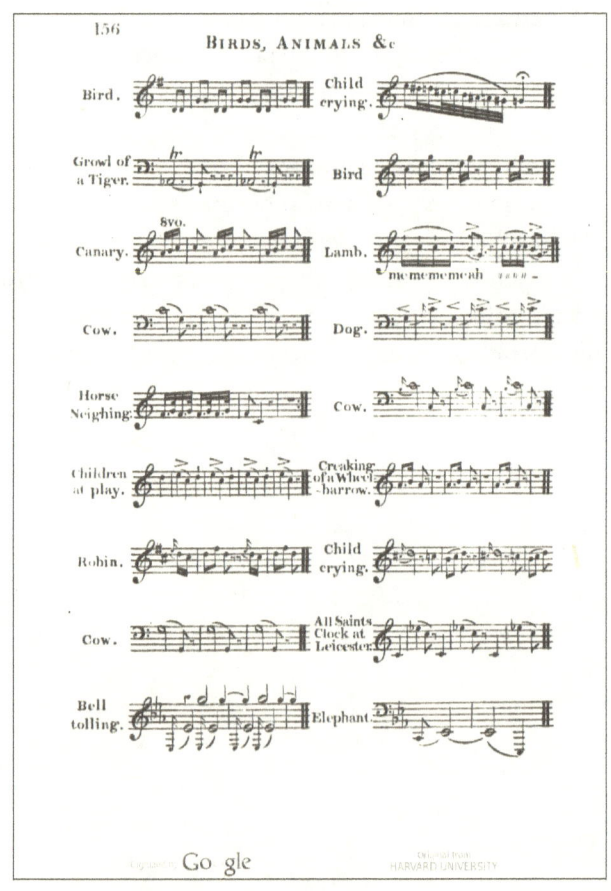

FIGURE 12. This is a notable page because of the eclectic sounds he gathers. Earlier examples are limited to one species (birds) or type of sound.

WILLIAM GARDINER'S *The Music of Nature* shows up in so many searches that it feels as if it echoes across the PPA. First published in 1832, the book defines language as "an art made up of sounds, by which we instantly communicate our ideas."[1] Gardiner's work is included in the category "Linguistic" because of its attention to the structure of language as expressed in oratory, though unlike many other works in the category "Linguistic," it does not include a "grammar." But as part of a broad history of linguistics, Gardiner's text advances a theory of language that nevertheless continues eighteenth-century discussions about language-origin theory found variously in Joseph Priestley, Lord Burnett Monboddo, James Beattie, and Hugh Blair, and it melds these with a sophisticated understanding of the sonic world: "In the dawn of society," early man progressed through stages of language acquisition like children, expressing wants and needs without language, "but as the mind developed, and our wants increased, means would be suggested, by the articulating powers to break these instinctive tones into particles of imitative sound; and in all probability the first words that were uttered bore some resemblance to the things described, as the boisterous roar of the sea would call for a boisterous expression."[2] Gardiner emphasizes the similarities between language and music as expressive: "Language, ... like music, is partly an imitative art, and has its origin in an effort to express the names of things by sounds. Its force will depend upon the use of the primitive tones, and its beauty upon the order in which various sounds are arranged. The present object is to speak of the English language, the basis of which is formed upon sounds of the most distant origin but stamped with great meaning and force."[3] Gardiner brings this eighteenth-century language-origin theory together with musical theory and theories of sound, and yet his main concern is about performance and meaning—both how to apprehend sound properly with the ear and how to perform sound eloquently (or roughly or badly) with the voice. Throughout the book, he argues that syllables resemble notes in music and thinks of measured language as musical composition (figure 13).

After considerably detailed forays into the problems with English, Gardiner expands his thoughts about vocal performance and aural apprehension for hundreds of pages. By the end of the book, he's made available his capacity for hearing music everywhere into a demonstrable score for any sound we might encounter (see figure 12). Gardiner's book qualifies, for us, as linguistic

1. Gardiner, *Music of Nature*, 44.
2. Gardiner, 31–32.
3. Gardiner, 34.

FIGURE 13. William Gardiner, *The Music of Nature* (London: Rees, Orme, Brown, Green, and Longham, 1832), 39. "The word *all*, in length of sound, may be represented by a minim; but the word *indivisible*, though composed of five syllables, will be spoken in a time equally short: consequently, each syllable in the last word is only one-fifth of the length of the monosyllable."

because it is protophonetic. It applies music and what we now call "sound studies" across the spectrum of vocal performance as well as details the ways that birds and animals are portrayed in music to bolster his thesis about music as the logical expression of the natural world. We classify the book as "literary" because Gardiner aligns with theories of English versification that discard the controversial longs and shorts of Greek and Latin and that adopt, instead, language about force and expression as accent in English music and speech.

It is a hodge-podge of a volume, but because of its generic capaciousness, it is a fitting synecdoche for the generic capaciousness of the PPA as a whole. If "poetry" is being judged as aesthetically pleasing because of the way a particular performer is trained to express or declaim it, how can we consider "aesthetics" without thinking through the specific historical moment when sound might have been considered pleasing depending on how close it came to the sound of one tone or another, or on how far it remained from the tone? What do we make of tone or discord when we put it next to the creaking of a wheelbarrow, the growl of the tiger, or the roar of the sea? The text presupposes that its readers are literate in musical notation. The ability to read musical notation, like the ability to read macrons and breves presupposing the recognition of Latin, signified membership in a social class: the social class that was being prepared to both uniquely create and uniquely apprehend the aesthetic universals of the world. Accent marks presupposed the recognition of emphasis in speech (codified by dictionaries and pronunciation guides for the layperson, even if these changes were also coded by dialect communities and shifting pronunciation). Phonetic speech guides and spelling reform movements attempted to do away with phonographic literacy. By the end of the nineteenth century, the linguists who codified the international phonetic alphabet (IPA) derived a system by which to measure sounds beyond what was possible in alphabetic characters, useful for them but not largely taught to students learning to read or pronounce. Gardiner's *Music of Nature* survives in the PPA and in our imagination of how language works—or how we often see its activation in poems: as if all sounds are of a distant origin that we can no longer hear, and as if under the rules of pronunciation and versification lurk some primitive art that will bring us to nostalgic (prelingual) past that, despite ourselves, we are always seeking. If that language sounds familiar it is because it is rewritten, in some way, into nearly every poetry handbook from the late twentieth century. When poetry is the music of nature, reading poetry should come naturally.

4

How We Express [Typographically Unique]

Pattern Recognition

The collection "Typographically Unique" is made up of works with pages that are currently computationally unreadable—pages that will not show up in text-based search results—and that are littered with diacritical marks. Both the collection and this chapter argue that what we see on a page can help us understand what we cannot see, how it can maybe get us closer to understanding what we are taking for granted behind the scenes of an interface, whether a screen or a page. How might we put opacity about "expression" in sound—a move from phonetic to semantic meaning—into conversation with how the visually apprehended digital image of a page does not correspond to the textual characters rendered computationally behind it (the textual characters that we rely on when we "search")? In this chapter, I put these questions into conversation with the new—and urgent—legal understanding that the scanned *image of the page* is another layer of "expression," as is the text generated automatically beneath it. But what kind of expression are we reading, where is it located, and when did it—or is it—taking place?[1] The author who wrote the original work, and the publisher who printed it, are both "out of copyright." But a new form of expression replaces the author's original expression in the digital age.[2] The expression at stake here is the new sense of digital "expression" of the scanned image of old pages, newly configured "works," as well as

---

1. I do not refer, here, to regular expressions or expressive programming languages, nor to the expressiveness of interactive media as in Wardrip-Fruin's *Expressive Processing*. One of the clearest accounts of regular expressions comes from Kernighan, "Regular Expression Matcher."

2. Cf. Saint Amour, *Copyrights*; Hofmeyr, "Colonial Copyright, Customs, and Port Cities."

Of | man's | first | diso|bedience | and | the | fruit | Of | that | for | bidden | tree | whose | mortal | taste | Brought | death | into the | world | and | all our | woe | Sing | Heavenly | Muse.

FIGURE 14. George Saintsbury, *A History of English Prosody from the Twelfth Century to the Present Day*, vol. 2 (London: Macmillan, 1908), 548. (This is not Saintsbury's scansion! This is Joshua Steele's scansion, which Saintsbury hates!)

the text beneath it. Google Books owns all these digitized images and the autogenerated text beneath them, whether they exist in hard copy in your university library or not. "Typographically Unique," therefore, brings together the pages Google cannot read to think about what computers can and cannot know about poetry (and why that unknowability plays right back into our cultural associations that poetry is "expressive" in some special way), and to defamiliarize what we think we know when we approach a poem written in the past.

The visible images of scansion marks on a page work to defamiliarize the act of reading poetry for us; they show us the layers of mediation that hover between our apprehension of poetry in the present and the possible readings of poetry in the past. The materials in "Typographically Unique" not only demonstrate the defamiliarization of historical sound but also argue for the theoretical and conceptual operations of reading and researching historical materials with page images online in the PPA, a process that should also act to defamiliarize what we think we know about poetry in the past. These pages are an accumulation of histories of reading, on the one hand, as well as an intervention into how poems are coded with several conversations about reading in their variously apprehended structures, on the other.

For instance, the lines in figure 14 are quoted by George Saintsbury, who scolds T. S. Omond's admiration for the prosodist Joshua Steele, whose scansion he presents here, from Steele's 1779 *Prosodia Rationalis*, as "contemptibly and impudently ridiculous." Already in this short, layered history, what Saintsbury names a "musical-mathematical supererogation, if not a musical-mathematical hallucination," we see how one man's rational prosody is another man's hallucination.[3] John Thelwall, whose scansion hews closer to Milton's

---

The field of law and literature, for example, examines often how literary characters are shaped by copyright law.

3. Steele, *Prosodia Rationalis*; Saintsbury, *History of English Prosody from the Twelfth Century to the Present Day*, 2:548.

" Of | Mān's fīrst | dīso|bēdĭēnce, | ꜰand thĕ | fruīt |
                                                  △ ∴
" Of | thāt for|bīddēn | Trēe, whōse | mōrtāl | tāste

FIGURE 15. John Thelwall, *Illustrations of English Rhythmus*
(London: McCreery, 1812), xlix.

Ov mánz férst disɷbédiens, and ðe frút	0-1-,½-0,01,00-0-,0-1-	(1)
Ov ðát fɵrbíd'n tré, hwuz mértal tást	0-½-,01,0-½-,0-1,0-1-	(2)
Brót dét intɯ ðe wúrld, and ól ɶr wó	½-1-,00-,0-1-,0-½-,0-1-	(3)
Wið lós ov 'Ɛd'n, til wun gráter mán	0-½-,0-1,0-0-,0-1,0-1-	(4)

FIGURE 16. Alexander Ellis, *The Essentials of Phonetics*
(London: F. Pitman, 1848), 77.

own line breaks (after "fruit" and "taste"), uses staves for foot division (not uncommon in the late eighteenth and early nineteenth centuries) (figure 15).[4]

Thelwall adds macrons and breves over vowel sounds (familiar to Latin students) and additional notations: the full triangle followed by a three-pointed triangle is the mark of a particular "cadence," which he describes as "a portion of tuneable sound (or of organic aspiration) beginning heavy and ending light."[5] This combination of elocution and meter is a complicated mix, and in other scansions Thelwall even adds musical notation. A right reading, in his account, takes a good deal of practice and breath control; verse is to be read not only with the eye (though it needs to be, since the symbols require it), but also with the careful modulation of the breath.

Alexander Ellis, in 1848, gives a phonetic respelling with accents, as well as a numerical key, in his *Essentials of Phonetics*, which takes even more practice and expertise to master than the system promoted by Thelwall (figure 16). (Though Ellis's phonetic speech did not catch on, it did form one basis of the field of phonetics.) His scansions begin to resemble binary code, but that little ½ is a "sub-accent," according to his rule; though we might "assume that sub-accents have the same effect on the ear as primary accents," that is "far from being the case" (translation mine).[6]

---

4. Thelwall, *Illustrations of English Rhythmus*, xliv.

5. Thelwall, xliv.

6. Ellis, *Essentials of Phonetics*. The "universal alphabet" Ellis included in his guide is explained also entirely in phonetic script, but, he states, "a universal alphabet can not be used by everyone, for not everyone has a universal knowledge of spoken sounds" (87; translation my own).

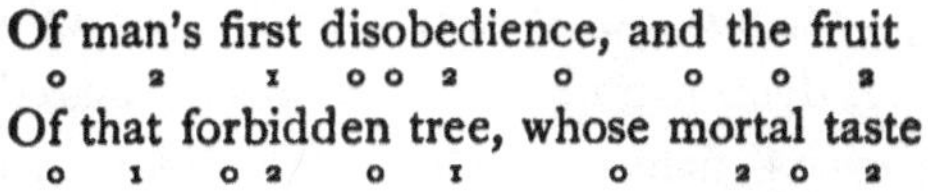

Of man's first disobedience, and the fruit
o 2 1 o o 2 o o o 2
Of that forbidden tree, whose mortal taste
o 1 o 2 o 1 o 2 o 2

FIGURE 17. Raymond Alden, *English Verse: Specimens Illustrating Its Principles and History* (New York: H. Holt, 1903), 4.

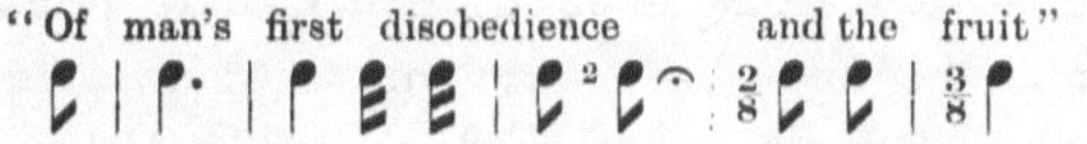

"Of man's first disobedience   and the   fruit"

FIGURE 18. William Thomson, *The Basis of English Rhythm* (Glasgow: W. & R. Holmes, 1904), 54.

By the early twentieth century, in 1903 (figure 17) and 1904 (figure 18), we find at least two entirely oppositional methods of scansion at play. Raymond Alden builds on Ellis's "more elaborate" system (in which Ellis eventually "recognized nine varieties of force of stress, which he named ... subweak, weak, superweak, submean, mean, supermean, substrong, strong, superstrong").[7] This quoted passage is Alden's translation of Ellis's revised and simplified scansion, from the *Transactions of the Philological Society*, 1875–76. Compare Alden's approval of three levels of stress to the scansion, the following year, of William Thomson, who argues for three levels, but three very different levels.

Thomson uses musical notation because it is "mutually intelligible." For Thomson,

> the understanding of a poem read so as to address the intelligence only must include a correct apprehension ... of the rhythm and the metre. And rhythm ... is said to be treated on the mid level, because there is an extreme on either side of this mean. On the low level, rhythm is treated mechanically as a scheme of sound rather than of sense. This is the rhythm that appeals to children and savages.[8]

He calls this the "heel" rhythm, as opposed to the "head" or "heart" rhythm. Thomson continues, "The high level, the other extreme, is that on which the emotions are addressed."[9] Whether Milton's rhythm participates in the heel,

---

7. Alden, *English Verse*, 4. Note, here, the collision of the scientific discourse of physics. One could map prosodic discourse onto a history of the sciences, with its changing nomenclature.

8. Thomson, *Basis of English Rhythm*, 51.

9. Thomson, 51.

head, or heart rhythm, Thomson does not say. These graphical representations of reading practices demonstrate that there was no shared lexicon of reading meter or rhythm, even if many scholars insist that there was, and that historical concepts of prosody are inextricably linked to the way that these various marks on the page, typographical symbols that are known mostly as diacritical marks, attempt to express these concepts.[10] These conceptual expressions, in turn, attempt to create shared meaning among different kinds of speakers and readers (whether or not they know Latin or read music, whether they apprehend rhythm with their head, heart, or heel).[11] Prosodists' and linguists' desire to uncover and display what they felt were implicit patterns in poetic language was an act of supplementing punctuation and pronunciation to elaborate and even exaggerate several other patterns that they felt were important to arriving at the correct understanding of the poem.[12] For each of these examples, the scholars believed—or hypothesized—that the correct marks could help readers recognize, and so understand, the correct pattern.

Though each of these attempts to code a line of poetry might seem alienating or off-putting (or perhaps familiar and comforting), the intention of these writers was to prove that their system would ensure that poems could be pronounced, heard, and transmitted a *right* way, in one way. The hope of the systems—of the prosodists and protolinguists who concocted and, in some instances, popularized them and lobbied for their uptake—was wide usage for students and speakers, greater accessibility to what they believed was the right way to read, speak, hear, and understand a poem's, and a language's, meaning. The collection gathers these various systems to show how inaccessible these attempts are, as well as to show how the marks themselves float away from the words and the poems and, in the digital environment, express something altogether different (figure 19).

10. Drucker, "Performative Materiality."
11. We could call this, as others have, a shared understanding of particular systems, like the accentual-syllabic system that uses macrons and breves translated from the Latin and the Greek, *a metrical lexicon* in the linguistic sense of lexicon, and yet even what was, perhaps in the early and mid-twentieth century, a shared lexicon is also historically specific and, for particular groups (linguists, most people who work on meter), is not an understanding that accurately maps onto how they believe language, or even meter, works. To call the most common diacritical marks for meter a lexicon we would need to qualify it is a deficient metrical lexicon—that is to say, people do use it and refer to it, but almost always with the understanding that it is not accurate and that a better or more sufficient system of diacritical marks might be possible.
12. See Martin, *Rise and Fall of Meter*, 44.

FIGURE 19. Close-up of the PPA homepage featuring the PPA logo and background image designed by Xinyi Li, with Gissoo Doroudian, *Princeton Prosody Archive*, version 3.12.1, 2018. Center for Digital Humanities at Princeton. Accessed June 4, 2024.

Scansion was primarily argumentative ("this is the way one ought to read a poem") and pedagogical ("here are the marks that will help you read it in this way"). As a method of interpreting a poem and of teaching how to read a poem, scansion is still widely used in the classroom despite it having fallen almost entirely out of contemporary critical discourse about poetry.[13] Even though it is still taught, there is no agreed-on method, no way of doing it that is particularly successful (though those who believe in one system over another in pedagogy *really* believe in their chosen methods). If I wanted to use a mark for stress in this manuscript, for instance, I could use " ′ " or "/" or "X," and I would have to give instructions as to how I wanted these marks to appear.[14] In the absence of any standard approach to teaching poetic meter, we

---

13. See the introduction in Glaser, *Modernism's Metronome*, on scansion falling out of favor with twentieth-century critics as they replaced "meter" with the even more abstract concept of "rhythm."

14. "On Scansion and Notation," in Perloff's *Infrathin*, n.p., is a recent example of this trend—a necessity to justify an often bespoke notational system in use in any introductory text (as well as more advanced ones, as in "Appendix on Scansion and Metrical Notation," in Glaser, *Modernism's Metronome*, 219). For a variety of contemporary marks for scansion, see Kinzie, *Poet's Guide to Poetry*; Finch, "Scansion Marks," 312; Nims and Mason, "Note on Scansion," 220 (in their *Western Wind*, which has been in print since 1974); King and Kurtinitis, *Being and Becoming*, 1023; Gross, *Sound and Form in Modern Poetry*, 2. I could go back through each decade, but this should be enough to give a sense of how pedagogical texts include short justifications for systems of scansion that are not alike. This contrasts with entire works devoted to the adoption of new systems in the twentieth century, such as Attridge, *Poetic Rhythm*; and, with poet Thomas Carper, the more classroom-friendly *Meter and Meaning*. I see both the scholarly and the pedagogical accounts of new systems of measure as a continuation of the historical work I gather in the PPA; in fact, they are often inspired by historical systems (e.g., David Aruffo bases

generally agree that the patterns we detect are *good enough* to make literary arguments about meter, despite the fact that there is always the possibility that someone else's ear might not hear the way ours does, or that someone else's understanding of meter might (and likely will) disagree with the pattern that we've detected and decided to mark a certain way, and on which we might base an argument. And though most scholars generally understand that our metrical lexicon is deficient, we seldom teach the history of the diacritical marks we choose. These "good enough" systems, particularly those that rely on accentual-syllabic meter and recourse to what we have named "Anglo-Saxon" rhythm, have long and complicated histories that we have chosen to put aside so that we can get across some larger story about poetic form.

Of course, expediencies of teaching require us to make all kinds of decisions about what is "good enough." Scansion in the classroom is an overdetermined topic, when we teach it at all, and it might be enough to name a historical metrical pattern and show our students what we think a writer intended or constructed and how a reader might detect and then express according to this pattern. That is, we can teach a concept of the "metrical contract" without diacritical marks. But if we want to teach the history of poetry, looking at these marks shows the history of broken contracts—places where some marks didn't make it into the lexicon. These broken contracts allow us to see the long history of disagreement about versification as well as to apprehend the paths by which the marks that may be familiar to us now (based on classical scansion) came to be popular (if still entirely deficient). It also reveals why and how scholars were invested in these ways of reading in the first place. Dwelling on the marks that we might recognize is as useful as dwelling on the marks that we might not.[15] By putting one system of scansion beside others, we can show students how unnatural, how arbitrary, one system of reading is as opposed to another. We can read a poem while also showing how reading poetry might present the history of reading.

This approach allows discussion of how some poems or traditions have been left out of the canon entirely (poems that rely on oral rather than textual

---

his *A Rational Guide to Verse: Scansion Made Simple* on the theories of Edgar Allan Poe; the accompanying workbook [Aruffo, *Rational Guide to Verse: Scansion Made Simple Workbook*] contains, according to its cover, "easy, step-by-step exercises!").

15. An extreme example of this is in *The Dickinson Composites*, a series of quilts that consist only of the variant handwritten marks—some diacritical—left out of modern editions of Emily Dickinson's fascicles: Bervin, "Dickinson Composites Series." See also Craig Dworkin's incredible *The Radium of the World*, for readings of unintentional marks of all kinds.

transmission, for instance), and about how it's okay—even interesting and important—if a poem doesn't "sound" right to one student, whereas it feels "natural" to another. (We can do this listening to performances of poetry, too, to think about defamiliarization in another way.) This process of approaching poetry via multiple possible trajectories and experiences of reading, both in the present and in the past, allows us to understand the constructed nature of our attachments to certain kinds of poems. The arbitrary systems of scansion in the typographically unique collection include—and purposefully make strange—"scansions" that readers of poetry might recognize beside new systems. They show some of the insidious ways that the systems we accept as "good enough" are themselves coded with bias, and how that bias accrues over time such that certain systems begin to carry the weight of fact, of history, of tradition. I don't ever want my students to believe that they do not have an "ear" for poetry because they cannot hear or read it according to someone else's system of measuring sound. What I do want is for them to think about why it might be easier for some students to "scan" than for others, and to think of these arbitrary marks as a way into the history of reading. Understanding these histories of reading is how we learn how to read a poem.

Close Reading and Distant Poetry

In late 2010, I first understood the promise of mass digitization as well as the fear that the kind of poetry I was interested in would be lost because of it. In October of that year, I attended the Victorians Institute conference at the University of Virginia, a place well known for its leadership in digital humanities. That year's conference was called "By the Numbers," and I listened to Dan Cohen give a keynote based on his research as part of the Google "Genius" program. This program had given him time, as part of Google Labs, to tinker with the not-yet-available Google Books Ngram Viewer.[16] When Cohen

---

16. The name of this grant is important; paralleling the words "Google" with "Genius" erases the projects that the so-called Genius investigators were researching and replaces the work itself with the concept of a person—in this 2008 case, white men, or groups of white men, who, aided by Google's implicitly genius technology, accelerate their original ideas. See Garber, *Loaded Words*; Gordin, *Well-Ordered Thing*, especially 166–97. T. V. F. Brogan argues that "genius" is a middle term in the evolution of the idea of inspiration and poetic ability from a belief in an external source (afflatus, or divine infection, and poetic frenzy, or divine madness) and an internal source (imagination and the subconscious). The only source for the extensive Wikipedia entry "Genius (literature)" is from Brogan's definition of "genius" in Preminger and Brogan, *New Princeton Encyclopedia of Poetry and Poetics*, 455–56. Cf. Redding, *Google It*. Google Books

flashed his slides showing the now famous n-gram confirming God's disappearance, the audience audibly gasped.[17] I wrote him an email during his presentation asking whether he could use his early access to the Ngram Viewer to search "prosody" and "meter" and "verse" in the Google Books corpus for me (this was before I understood the racehorse problem). It was both disorienting and exciting to see what Cohen was doing with n-grams. These new graphs and methods seemed to make visible a method of tracing long periods of conceptual change through distant reading (if we trusted what books were in the corpus, and we trusted what was being searched). I had come to the conference to think through how to tell the story of these prosodists who kept referring to one another and arguing, referencing one another in a print community that seemed to spill over into school textbooks and other formats like the newspapers and periodicals that weren't yet searchable at my library. They were arguing about how to count—how to measure—verse in English; my paper was titled "Counting the Counters." Though I was not completely enamored with the methods (I worked on poetry, after all), I recognized the impulse to measure culture by numerical means. The obsessive quantifiers of poetry and prosodic discourse from the nineteenth century had already taught me that the desire to quantify had a longer history than Google. Could the broader contours of literary history that these millions of books promised help

---

Search had been called Google Print prior to November 2015. BackRub was named for its ability to analyze "back links" that pointed to a given website. Even in 1996 they were committed to building a searchable digital library of the world's books, and Page returned to the project in 2002 when he asked Marissa Mayer, Google employee no. 20 and Google's first female engineer, to help test the idea by turning pages to the beat of a metronome as he snapped digital photos. It took him forty minutes to photograph all the pages of a three-hundred-page book. Norman, *History of Information*, also cited in Brandt, chapter 9, "The Ruthless Librarians," in *Google Guys*. A Google-produced video titled "Google Books: 15 Years of Preserving Knowledge from around the World" features University of Michigan librarian for philosophy Scott Dennis juxtaposing the Google Books effort as that which would save earlier texts from their inevitable fate: "This will eventually turn to dust. We were in danger of literally losing every copy of some of these books from the nineteenth century. Google went through all of this. I can walk through here now and we know that it's been preserved." After cutting to a female engineer talking about Google's mission statement and access to information, a crowd cheers for a rock star (Google) who is also a PhD student, and Google Books allows him to continue his research while touring with the band: "it saved my back from carrying so many books around" (October 17, 2019, https://youtu.be/zz_vG9b9dv0).

17. D. Cohen, *Searching for the Victorians*.

me situate the more local contours of prosodic discourse within the history of English?[18]

That moment of shock at the n-gram in Virginia was captured by Patricia Cohen, who published a number of articles in a series (Humanities 2.0) about the shifts in research ushered in by Google Books in 2010.[19] The articles focused on how "technology is transforming the study of literature, philosophy, and other humanistic fields that haven't necessarily embraced large-scale quantitative analysis." The "powerful digital tools and databases" were, at the time, tracking word frequency of two dozen words, including "God," "love," "work," "science," and "industrial" in British book titles from 1789 to 1914: "We can finally and truly test these and other fundamental claims that have been at the heart of Victorian studies for generations."[20] Dan Cohen's project "Reframing the Victorians" was one of twelve projects that Google approved in its efforts to attract digital humanities scholars to the Google Books corpus.[21] John Orwant, who was at the time the engineering manager for Google Books, Magazines, and Patents, "said the plan was to make collections and searching tools available to libraries and scholars free. 'That's something we absolutely will do, and no, it's not going to cost anything.'"[22] I felt strange being quoted in the article; I remember vividly that I was at the University of Michigan for a meeting of the historical poetics reading group when it came out.[23]

Most of us in the historical poetics reading group were already working on one form or another of remapping the contours of literary history, whether it

---

18. Underwood, "We Don't Already Understand the Broad Outlines of Literary History." The discussion on weights in the comments is especially prescient for thinking about how to understand what "history" is represented in the Google Books corpus. Cf. D. Cohen and Gibbs, "Conversation with Data." Crane's classic "What Do You Do with a Million Books" anticipated many of the issues that emerged in the Google Books era, as did Clement, Steger, Unsworth, and Uskhalo, "How Not to Read a Million Books," an early, now defunct, text-mining project. Sculley and Pasanek suggest how to proceed with caution in "Meaning and Mining."

19. P. Cohen, "Analyzing Literature." Cf. counterarguments in Fish, "Digital Humanities and the Transcending of Mortality"; and Fish, "Mind Your P's and B's."

20. P. Cohen, "Analyzing Literature."

21. Other projects included Andrew Stauffer's JUXTA Collation Tool; and David Mimno and David Blei's *Open Encyclopedia of Classical Sites*; see "Our Commitment to the Digital Humanities," Google, July 14, 2010, https://googleblog.blogspot.com/2010/07/our-commitment-to-digital-humanities.html.

22. P. Cohen, "Analyzing Literature."

23. https://www.historicalpoetics.com/public-events/dialect-poetry/.

was looking at women poets and the poetess anew, the circulation of global print and its impact on literary forms, the melodrama as a genre, or the formats of print and how the politics of reprinting impacted how literature was circulated. Many of our interests took place beyond the broad contours of English literary history already—the poetess, poetry from the colonies, poetry in translation, reprinted poetry.[24] But in that particular meeting of the working group, we were discussing dialect poetry. The kind of reading that we did together in that room in Michigan, discussing the multiple levels of mediation that go into the performance of dialect in print, was also taking place via the multiple levels of mediation that allowed us to find the works to begin with. We knew what we were searching for when we were searching online, but had we started our search without that knowledge, any words we used with marks for dialect on the printed page would not have shown up. Meredith McGill and Andrew Parker had already cautioned that the media landscape was flattening format, writing that "printed books of radically different sizes, circulations, and cultural weight are made equally available to readers, delivered to our computers through interfaces that render these texts not only similarly sized but also eerily rescalable."[25] Oral culture was largely already invisible in the print-heavy field of literary studies; now the print records of oral culture, the marks for performance, elocution, and the long tradition of writing poetry in dialect would be rendered invisible as well.

For that meeting, we read Paul Laurence Dunbar, James Hamilton, William Barnes, James Russell Lowell, and James Whitcomb Riley, among others; many of these works were digitized by Google, one by ProQuest; and several were scanned by members of the group. All of them were littered with marks for dialect, records of imaginary sound that gestured to the various communities that might recognize those sounds as such or, to put it another way, marks for sounds in dialect as modes of recognition but for fantasies of imagined communities. Staging of ethnic and racial types were mediated through conditions of print—Dorsetshire and Hoosier dialects, folksy pseudo-ballads, nostalgic fantasies about sounds disappearing, the ambivalence of naturalization and denaturalization in Dunbar's verse—in texts that were both discomfiting and charming. All of these were ways to read together what these poems might be telling us about dialect itself, the marks for sound in text that were not only

24. Underwood, "We Don't Already Understand the Broad Outlines of Literary History."
25. McGill and Parker, "Future of the Literary Past," 962; see also McGill, "Format"; McGill, "Literary History, Book History, and Media Studies"; Meredith McGill, "Introduction: The Traffic in Poems," in McGill, *Traffic in Poems*, 1–12.

capturing the concept of sound but activating it to signal—to index—a concept of language that did not feel immediate but felt powerfully located in the event of its imagined performance in the past. Sometimes print conventions of "vulgar" dialect masked the "sophistication" of poetic forms; often, introductory material in the historical volumes proved crucial to our understanding of what the various poems, from both sides of the Atlantic, were narrating. But the sense stayed with me that poems like these—not canonical poems that had been widely anthologized (with the exception of the poetry by Dunbar), but poems that were speaking specifically to rural locations, to smaller communities in particular—were even more vulnerable to technological erasure because of the marks above them that already signaled their resistance to capture.

In 2010, the only projects that I knew about that were even attempting to work with poetry and distant reading were coming out of the Stanford Literary Lab.[26] I was relieved I didn't have to take a side in the debates about close versus distant reading. The histories of a different variety of close reading that I tracked, with their marks and oddly formatted books, were not easy candidates for the distant reading approaches that I was seeing. I could find media archaeologies and theories of electronic poetry, hypertext poetry, and poetic experimentation, but except for the Stanford group, poetry and distant reading, at least in the United States, did not seem compatible.[27] Poetry resembled

26. Here, again, I mean historical poetry, not poetry produced in electronic formats. Literary scholars pay more attention to archival and institutional mediation via someone's poetic account of it rather than in their own research practices, with the exception of book historians and digital humanists. Cf. Dworkin, *Radium of the Word*; Dworkin, *Dictionary Poetics*; Dworkin, *No Medium*; and Dworkin, *Reading the Illegible*, for a genealogy of material reading practices related to contemporary poetics. Most of the experimental work that undermines the medium of the monograph either is based on electronic literature—Hayles, *How We Became Posthuman*; Hayles, *My Mother Was a Computer*; Hayles, *How We Think*; Hayles, *Postprint*; and Raley, *Tactical Media*—or creates it: cf. Montfort, *10 PRINT CHR$*; and the Software Studies series (MIT Press), edited by Nick Montfort et al., starting in November 2012. I am not able to trace the interesting overlaps between critical software studies, critical platform studies, critical code studies, and critical data studies—each have their own conversations, traditions, and discourses. However, I am interested in how, other than Dworkin, most of this work (including Matthew Kirschenbaum, whose reading practices melding book history and digital literacy infuse my own) focuses on contemporary rather than historical literature. It is our differently—not newly, but differently—mediated access to the literature of the past that is my main concern here.

27. The chapter "Potential Readings," in Ramsey, *Reading Machines*, posits several approaches to poetry reading that are concerned with tampering, tinkering, and reading anew.

advertisements in newspapers, and so it was not an easy task to train a computer vision model to detect them. Poems didn't work as bags of words. The field felt mired in debates about digital humanities at the abstract levels of "close" versus "distant" reading with little attention to the fact that our research had become almost entirely digitally assisted.[28] As I discussed in chapter 2 (in the section "Poetry after Punch Cards"), the way we read poetry in the Google Books era was to transcribe it and TEI code it in digital poetry collections across the web, whether a single-author database or poetry beautifully indexed and transcribed from the pages of newly digitized periodicals.

There were exceptions: Laura Mandell focused on improving optical character recognition (OCR) for eighteenth-century texts developing systems of full-text correction for early modern texts (EMOP) and crowd-sourcing platforms for correcting manuscript data.[29] Melissa Terras's work on Transkribus continues to accelerate the use of handwritten text recognition (HTR) to

---

Ramsay draws on Samuels and McGann, "Deformance and Interpretation," which also appears as chapter 4 of McGann, *Radiant Textuality*. The first distant reading application to poetry that gained a wide and influential readership was Long and So's "Literary Pattern Recognition." See also The Trans-historical Poetry Project (Stanford Literary Lab, 2016, https://litlab.stanford.edu/projects/transhistorical-poetry/). Natalie Houston, "Toward a Computational Analysis of Victorian Poetics," summarizes her three related projects: (1) the database project "The Field of Victorian Poetry" (1840–1900), which focused first on network relationships among poetry publishers; (2) a project related to the issues of OCR, which I discuss in this chapter, "The Visual Page as Interface," aimed at drawing attention to "unremarked material aspects of ordinary books of poetry," though the application VisualPage that she was developing in collaboration with Neil Audenaert (to retain page layout in document-image analysis in order to extract features such as line-length, margin size, line indentation, and the ratio of text to white space) was never released; (3) a project, "Understanding Poetic Style," that aimed to explore "how large-scale computational analysis of linguistic patterns can offer new approaches to understanding genre, form, theme, and trope; influence, and intertextuality; and cultural poetics broadly conceived" (508). See her descriptions of these projects in Houston, "Re:Search Technologies"; Houston, "Exploring the Idiom of Victorian Rhyme"; Houston, "Modeling the Poem on the Page"; Houston, "Distant Reading and Victorian Women's Poetry"; Houston, "Reading the Visual Page in the Digital Archive."

28. Among many others, see Fitzpatrick, "Do 'the Risky Thing' in Digital Humanities"; several articles by William Pannapacker, starting with "On 'The Dark Side of the Digital Humanities' "; and Matthews, "Millions of Sources."

29. Further, the issue of what image-based textual reading means in the digital environment is a discussion that has been going on for at least twenty years: Mandell, "Marking Texts in Many Dimensions"; McGann, "Culture and Technology: The Way We Live Now, What Is to Be Done?"; McGann, "Literary Scholarship and the Digital Future"; and McGann, "What Is Text?" Kirschenbaum, "Editor's Introduction," convenes a special issue of *Computers and the Humanities* ("Image-Based Humanities Computing") and provides a glimpse of the field

make digitized images of manuscripts more accessible, and scholars have also started using a tool called eScriptorium to facilitate text recognition on handwritten pages. In 2018, David Smith and Ryan Cordell, co-PIs on the Viral Texts project, published a landmark report on the state of OCR, "A Research Agenda for Historical and Multilingual Optical Character Recognition." There, they characterized a sense of collective apathy around the poor quality of OCR in historical documents.[30] The algorithms that were trained to detect characters were trained on clean, typewritten business documents from the 1960s, not on messy historical newspapers, historical typefaces, or historical typographies like the long S. The prevalent mood among humanists in the preceding Google Books decade seemed to be the same as that among the computer scientists—the OCR was "good enough" to conduct historical research since, after all, even if the machine missed one instance of a word, it would be common enough in the document, as Cordell points out, to be read accurately by the machine somewhere else. Were scholars to pay closer attention to the problems of OCR, or to any of the ways their digitized pages were mediated, could they then, in Cordell's approach, think critically about the distance between what they are able to read (a translation into text of the image of a word) and the historical conditions and stories that accrue to that original page as well as all the circuits it took for it to be visible to you on your screen?[31] Paul Fyfe also explored the histories of transmission that brought nineteenth-century newspapers to microfiche machines and then into the corporations that sold them back to us, or, as he elegantly wrote, "how Victorian data gets to now."[32] Book history, media archeology, and domain experts were theorizing the new landscape of literary studies, but my data still felt different—discourse about poems in addition to poems in excerpted forms as examples, made illegible to both human and computer eyes by layers of additional marks. What was the purpose of turning these already odd characters into machine-readable odd characters?[33]

---

in 2002. McGann and Drucker, "Images as the Text"; McGann, "Who's Carving Up the Nineteenth-Century?"

30. D. Smith and Cordell, "Research Agenda."

31. Cf. Cordell and Smith, *Viral Texts*. *Viral Texts* is the digital manifestation of Meredith McGill's argument in *American Literature and the Culture of Reprinting*, so it is no wonder his bibliographic approach appeals to me.

32. Fyfe, "Archeology of Victorian Newspapers," 546. See also Milligan, "Illusionary Order"; Kirschenbaum, *Mechanisms*; Kirschenbaum, *Bitstreams*. For a snapshot of the field in 2014, see Kirschenbaum and Werner, "Digital Scholarship and Digital Studies."

33. See Muehlberger et al., "Transforming Scholarship in the Archives."

The n-gram meeting followed by the historical poetics meeting on dialect cemented my concern that the squiggles, marks, numbers, and phonetic systems that littered many of the handbooks and prosodic manuals I had collected were unreadable, and more frustrating, that the poems that these handbooks and grammars used as examples—not to mention all the dialect poems we had just read—would be rendered invisible as well. For OCR to work effectively, it needed to be trained on patterns that are similar: all "A" images, for instance, should match as much as possible to fine-tune the algorithm's successful identification of that letter. For computer scientists, OCR was "solved" in the sense that it was good enough for mass digitization; why did a few diacritical marks matter? The features that these systems are trained to recognize and extract are characters (letters) and words; they are "image-based sequence recognition tasks" within computer vision, and I wasn't interested in making the odd characters readable by human or machine, because I understood that to read them, I needed all the culturally and historically specific information that I had just learned reading these poems with the historical poetics reading group; merely translating the poem more effectively into binary codes would not deliver that. It would also not deliver the confusion and misapprehension that create so much of the interpretive possibility, or what allowed them to make a critical impression as a way of reading both in the past and in the present at once. Scansions are not objective; dialect poetry does not correspond 1:1 to speech expression. The fact that technology has recently simplified language into a predictive tool that stands in for expression is not lost on me. But then, because I was both curious about and frightened by what technology meant for poetry's data, my questions focused on how to preserve the poetry of the past *as* unreadable, that is, unreadable without the important cultural contexts that the marks on the page were always pointing me toward. Just because we don't see diacritical marks when we read does not mean we don't import our own.

Reading Expression at the Interface

The poet's perceived expression in a poem is mediated by the critical apprehension of that poem as an object with expressive potential for the reader, or the imagined readers the critic projects. We interpret poetic expression via interpretive practices that imagine all kinds of abstract communication networks and information circuits. Even when the poet (or author) is not part of that equation, the patterns that we are trained to detect and out of which we make meaning "express" that meaning to us. We need a new theory of expression in poetry in the wake of "expressive use." From book history to software studies, the word "expression" is a central theoretical term, whether the most literal sense of expression in performance, its metaphorical use in criticism (consolidated under the fiction of the "speaker"), the expressive possibilities of apprehended patterns, the computational operations of regular expressions (operationalized lexical patterns), or the limited ways we are allowed to apprehend visual patterns on a digitized page in the current moment (expressive use).[34] Whether the author who wrote the original work and the publisher who printed it are both "out of copyright" does not matter, because the new "expression" made possible, or impossible, by the digitized image and its underlying code are now owned by corporations who are not the writer or the reader.[35]

Whereas the computer interface often masks the complicated markup and technological processes that facilitate our ability to easily read what appears on the screen, scansion foregrounds technical symbols and complicated diacritical marks to try to teach us *how* to read. The "proper expression" of a poem is usually imagined to be nontextual, or off the page in some sonic and social realm. Scansion does not always mean that we can or should be able to read "expression" properly, but it does mean that we can see how someone was trying to translate expression into directions for utterance that appear above a word—scansion, diacritical marks, and dialect marks are *textual* forms that rely on the possibility of an imagined vocal expression in order to work. Marks for scansion on manuscripts might be employed to make the intended reading plain—here is how the poem "should" be expressed. This textual apprehension is different from the marks above a dialect poem, which rely on the already interpolated concept of a "standard" national and class pronunciation (facilitated by other printed diacritical marks for pronunciation) to comment on those concepts. As historical residue and as evidence of our distance from the

34. For an account of copyright and reading in the digital age, see Tenen, *Plain Text*, especially chapter 3, "Form, Formula, Format," 93–124, and chapter 4, "Recondite Surfaces," 131–57.

35. McGill, "Copyright and Intellectual Property," is yet another arena where McGill (in a review of Decherney's *Hollywood's Copyright Wars: From Edison to the Internet*, 2012) calls for book historians and comparative media historians to work together: "rather than a reliable, external guide to the history of print ... copyright law should be read as internal to the history of media" (412). The same year that McGill published this article, Denny Chin dismissed the Authors Guild lawsuit against Google Books, ruling that Google's book scans constituted fair use under the law.

original texts, both kinds of marks present layers of opacity we need cultural context to read. Typographically unique symbols and diacritical marks on poems are opaque to contemporary readers; they should inspire us to think critically about the distance between our methods of reading and methods and contexts of reading in the past.

Similarly, OCR does not allow us to "recognize" the history of the characters it puts before our eyes: it is a method by which a computer is trained to read and render seemingly transparent the correspondence between the image of the page on which letters are printed and the text of those letters that exist somewhere else and are then translated into binary code. In this way the computer interface is the opposite of scansion, yet the kind of computational expressions that undergird our ability to read texts *about* expression on a historical digital page might provide a metaphor for the kinds of cultural information relevant to knowing how to read diacritical marks on poems. Many theories of the interface imagine it to be a layer—we see the page, then we click "beneath" to reveal the text that we can see as not corresponding exactly to its format on the page—instead of the image of a poem formatted as we might expect, we see the machine-encoded text itself, often formatted quite differently from what we might expect.

In 2017, Cordell laid out the pitfalls for humanists of merely bemoaning the difficulty of relying on OCR technology as if it could provide a 1:1 correspondence between the text file and the page image. He wrote, "To adequately theorize *any* research conducted in large-scale text archives—including research that includes primary or secondary sources discovered through keyword search—we must avoid the myth of surrogacy proffered by page images and instead consider directly the text files they overlay."[36] (In non-OCR poetry transcriptions, we also don't see the markup that is telling the computer how to format that poem with indentations, capital letters, and spacing.) Even what we imagine is the "real" layer of the text "beneath" the image file is still obscuring the several additional layers necessary to make us believe that what we encounter through the digital interface is the same as reading a book. Or, put differently, OCR is one of the many ways we are alienated from the procedures of transforming a physical book into its digital surrogate, made up of image files and text files and metadata, what Matthew Kirschenbaum called, in 2013, the .txtual condition.[37] Theorizing our relationship to the digitized page is

36. Cordell, "'Q I-jtb the Raven,'" 193.
37. Kirschenbaum, "The .txtual Condition."

complicated work; the immediately available expression on the digitized page's electronic "surface" is, for most scholars, good enough. To argue that literary scholars should become aware of the expressive capacities of a search's navigational "interface" in addition to the expressive capacities of a digitized page is an even bigger challenge. The PPA makes several arguments in its design that structure the researchers' relationships with the material structures of the database and the material texts that populate it.[38]

One of those arguments is that the history of expression might teach us, now, about our complicated relationships with the term. "Expression" litters seventeenth-century rhetoric manuals and appears in numerous tracts on the "art of speaking" throughout the seventeenth and eighteenth centuries. These formed the background of the more well-known "rhetoric and elocution" texts in the late eighteenth and early nineteenth centuries, which rose alongside new theories of pronunciation appearing in eighteenth-century dictionaries (with accompanying diacritical marks to guide proper pronunciation). In the nineteenth century, expression appears in overlapping discourses: it becomes the name for a branch of vocal training based on new philosophies of the human voice, so in that context "expression" means proper vocal training for dramatic or musical performance. Expression also continues along the lines of proper pronunciation as phonology and lexicography develop as concurrent conversations about how to mark standards for sound, and it is in this climate that varieties of dialect poetry proliferate. In the nineteenth century (though beginning in the eighteenth), more texts about proper expression for foreign speakers and those who wanted to sound as if they were a part of a certain class appeared—the prehistory of what would later become a well-known example of Eliza Doolittle learning the art of elocution in *Pygmalion*. In the twentieth-century schoolroom, expression was linked to recitation and was often seen as a terrible way of teaching poetry. E. A. Lamborn wrote in 1922, "there is one thing worse than reading poetry 'with expression': it is reading poetry dramatically."[39]

Whereas students may have been taught to "express" a poem in a certain way, following one method of elocution or another without any thought to the poem's inherent structures, critics in the early twentieth century leaped to

---

38. Cf. Mak, *How the Page Matters*. One might also look to the fields of HCI (human computer interaction) and science and technology studies for a deeper understanding of "user interfaces." Drucker, *Visualization and Interpretation*, sits at this interdisciplinary intersection. For the intersection of interface and manuscript studies, see Trettien, *Cut/Copy/Paste*.

39. Lamborn, *Expression in Speech and Writing*, 95.

defend poetry against *too much* expression, so as not to ruin what was increasingly being understood as the ineffable qualities of poetry's power. When critics talked about poetry in the early twentieth century, they often pitted the perceived "standards" of how poetry was taught according to certain rules of elocution (which sometimes did and sometimes did not follow popular ideas about versification) against much more abstract standards and rules about "natural expression." Or, to put it another way, oral recitation was yet another category that, like accentual-syllabic meters, was abstracted into something rote, mechanistic, and fundamentally opposed to the supposed freedom of "natural" rhythms and voices, even when those natural rhythms and voices were nevertheless trained to sound natural within a particular standard of pronunciation. And despite the continued exploration of what poems expressed and how they expressed it, much twentieth-century criticism is still divided among those who are interested in the poem in performance, those who are interested in the science of sound in linguistics, and the alternative to addressing the ideologies behind "natural" rhythm for English speakers—the concept of an abstract "speaker," and the idea that "poetry" was ineffable (but only certain kinds of poems).[40]

What does this do for how we read poems on the page? The digital and the print page differently materialize the problem of expression, but the theoretical abstraction of expression ignores both differently mediated conditions. When we rely on the impossibility of voicing a poem or a word as the subtext to our insistence that we are connected to an imaginary utterance in the past, we lose the opportunity to think about the material differences between the many concepts of expression layered in those texts. Yet when critics rely on a poem's ineffability or impossibility of being vocalized, they nevertheless rely on what they perceive to be the stability of prosodic effects: "echoing of rhyme, assonance, or alliteration, and rhythmic patterning," in Jonathan Culler's argument. In addition to "voicings," Culler calls these effects the "fundamental dimension of lyric," yet he mutes the fact that all these effects are textually mediated and each is historically contingent.[41] The ongoing lack of agreement, for instance, on how Gerard Manley Hopkins would have performed his poetry is a case in point.[42] Angela Leighton uses Culler's division between "voice"

---

40. On "the speaker," cf. Martin, "Writing of Sound"; on the speaker, "lyric," and people, see Jackson, *Before Modernism*. On the naturalization of rhythm, see Glaser, "White Things."

41. J. Culler, *Theory of the Lyric*, 35.

42. See Martin, "Prosody and Meter." See also Martin, *Rise and Fall of Meter*.

and "voicings" to sidestep any discussion of performance.[43] The possibility of your voice taking the place of an author's voice, or, rather, having the entire poem *take place nowhere*, is what Jackson powerfully names "the fiction of the lyric speaker," which "locate[s] the poem's conversation in a fictive space in which you and I can share intimacies and priorities without having to share personal information."[44] In this space—the *only* location where sound might be imagined as stable; where rhyme, assonance, alliteration, and rhythmic patterning never change; where you may disregard the poem's varieties of prosodic or linguistic meaning so as to quickly move past how any prosodic effects may have been perceived in the past—in this place the universal speaker lives. And this is how and why one project of historical prosody and historical poetics is to rethink this concept altogether: this concept of "voice" and "speakers" is what allows scholars who say they are talking about sound in poetry to set aside, Leighton explains, "not only drama and performance poetry, but also much of the heritage of black writing, from Langston Hughes to Patience Agbabi—writing which calls on the voice rather than on what Griffiths and Culler call 'voicing,' and whose logical end is the live audience rather than the solitary reader." But whose logical end does Angela Leighton mean, here? "My excuse then," she wrote, "is that this book focuses on the sound that, in a sense, stays silent on the page while shaping the labor of the ear through which it might, nevertheless, be heard."[45] A poetry held apart from drama, performance, and much of the heritage of Black writing is not one that interests me very much. Or, rather, Leighton's method provides a convenient excuse to disregard any poem that destabilizes the abstraction of expression, that closes the distance from a past "utterance" that might be considered "universal" and to make entirely stable any prosodic effects that might back up that translation. Why are the scansion marks that try so urgently to inscribe the possibility of expression so silent when the material artifacts of sound are everywhere to be seen?

The pages in the "Typographically Unique" collection foreground the constructed, the artificial, the arbitrary. They show the diversity of diacritical marks and typographical variation to teach researchers about the opacity of reading in a landscape in which we should not trust the underlying text of the page image. How could a simple keyword search transparently reveal the complexity of human expression (in all its valences) in the first place? How could

---

43. Leighton, *Hearing Things*, 7.
44. Jackson, "Historical Poetics and the Dream of Interpretation," 293.
45. Leighton, *Hearing Things*, 18; cf. Griffiths, *The Printed Voice of Victorian Poetry*.

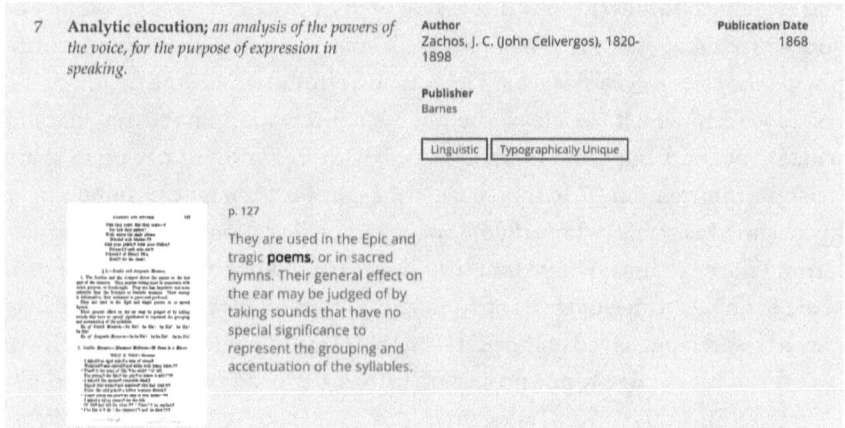

FIGURE 20. Screenshot of J. C. Zachos, *Analytic Elocution, an Analysis of the Powers of the Voice, for the Purposes of Expression in Speaking* (Barnes: New York, 1868), as a PPA Record, on p. 127, *Princeton Prosody Archive*, version 3.12.1, 2018. Center for Digital Humanities at Princeton. Accessed June 4, 2024.

a written character? Figure 20, figure 21, and figure 22 provide examples of the messy materiality of expression.

I reproduce the record here from one of the 705 records (as of 2024) in "Typographically Unique." Zooming in on this page, you can see what it is that the page "expresses": two examples of a particular system of scansion, based both on the accentual syllabic foot system (iambic) and on a ninety-beats-per-minute instruction. Looking more closely at the text displayed at the bottom of the page, we see the image in figure 21.

This image of the beginning section of a poem that appears on page 127, or page image 133, of *Analytic Elocution: An Analysis of the Powers of the Voice, for the Purpose of Expression in Speaking.* The physical copy of this book is at the University of Virginia Library, and the book was published in 1868. It was digitized by Google on December 17, 2010, and we included it in the PPA since it is part of the HathiTrust Research Library, adding it to our curated collection around 2014. Figure 22 shows what the text behind this image looks like in the HathiTrust Research Library "text only" view (you can see how the computer renders Zachos's eighth-note rests as the Arabic numeral 7).

Several texts in the PPA could provide interesting case studies for the bibliographic and computational work of detecting how particular texts travel

WHAT IS TIME!—Marsden.

I ásked·¶ an áged mán,¶ a mán of cáres,¶
Wrínkled·¶ and cúrved,¶ and white with hóary háirs ;¶¶
" Tíme¶ is the wárp of life,"¶ he sáid,¶ " O' téll
The yóung,¶ the fáir,¶ the gáy,¶ to wéave it wéll !"¶¶
I ásked·¶ the áncient¶ vénerable déad,¶
Ságes¶ who wróte,¶ and wárriors¶ whó had bléd ;¶¶
From· the cóld gráve¶ a hóllow múrmur flówed,¶
" Tíme¶ sówed the séed¶ we réap in thís abóde !"¶¶
I ásked a dýing sínner,¶ ére the tíde
Of life¶ had léft his véins :¶¶ " Tíme !"¶ he replíed,¶
" I've lóst it !¶ áh· ! the tréasure !"¶ and· he díed.¶¶¶

FIGURE 21. Close-Up of "What Is Time," in J. C. Zachos *Analytic Elocution, an Analysis of the Powers of the Voice, for the Purposes of Expression in Speaking* (New York: Barnes, 1868), 127.

SCANNING AND RHYTHM. 127 Fdst they come, fdst they come—1 See how they gather! Wide waves the edge plume, Blended with heather.77 Cast your pldids,7 drdw your blddes,7 Fdrward,7 each mdn set !7 Pibroch 7 of Donuil Dhu, Kn6117 for the (inset! § 2.—Iambic and Anapestic Measure. 1. The Iambus and the Anapest throw the accent on the last part of the measure. They express feeling more in connection with mind, purpose, or forethought. They are less impulsive and more reflective than the Trochaic or Dactylic measure. Their energy is deliberative, their sentiment is grave and profound. They are used in the Epic and tragic poems, or in sacred hymns. Their general effect on the ear may be judged of by taking sounds that have no special significance to represent the grouping and accentuation of the syllables. Ex. of Iambic Measures.—ha Hd! ha Ha! ha Hd! ha Hd! ha Hd! Ex. of Anapestic Measures.—hahaHd! hahaHd! ha ha Ila! 2. Iambic Measure.—Movement Moderate—90 Beats in a Minute. WHAT IS TIME!—Maksdkn. I dsked7 an dged mdn,*? a man of cares,*? Wrinkled7 and ciirved,7 and white with hoary hdirs;7"? « Time7 is the warp of life,"7 he sdid,7 "O' tell The young,7 the fdir,7 the gdy,"? to weave it well !"7"? I dsked 1 the dncient*? venerable dead,7 Sdges7 who wrdte,*? and warriors7 wh6 had bl£d ;7"? From* the wild grdvc*? a hollow murmur fldwed,*7 "Time7 sowed the seed7 we reap in this abode!""?"? I dsked a dying sinner,7 ere the tide Of life7 had 16ft his veins :«?7 "Time!"'? he replied,7 "I've ldst it!7 dh' ! the treasure !""? and' he died.*?7 7

FIGURE 22. "Text-only" view of *Analytic Elocution, an Analysis of the Powers of the Voice, for the Purposes of Expression in Speaking* (New York: Barnes, 1868), 127.

through the various institutional workflows of digitization and machine-readability frameworks. It is not a bug, but a feature, that the uniqueness of scansion renders these pages difficult—or impossible—for a human voice to "express" even if the books and articles in "Typographically Unique" were intended to improve the reader's ability to express the English language and poetry more fluently. We intend for you to stumble onto these images and to stumble with them. You cannot find the words in the poems because the computer cannot find them, but you can see the images of them now that you know how to look for them. If that convoluted pathway makes you think about the ways that both historical poems and contemporary digital pages are mediated, then we have at least made part of the argument of the PPA clear.

Snippets and Thumbnails, or Who Owns Poetry's Data?

If you put two hundred digitized pages of a poetry handbook next to one another on a large enough screen, you can see from a distance which ones have poems on them. If you step a bit closer, you might also see which of those poems, or, more likely, extracts of poems, offset a bit on the page, have marks on them. To create the first "Typographically Unique" collection, Ben Johnston hired an undergraduate to do just that with the page images we had collected: "distant reading," for that student, meant stepping far enough away from the large screens of collected pages and seeing from a middle distance which page might have poems with marks.[46] To find new examples of texts that are unreadable by OCR, researchers on the PPA team considered which words might be searchable around, above, or beside quoted poems or full poems with diacritical marks, and whenever we would find one, we would make sure to mark it for the "Typographically Unique" collection. (This same designation applied to tables, drawings of mouths and larynxes, and illustrations of gestures.) Many of the books that had "expression" in the title were typographically unique. But who owned these sources? We knew that Chadwyck-Healey "owned" the poems in its database, but these materials *about* the poems, which were all out of copyright, were owned by the companies that digitized them.

From 2009 to 2014, as we were first putting together these texts and trying to figure out how to create the project that would allow others to see these scansion marks and read the history of how poetic meter was taught and debated, the field of nineteenth-century studies was theorizing new reading practices and thinking carefully about what the digital age would bring to the study of the nineteenth century; activist scholars like Andrew Stauffer,[47] Dino

---

46. Now there are training models to find poetry on page images, with or without the marks, but before we had access to transformer technology, we had to trust our eyes.

47. Stauffer, "Nineteenth-Century Archive": "Even as the nineteenth-century printed record was being produced, people were overwhelmed by its sheer scale, and ever since we have of necessity relied on partial reading, specialized attention, and representative sampling for our interpretations of the cultures that produced it. Yet now, with the advent of multi-million-text repositories such as the Google Books corpus and the HathiTrust Digital Library, or more specifically (and for a fee) ProQuest's C19 database of 23 million nineteenth-century items and Gale-Cengage's ambitious new Nineteenth Century Collections Online, we are in a position to revise upward exponentially the number of texts that we bring to bear on our hypotheses. Algorithmic searching and text mining can guide us towards new patterns and connections that are only visible through the power of digital processing.... We can learn much about historical

Felluga,[48] and Laura Mandell built collective communities of practice to share information and connect digital scholarship across institutions.[49] There were rich responses that drew on and expanded the remit of media theory and sociology, as well as the idea that new platforms would be needed to support and adequately theorize the vast new availability of nineteenth-century materials. And yet these calls for action and engagement were not followed through—part of the collective apathy David Smith and Ryan Cordell diagnosed in 2018;[50] this apathy is likely why calls to support library infrastructure and digitization workflows often fall on deaf ears. Just as the necessary labor of historical contextualization that historical prosody requires imposes on the researcher to put aside their immediate response to a poem or cultural object, so too could the thick description of technical detail—even in this chapter—alienate scholars from the necessity of engaging with their mediated research environments. When it comes to confronting and navigating new technologies in the humanities, we reward a performative helplessness around it rather than a theoretical apparatus to reverse the collective apathy around the material conditions of book production and digital knowledge infrastructures. Our administrations provide no incentive to mobilize, work collectively, or to think

---

discourse through keyword searching—or at least, we can be pointed in countless promising directions for further reading" (336). See also Stauffer, "Introduction": Reading by machinery "has thus far been incompletely theorized; its practical consequences are still emerging. We all know that digital cataloguing, representation, storage, and searching of Victorian texts as well as their attendant scholarship are altering the vernacular and methodologies of the tribe" (64).

48. See Felluga, "Addressed to the nines," who advances his theory of the skeuomorph ("aspects of the book as we know it, like aspects of manuscript culture or oral culture, will persist as skeuomorphs even when put to use for alternative purposes") and argues that "we must take into account both the material and ideological limitations of our current cultural moment as we instantiate a repository of digital nineteenth-century scholarship" (311); and Felluga, "branching Out," which provides its own genealogy of the subgenre of writing about new research protocols and describes the branch project as offering "a new approach to history itself, suggesting that any given bit of historical information can branch outward in often surprising directions" (53). The essay ends with a particularly powerful assertion that the challenges of evaluating digital scholarship unfairly limit its possibilities for junior scholars in the field. See also Felluga, "Eventuality of the Digital."

49. Mandell, "Digitizing the Archive"; Mandell et al., "Navigating the Storm"; see also Heil and Samuelson, "Book History in the Early Modern OCR Project"; Torabi et al., "Early Modern OCR Project," 23; Gupta et al., "Automatic Assessment." See also Hill and Hencghen, "Quantifying the Impact"; and Schoen and Saretto, "Optical Character Recognition"; and Katie Trumpener's response to Franco Moretti in "Critical Response I."

50. D. Smith and Cordell, "Research Agenda."

through the shifting grounds of knowledge infrastructures in our increasingly conscripted and corporatized research environments. Monographs are rewarded, but they also keep us isolated by design.

Several scholars have provided useful broad sweeping histories of digital modes of reading, theorized new research protocols, and described specific digital projects that might advance or change the way that we ask questions in the discipline.[51] For most of these scholars, the concept of creating a new platform was motivated in part by the understanding that we would not have adequate or equal access to the materials that had been digitized, an understanding that motivated me as well. As Stauffer wrote in 2012, "to understand the complex meaningfulness of nineteenth-century literature in its social, human character, we have to attend to the interface, which includes both the hardware of the physical book and the software of the many processes shaping its material forms and formats in an historical frame of reference."[52] His crowdsourced project *Book Traces* preserves books that have the annotations of historical readers by inviting participants to upload images they find in the stacks. In the best instances, scholars had conversations about preservation and access with the librarians who had already been building workflows for digitizing materials and platforms for accessing them. Librarians had to also navigate an explosion of federally funded digitization projects—with funds often going to scholars with little to no understanding of sustainable information infrastructure rather than to libraries—just as they had to decide how to fund the proliferating available subscriptions to proprietary databases of digitized historical materials.

Because Princeton University Library was a member institution of the HathiTrust Research Library, we were able to negotiate access to the bibliographic metadata, the page images, and the full text and rehost it on our platform. Though it took nearly a year to establish the agreement, our access to the bibliographic API (application programming interface) *and* page-image and text APIs relied on our ability to prove that we were substantially transforming how these materials were being used. We initially requested a small collection of "typographically unique" materials to display, but as we learned more about how our project would present a "transformative use" case for the

---

51. Cf. Pasanek and Sculley, "Mining Millions of Metaphors"; Drouin, "Close- and Distant-Reading Modernism"; Martens, "Literature, Digital Humanities, and the Age of the Encyclopedia"; D. Cohen, *Searching for the Victorians*; Mimno, "Computational Historiography"; Heuser and Le-Khac, "Learning to Read Data."

52. Stauffer, "Nineteenth-Century Archive," 336.

copyrighted digital surrogates and therefore would fall under academic fair use, we decided we would build the database that became the first version of the PPA, with "Typographically Unique" as one of several curated collections. Thumbnail images allowed us to continue adding material to the "Typographically Unique" collection,[53] and snippets of text could often show us where OCR was particularly bad, in addition to providing enough contextual information so that we wouldn't have to click back into HathiTrust to look at a full work.[54] Even though it still makes us laugh, part of our agreements were intended as noncompetition clauses with Google. In *Feist v. Rural Telephone Services Company* (1991), the ruling reads: "Copyright assures authors the right to their original expression, but encourages others to build freely upon the ideas and information conveyed by a work.... This principle, known as the idea/expression or fact/expression dichotomy, applies to all works of authorship.... This result is neither unfair nor unfortunate. It is the means by which copyright advances progress of science and art."[55] After the Authors Guild filed (and lost) a suit against Google (2005), it targeted the HathiTrust Digital Library (2012 and 2015) to restrict users from reading digitized versions of text in copyright online. When we began our collaboration with HathiTrust in 2012, we already knew our collection would be restricted to books that were out of copyright, but we were not prepared for HathiTrust's intense attention to potential litigation.[56] Because of the legal determinations of the copyright cases against HathiTrust and Google, snippets and thumbnails did not violate the consumptive/expressive use clauses and therefore qualified for fair use—a snippet of text, like a small sample of a song or a film, was permissible.[57] Combined with the small thumbnail—just good enough to see whether there were any marks on the page—the snippet and thumbnail interface is now the main way researchers interact with the material inside the

53. *Perfect 10, Inc. v. Amazon.com, Inc.*, 508, F. 3d 1146, 1165 (9th Cir. 2007) justified as transformative fair use purpose the use of a digital thumbnail copy of the original to provide an internet pathway to the original.

54. "A snippet is a horizontal segment comprising ordinarily an eighth of a page. Each page of a conventionally formatted book in the Google Books database is divided into eight nonoverlapping horizontal segments, each such horizontal segment being a snippet." *Authors Guild v. Google*, U.S. Court of Appeals for the 2nd Cir., December 3, 2014, Petition for Writ of Certiorari, December 31, 2015, 8a (docket no. 13-4829-cv).

55. *Feist Publications, Inc. v. Rural Tel. Serv. Co.*, 499 U.S. 340 (1991).

56. We were very prepared, on the other hand, by the time we negotiated an MOU with Gale-Cengage over ECCO several years later.

57. US Copyright Office Fair Use Index.

PPA.[58] Our interface design, therefore, puts the snippet of machine-readable full text directly beside the thumbnail image of the page. Marks for scansion on the page appear beside their subsequent OCR errors; two otherwise invisible histories of reading, side by side.

Why Computers Can't Scan

Using a computer to map the tensions among computational approaches to poetry before the advent of the modern computer—as I did in the PPA—appeared exempt to the processes of computational literary study. The distance between the historical computational approaches that relied on authors counting syllables, for example, and the new computational approaches that counted syllables or lines at a much larger scale appeared a continuation rather than a rupture. Metrical forms—no matter how precise—have always been viewed as mechanistic and rule bound, and part of the desire to create an adequate system to measure the flexibility of English was, and is, a desire to explain what happens when a poet has read enough poetry so that some of the rules have become, to that person, natural seeming, natural feeling. This can take the shape of a particular rhythm in a poem or a reading practice that is attuned to the kinds of meters that would have been circulating in the historical discourse or in the soundscape. Noticing when a particular rhythm in a line of a poem might be imitating or poaching or altering other meters can give us, the interpreting readers, a sense of what metametrical conversations are taking place in the poem.

Meters are patterns that we learn, replicate, and recognize, and from which we make meaning. Marks for versification and pronunciation, performance and dialect express some of what we still need to learn about how to read the poetry of the past in context. Historical prosody can also show us the long history of how the patterns of poetry have been simplified into the binary values of "strong" and "weak" as well as the more nuanced attempts to avoid that simplified form. Though it is not at all comprehensive, I provide here a brief tour of a few distant reading approaches to poetry (both with and without scansion) to show the persistence of our cultural obsession with demystifying, through empirical means, the formal and combinatorial possibilities that go into the making and reading of poems.

Though Adelaide Crapsey will be remembered for popularizing the syllabic verse form the "cinquain" (2 / 4 / 6 / 8 / 2), she tabulated percentages of

---

58. McSherry, "Big Win for Fair Use."

A STUDY IN ENGLISH METRICS 21

TABLE I.

MILTON		Total No. of words	Per cent Mono-dissyllabic	Per cent Polysyllabic
Paradise Lost	I	5,960	91.67	8.33
	II	7,917	92.24	7.75
	III	5,566	92.07	7.92
	IV	7,700	92.74	7.24
	V	6,804	92.01	7.99
	VI	6,773	90.95	9.03
	VII	4,774	91.40	8.58
	VIII	4,921	91.45	8.53
	IX	9,010	93.01	6.98
	X	8,370	91.74	8.24
	XI	6,859	92.48	7.50
	XII	4,930	91.78	8.21
Total		79,584	92.03	7.95
Samson Agonistes				
Dialogue		9,465	92.04	7.94
Choruses		3,427	90.92	9.08
Total		12,892	91.75	8.23

FIGURE 23. Adelaide Crapsey, from *A Study in English Metrics* (New York: Alfred A. Knopf, 1918), 21.

monosyllabic, disyllabic, and polysyllabic words to try to "venture the suggestion that an important application of phonetics to metrical problems lies in the study of phonetic word-structure" (figure 23).[59] She wrote, "I have given first (in tentative formulation, of course) a specific conclusion with supporting data, and second a brief indication of the reasons for maintaining the general position."[60] To use numerical data was not an uncommon practice, and poems were measured not only by scansion marks but also by tabular data, as an excerpt from "The Order of Rimes in the English Sonnet" by L. T. Weeks demonstrates (figure 24).[61]

Early twentieth-century psychological experiments tried to record different responses to poetic rhythm with new equipment, but these experimental

59. Crapsey, *Study in English Metrics*, 13.
60. Crapsey, 13.
61. Weeks, "Order of Rimes in the English Sonnet."

Octaves	sestets cde fcd 1	cfe efc 2	cde eff 3	cfc fec 4	cdc ffe 5	eff ecd 6	eff efc 7	eff eff 8	eef efe 9	eef efc 10	eef fcd 11	eff egg 12	eff gez 13	eff gee 14	eff fgg 15	eef fgg 16	eef gfg 17	eef ggf 18	cde fgc 19	cde gfg 20	cde gfd 21	eff gfg 22	efg efg 23	efg feg 24	efg egf 25	efg fge 26	efg gef 27	efg gfe 28	29	Combinations	Octaves
1 ABBA ABBA	820	21	27	16	111	239	171		5	13		1	15	25	158	48	22	13	24		76	366		88	31	26	775	130		84	48	73	51	29	3477
2 ABBA BAAB	3				1			1					5	2						1	2					3								8	18
3 ABBA ABAB	9				2	2	1						1	1	1					8	1	1		7	3		1	2	1		15	41
4 ABBA BABA							1			1	2	2								5		1	1	1		1	1		1		11	17
5 ABBA ABAA																				2					1					2	3
6 ABBA BBAB												2																		1	2
7 ABAB ABBA	3				3		6					2								1				2	2					7	19
8 ABAB BAAB	3			2	2	3						11	2							4				4	1	3	1	2	3	13	41
9 ABAB AABB						1																		1						2	2
10 ABABA AABA	2												1																	2	3
11 ABAB ABAB	11							4				5	26	2			5	34	2	1		2		1				11	93
12 ABAB BABA	5			1	1	3			1	2	1	2			3	7	1		1	1			1	14	30
13 ABBA ACCA	50	1	1		19	13	25	2		1	2	67	9	4	1	1	16	73	15	15	5	49	16	24	11	12	6	25	438
14 ABBA CAAC	1															1			1						3	3
15 ABBA ACAC	3						2					5				2	1				1		6	14
16 ABBA CACA	1		2								3							1			5	9
17 ABAB ACCA	1					1				1			1	3	1		1			7	9
18 ABAB ACAC	4		1								1	3		2			6	11
19 ABAB CACA								1			1	1				3	3
20 ABBA BCCB	2					2					1	2			4	7
21 ABBA CBBC	1				1		2			1	1	1	2	1	8	10
22 ABBA CBCB						1		2	3			1	3	6
23 ABAB BCCB			1			3			5	1	2	1	2	8	16
24 ABAB BCBC	26				8	1	110	5	1	4	1	1	9	157
25 ABAB CBCB		1	5		1	2		4	1	2	7	15
26 ABAB CCBC		2					1			2	3
27 ABBA ACCB			1	2			2	3
28 ABBC CBBA		1				1	2	2
29 ABBA CDDC	4	1	6	3	3		59	1	1	1	4	24	7	1	8	3	3	1	1	18	131
30 ABBC CDDA									1	1	1	3	3
31 ABAB CDDC			2	4		1	8	2	1	6	18
32 AABB CCDD					18	1	2	19
33 ABAB CDCD	7	2		1	4	3	1	2	1279	5	1	1	11	1306
34 ABAB CCDD		1		2	1		3	4
35 ABBA CDCD					1	1	2	1	4	5
Total sestets	956	29	28	28	147	266	213	9	17	4	16	35	342	97	32	35	27	110	1952	127	52	33	872	165	121	65	93	67	5940

Total number of combinations of octave with sestet, ... 262

Sonnets in blank verse,	12
Sonnets with octave rime carried over into sestet,	140
Sonnets with four-stressed lines (S. T. Coleridge and H. H.),	2
Ten-lined sonnets from "Laura," 1594,	60
Twelve-lined sonnets from "Laura," 1594,	60
Thirteen-lined sonnets,	6
Fifteen-lined sonnets,	9
Sixteen-lined sonnets,	50
Eighteen-lined sonnets,	4
Total number of sonnets studied in this paper,	6283

FIGURE 24. L. T. Weeks "The Order of Rimes in the English Sonnet," *Modern Language Notes* 25, no. 6 (1910): 179.

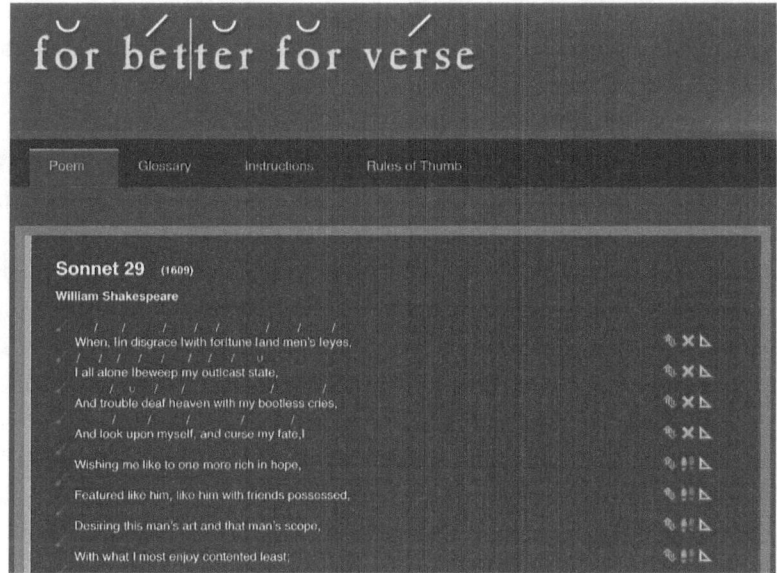

FIGURE 25. "For Better for Verse," Herbert Tucker and Scholar's Lab, University of Virginia, prosody.lib.virginia.edu. Accessed June 4, 2024.

forms, replete with racial ideologies of rhythm as part of the experiments, were distinct from the development of phonetics as an object of study.[62] All these graphical displays are collected alongside marks for scansion and other images in the "Typographically Unique" collection.

Collecting poetry's data is also a necessary interpretive step before building a metrical generator. Jason Hall has described the long history of automaton versifiers that fix language into the pattern that the concept of metrical feet provides. For John Clark's Eureka Latin hexameter machine, for instance, which was operated by a lever and produced Latin hexameters, Hall clarifies that it was not a Latin verse machine as much as a "fixed foot fabricator."[63] Compare this concept of a "fixed foot fabricator" with more contemporary examples of computational approaches to scansion, like Herbert Tucker's teaching tool, shown in figure 25. Transcribing historical poetry and then relying on the expertise of Tucker's ear, the interface of this scansion tutor codifies Tucker's expert interpretation of the metrical form into its display.

62. Golston, *Rhythm and Race*; see also Scripture, *Elements of Experimental Phonetics*; Wallin, "Experimental Studies"; and E. Jones, *Turn of Rhythm*. Most pre-1928 works cited in Golston, *Rhythm and Race*, and in E. Jones, *Turn of Rhythm*, are available in the PPA.

63. Hall, *Nineteenth-Century Verse and Technology*, 130 and 142.

"For Better for Verse" allows students to practice marking accents and foot divisions, giving them a green checkmark when they succeed or a red x if they do not.[64] You cannot produce your own versions of Tucker's scansions, but he does include some notes about why one poem might have a trickier solution than others. Tucker is a good reader because he has read so many poems over the course of his career; detecting metrical patterns takes wide reading, not wide scanning, to master. There is, in the end, little difference between instructions to read certain poems only in one rule-bound way (like a sonnet) and writing an algorithm for generating a sonnet: these are executable functions, and it doesn't matter much whether a machine or a human executes them. The same goes for writing. A machine will write a better sonnet if it *reads* a million sonnets as its training data, rather than if we feed it the rules and ask it to execute. And yet whose expression is that output? And what does it express?[65]

Charles Hartman's "Scandroid" is another program with an interactive tutorial; Hartman calls it a "self-teaching tool ... suitable for some kinds of research on metrics" (figure 26). Though it teaches traditional foot-based scansion, some of its techniques and principles of construction derive from recent decades' work in generative phonology.[66] He considers lexical stress in the Scandroid manual (citing linguists Kristin Hansen and Paul Kiparsky), and a careful user of the program would be able to detect it. (Ryan Heuser's fantastic "Prosodic" is an even more explicit "metrical-phonological parser.")[67] Setsuko Yokoyama provides a useful historical overview of computational prosodic generators, which all, in some way or another, rely on justifications or assumptions about what unit of measure is most appropriate—each of the computational examples contain an implicit or explicit "note to scansion." She concludes that even with sound recordings, "digital technologies may ... help address the notion surrounding 'authoritative' voices and intonational contours that are culturally constructed." Even our perception of sound, she writes, is historically conditioned.[68] (And contemporary scholars are ap-

64. Herbert Tucker, "For Better for Verse," https://prosody.lib.virginia.edu/, accessed September 26, 2024.

65. Cf. Stephens, *Poetics of Information Overload*, and Perlow's *The Poem Electric*, for readings of poetry's relationship to data, information, and information technologies; Funkhouser, *New Directions in Digital Poetry*; Reed, "Idea Eater"; and Funkhouser, *Prehistoric Digital Poetry*, for electronic poetry. See also Walsh et al., "Sonnet or Not, Bot?"; and Martin and Heuser "Historical Prosody and Mechanical Form."

66. Hartman, *Scandroid Manual*.

67. Ryan Heuser, "Prosodic." https://github.com/quadrismegistus/prosodic.

68. Yokoyama, "Digital Technologies for Exploring Prosody."

```
┌─────────────────────────────────────────────────────────┐
│ ○ ○ ○                    the Scandroid                   │
├─────────────────────────────────────────────────────────┤
│   /     /|x     /  |   x  %  | x /| x     /             │
│ Close bosom-friend of the maturing sun;                 │
│              ( Scan )  ( Step )  ( Save )  ( Cancel )   │
├─────────────────────────────────────────────────────────┤
│ words in the dictionary: /of//the//ma/tur/ing/          │
│ read other words as: /close/ /bo/som/ /friend/ /sun/    │
│                                                          │
│ PRELIMINARY MARKS    (CAPS = stressed)                  │
│ dict. word stresses:  / of / the / ma TUR ing /         │
│ calc. word stresses:  / CLOSE / BO som / FRIEND / SUN / │
│ any ambiguous stresses will be resolved in the next step│
│                                                          │
│ CHOOSE ALGORITHM                                         │
│ the Scandroid knows two approaches to dividing the line into feet; it has tried both, and chosen │
│ Algorithm 1 (Corral the Weird)                           │
│ (you can force the choice; see the Scan menu)           │
│                                                          │
│ FIRST TESTS      <begin Algorihm 1: Corral the Weird>   │
│ check line for first/last feet of abnormal length:      │
│ found none                                               │
│                                                          │
│ FOOT DIVISION                                            │
│ the line (or what's left over after any first/last feet) has the number of syllables expected in this meter, │
│ so simply divide into normal-length feet                │
│                                                          │
│ PROMOTIONS    ('%' used here rather than usual '(/)')   │
│                                                          │
│          [if you use this as a sample for the Scandroid, you'll │
│          need to edit dictionary for these words at least:      │
│          maturing (ma TUR ing), conspiring (con SPIR ing),      │
│          barred (BARRED)]                                │
│                                                          │
│                        To Autumn                         │
│                                                          │
│ Season of mists and mellow fruitfulness,                │
│    Close bosom-friend of the maturing sun;              │
│ Conspiring with him how to load and bless               │
│    With fruit the vines that round the thatch-eves run; │
│ To bend with apples the moss'd cottage-trees,           │
│    And fill all fruit with ripeness to the core;        │
│       To swell the gourd, and plump the hazel shells    │
│    With a sweet kernel; to set budding more,            │
│ And still more, later flowers for the bees,             │
│ Until they think warm days will never cease,            │
│    For Summer has o'er-brimm'd their clammy cells.      │
│                                                          │
│ Who hath not seen thee oft amid thy store?              │
│    Sometimes whoever seeks abroad may find              │
│ Thee sitting careless on a granary floor,               │
│    Thy hair soft-lifted by the winnowing wind;          │
│ Or on a half-reap'd furrow sound asleep,                │
│    Drows'd with the fume of poppies, while thy hook     │
│       Spares the next swath and all its twinèd flowers: │
│ And sometimes like a gleaner thou dost keep             │
│    Steady thy laden head across a brook;                │
│    Or by a cyder-press, with patient look,              │
│       Thou watchest the last oozings hours by hours.    │
│                                                          │
│ Where are the songs of Spring? Ay, where are they?      │
├─────────────────────────────────────────────────────────┤
│          ( Load New ) ( Type New ) ( Reload Dict ) ( Save Text ) │
│ metron: IAMBIC          feet per line: PENTAMETER       │
└─────────────────────────────────────────────────────────┘
```

FIGURE 26. Screenshot of the Scandroid Version 1.1. Charles O. Hartman. https://academic.hartman.digital.conncoll.edu/Assets/Scandroid-screenshot.jpg. Accessed June 4, 2024.

proaching poetry via new technologies of distant listening.)[69] Again, if we see the longer history of poetry and measure, these computational approaches are only the most recent examples of a long and interesting counternarrative to what is largely perceived to be unknowable or ineffable about "poetry," in fact, we might argue that they bring us right back around to the uses of versification to measure and categorize what counts as the literary.[70]

Poems are a test case for artificial intelligence now, just as they were a test case for intelligence in the past. The history of prosody is full of guides that attempt to make versifying easy, and the internet is full of poetry separated from its page image and fed into pedagogical guides teaching fixed forms, teacher guides, introductions to poetry. Most of these are abstractions of meter into accentual-syllabic feet, but others, as I have shown, are not. Poetry's commodity value for artificial intelligence has little to do with whether an algorithm can produce a text that we will recognize as a poem, or whether it can produce something we might read as a poem no matter what it was trying to produce. Michele Elam concludes, "at its best and perhaps most interesting, AI-generated literature and art might capitalize on how meaning is already and always an ongoing, mutually constitutive, interpretive event."[71] When Ryan Heuser presented a paper on why ChatGPT wasn't very good at scansion, he quickly realized that the problem wasn't that ChatGPT couldn't scan; it's that no one in the audience could agree on the scansion of the line he was using as an example.[72] Computers can't scan (yet) because the matter of meter and rhythm means entirely different things to different communities. The elements of prosody that reveal an archive of reading practices—from linguistic change and cultural meaning—capture, in the moment you encounter it, the poem's ability to be in the past and in the present at the same time. It is the image of this history that historical prosody protects.

---

69. For fascinating work at the intersection of sound studies and poetry, see Clement *Dissonant Records*; Mustazza, "Machine-Aided Close Listening"; MacArthur, Zellou, and Miller, "Beyond Poet Voice"; and MacArthur, Rambsy, et al., "101 Black Women." For an earlier history of recorded poetry, see Camlot, *Phono-poetics*.

70. There are too many models of autogenerated poetry to list. Here are a couple that preceded GPTs: Bryan Winston, "Blackout Poetry Maker," https://glitch.com/~blackoutpoetry; Rory Green, "Generative Poem Template," https://glitch.com/~generative-poem-template. See also Slater, "Post-automation Poetics"; and Elam, "Poetry Will Not Optimize."

71. Elam, "Poetry Will Not Optimize," 295.

72. Conversation with Ryan Heuser, whose program "Prosodic" is the closest to being able to teach a computer to scan according to a more sophisticated, less reductive linguistic method.

EXHIBIT E: ILLUSTRATION

John Thelwall. *Selections for the Illustration of a Course of Instructions on the Rhythmus and Utterance of the English Language: With an Introductory Essay on the Application of Rhythmical Science to the Treatment of Impediments, and the Improvement of Our National Oratory; And an Elementary Analysis of the Science and Practice of Elocution, Composition, &c.* J. M'Creery, Black-Horse-Court; and Sold by Messrs. Arch, Cornhill; Ridgeway, Piccadilly; Kent, Holborn: and Harwood, Great Russell-Street, 1812 (figure 27).
[Typographically Unique] [Literary] [Linguistic] [Original Bibliography]

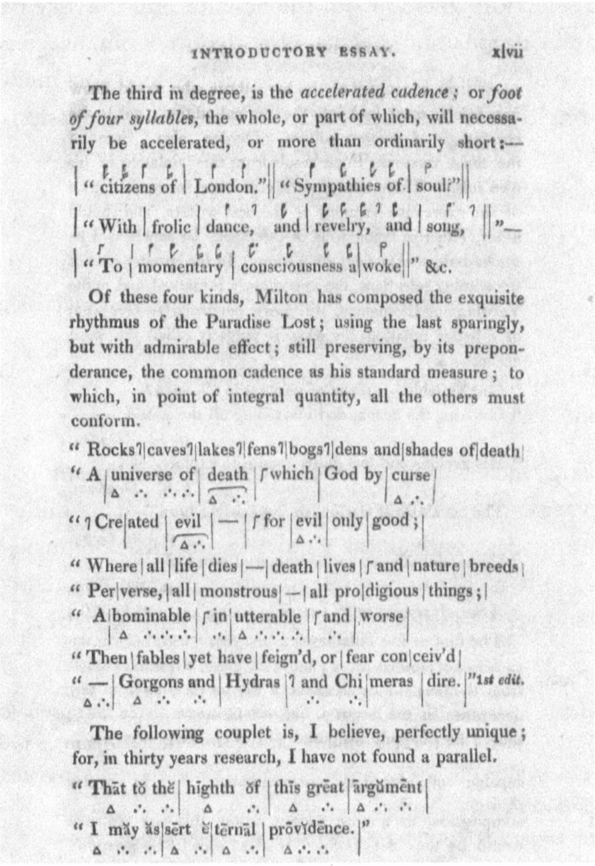
INTRODUCTORY ESSAY. xlvii

The third in degree, is the *accelerated cadence;* or *foot of four syllables*, the whole, or part of which, will necessarily be accelerated, or more than ordinarily short:—

| "citizens of | London." || "Sympathies of | soul?" ||
| "With | frolic | dance, and | revelry, and | song, || "—
| "To | momentary | consciousness a|woke ||" &c.

Of these four kinds, Milton has composed the exquisite rhythmus of the Paradise Lost; using the last sparingly, but with admirable effect; still preserving, by its preponderance, the common cadence as his standard measure; to which, in point of integral quantity, all the others must conform.

"Rocks|caves|lakes|fens|bogs|dens and|shades of|death|
"A | universe of | death | which | God by | curse |
"Cre|ated | evil | — | for | evil | only | good; |
"Where | all | life | dies | — | death | lives | and | nature | breeds |
"Per|verse, | all | monstrous | — | all pro|digious | things; |
"A|bominable | in|utterable | and | worse |
"Then | fables | yet have | feign'd, or | fear con|ceiv'd |
"— | Gorgons and | Hydras | and Chi|meras | dire. |" *1st edit.*

The following couplet is, I believe, perfectly unique; for, in thirty years research, I have not found a parallel.

"Thăt tŏ thĕ | highth ŏf | thīs grēat | ărgŭmēnt |
"I măy ăs|sērt ĕ|tērnăl | prōvĭdĕnce. |"

FIGURE 27.

Thelwall's "Introductory Lecture" is known as one origin story for British speech therapy, and he is among a long line of writers who blended the elocutionary and rhetorical aspects of oratory with a corrective for a variety of perceived ailments.[1] Thelwall's is the most well-known text in the exhibits. He associated with famous philologist Horne Tooke, and he was tried for treason for his revolutionary activity with the Corresponding Society.[2] He features prominently in accounts of William Wordsworth, Samuel Taylor Coleridge, and William Godwin's radical years.[3] The physical basis for his prosody, its grounding in breath and sound in addition to music, is allegorized in his own writing and continued in the writing of many scholars of Romanticism. Prosody's ability to augment aesthetic appreciation coexisted with its status as a science in the eighteenth century, one that Thelwall felt he was engaging with and adding to, according to scholars Courtney Weiss Smith and Joshua Swidzinski.[4] The selection "Elements of the Science and Practice of Elocution, Rhythmus and Composition" begins, "The theory of human speech is an important branch of Natural Philosophy."[5] For all the focus on Thelwall's "thinking through one's body" and attention to "the throb and remission of the pulse, the ebb and flow of the breath, and the stroke and counter stroke of the pendulum," he nevertheless tried to ground his theories in what he believed to be scientific and physiological fact.[6] His recourse to the "primary law of pulsation and remission" via the organ of the voice still reverberates through contemporary discussions of rhythm. But it is not natural. Thelwall's method was prescriptive and required several additional marks on the page in order to properly guide the voice. Here is how he describes his method of pedagogy, in his section "Praxis":

> In exercising himself upon these successive articles, the student is expected to scan every cadence into its correct quantity; to score out every passage into its proper bars, with all the regularity of a piece of music; and to read them over, reiteratedly, under the regulation of a time beater,—sometimes solo, and sometimes in chorus; sometimes accompanied by the voice of the

1. Rockey, "John Thelwall."
2. See Thelwall, *Poems Written in Close Confinement*; see also Thompson, *John Thelwall in the Wordsworth Circle*; and Wolfson, *Romantic Interactions*. Julia Carlson considers Thelwall's marks on Wordsworth's poem *The Excursion* in chapter 7 of *Romantic Marks and Measures*.
3. Roe, *Wordsworth and Coleridge*.
4. C. Smith, *Empiricist Devotions*; Swidzinski, "Poetic Numbers."
5. Thelwall, *Selections*, xxvii.
6. See the introduction to Thompson, *John Thelwall: Selected Poetry and Poetics*.

tutor, and sometimes without such guidance;—while the critical ear of the tutor, watches every tone and every quantity, not of the cadence and the syllable only, but of every element; so that the liquids, in particular, may sustain their due preponderance of quantity and inflection: which is the only efficient preservative against a tuneless cluttering, on the one hand, and that soporific drawl and drone, or that vulgar sing-song style, on the other, which so often disgust the ear in reading, and occasionally even speech.[7]

In Thelwall we have many strands of prosodic reading practices at once—derived from eighteenth-century natural philosophy, read as a Romanticist with a grounding in natural pulses that could lead to societal influence, and echoing through the nineteenth century to Patmore and others who would revisit his work to connect the measurement of English poetry to the properly trained English body.

There is very little in Thelwall's method that is not also found in Joshua Steele's manual, published in 1775 (figure 28).[8] Thelwall only adapts it a bit and renames some of the terms with an overlay of physiology. Thelwall's text reminds us that even the figures who stand out as original prosodists are in conversation with—and are likely building on—the work that came before them. Goold Brown provides an extended network of prosodic critics in his *Grammar of Grammars* as both citations and discussants, and Edward Bysshe translates (without acknowledging) Claude Lancelot (which Charles Gildon calls out 1721), but his rhymes and rules get reprinted in Thomas Hood's 1869 *The Rules of Rhyme*, which is then reprinted several times as *The Rhymester*. "History" and "tracing" and "narrative" are in many ways the wrong words, but "network" also doesn't quite work. Prosodic discourse is recursive, iterative; and Thelwall shows this not only in the way he adjusts and adapts Steele's peculiar symbols, but because of the way that Steele's adapted symbols become part of the history of Romantic poetic meters, with desire for a poetic expression that is at once unmediated and natural at the same time.

To map a recursive, nonteleological discourse about English poetic meter requires something like a digital archive. Data structures carry implicit and explicit connections between items in a database, and these are built into the way that the researcher can discover material. Rather than search only by author or title, the PPA encourages researchers to explore by keyword or

7. Thelwall, *Selections*, xxii.
8. Steele, *Essay toward Establishing*, 28.

[28]

shall be nearly divided under the several degrees of emphasis of heavy (△), light (∴), and lightest (..); as thus,

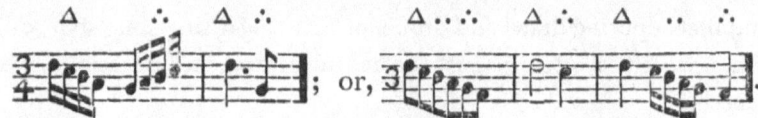

Having premised so much, I will now give a general precept and example in the following sentence:

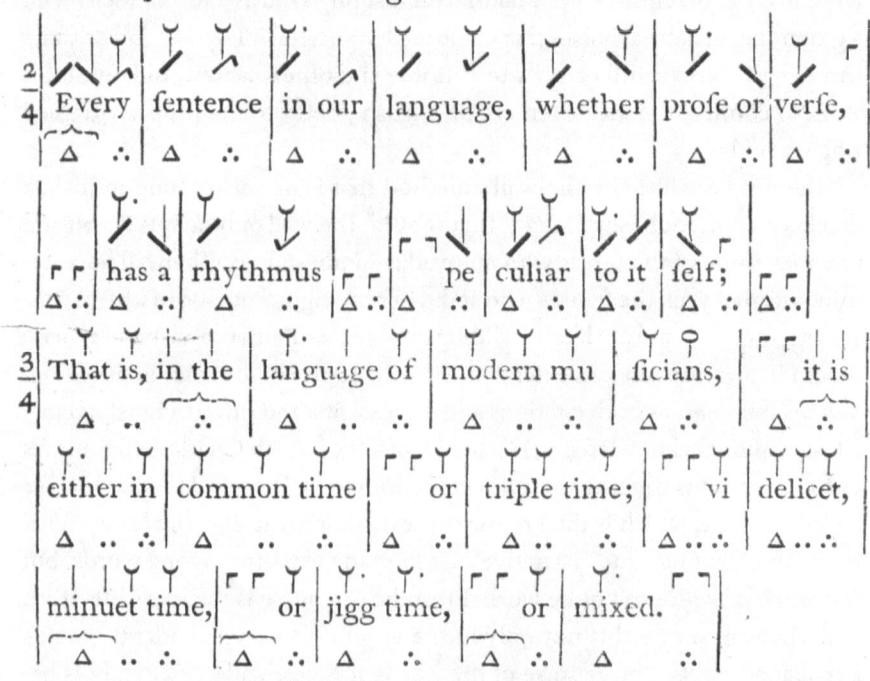

FIGURE 28. Joshua Steele, *Prosodia Rationalis: Or, an Essay toward Establishing the Melody and Measure of Speech, to Be Expressed and Perpetuated by Peculiar Symbols* (London: J. Nichols, 1779), 28.

collection rather than go straight to what they might be looking for. The search includes both full-text data and metadata, so authors' books appear alongside other authors who have mentioned them. It's not a citation network, but it aims to reveal connections between thinkers and concepts. Researchers can choose one collection or several as they search, but the structure of search requires a bit of meandering, a bit of scrolling, and even, we hope, some serendipity.

It would be impossible to replicate the experience of overlapping discourses that we tried to build into the PPA in a monograph. T. V. F. Brogan, the author whose work inspired and preceded the PPA, confronted the same limitations of the monograph in his own attempt to tell the story of prosody as an archive over forty years ago. Because of his work, I learned that there was more to the story of English meter than I had been taught, and I also learned that the affordances of technology might be the only way to teach others about the vast possibilities of English prosody's recursive stories.

5

How We Argue
[Original Bibliography]

Elements and Structures

"Original Bibliography" presents a historical snapshot of the texts that were available to T. V. F. Brogan at the time he compiled his reference guide, in the late 1970s, using traditional library catalogs, before the era of online catalogs and digitized searching. The collection formerly known as "Brogan" consists of all the works that appear in sections "A–K" of Brogan's *English Versification, 1570–1980: A Reference Guide with a Global Appendix* (*EVRG*), published by Johns Hopkins University Press in 1981. This chapter also outlines how he reimagined the reference guide, in the late 1990s, as a hypertext resource, and how his ongoing research in both prosody and technology positioned him to spearhead and oversee the monumental undertaking of editing what would become, in 1993, *The New Princeton Encyclopedia of Poetry and Poetics*.[1] In each of these moments, he was confronted with disciplinary and technological barriers that required him to reimagine what was possible within the existing information ecosystem.

---

1. The first "edition," titled *Encyclopedia of Poetry and Poetics*, edited by Preminger (and listing Warnke and Hardison as associate editors), was published in 1965, followed by an enlarged edition in 1974, also edited by Preminger (again listing associate editors Warnke and Hardison), which became known as the second edition. *The New Princeton Encyclopedia of Poetry and Poetics*, edited by Preminger and Brogan, was technically the third edition, but only the 2012 *Princeton Encyclopedia of Poetry and Poetics* (edited by Greene and Cushman, and listing Cavanagh, Ramazani, and Rouzer as associate editors) removes the "new" in the title and advertises itself as the fourth edition.

This chapter, then, is about exceeding the resources and methods of the available organizational structures for our research, and the frustrations of using technology to try to make those arguments in new ways, but it is also about what we learn by this process—what new connections and epistemologies emerge in moving away from the narrative structures of linear arguments in monograph form. Our relational database, inspired by Brogan's work, attempts to model a structure of discovery and reveals what the historical data about poems can teach us about reading poetry in the remediated digital environment. Both this book and *EVRG* attempt to critique the largely invisible knowledge structures that uphold modern literary criticism, and the institutional infrastructures on which they are built, by proposing new ways of navigating scholarly materials and imagining different models for scholarship. Brogan's work is a case study of how the model of an autonomous single author gathering resources and making claims in an argumentative monograph is not, and has not been, the only way that knowledge about poetry's data circulates and influences how we read poems. His career, from the compiler of a multi-argument reference guide to the editor of *The New Princeton Encyclopedia of Poetry and Poetics*, was on the margins of a profession that preferred his labor to remain invisible and adjunct to the mission of the academy. Our disciplinary lack of recognition for models of knowledge production that are not monographs means that these alternative models—reference guides, databases, and yes, even (and especially) teaching—have a profound yet undercredited influence on what we do and how we approach our work, partly because they, too, have arguments that we do not know how to read.[2]

Imagine undertaking a project like the one Brogan decided to undertake in the 1980s, knowing that the analog structure for a comprehensive reference guide needed to reflect the subject's historical and contemporary complexity:

> This book is intended to collect, list, classify by subject, summarize, describe, generally evaluate, cross-reference, and index by poet and by author all known printed studies of English versification from their origin in the Renaissance, Roger Ascham's *The Scholemaster* in 1570, up to January 1980, the year 1979 being the last for which complete bibliographical indexing is available.[3]

---

2. See, for instance, Heffernan and Buurma, *Teaching Archive*.
3. T. V. F. Brogan, *EVRG*, xiii.

Brogan began this project with what he described in a 2010 interview as an "enormous card file—a plywood box with five thousand cards in it, about two feet wide by three feet deep, 4 × 6 notecards."[4] He refers to the plywood box as a "file," and he keeps the structure of cross-referencing on the notecards themselves. Collect, list, classify by subject, summarize, describe, generally evaluate, cross-reference, index by poet and by author: though these are now methods with protocols in research data management, they are still not considered central to our project as literary scholars. Brogan's research guide did not count as a dissertation, just as I know that graduate students who undertake similar data-gathering projects are often advised to minimize the story of that labor, to put the interpretive data work into an appendix if they acknowledge it at all. This labor is adjunct to what is still seen as the real work of a dissertation or a monograph, rather than credited as interpretive and transformative on its own—not because it does not deserve this credit, but because the profession has not bothered to learn enough about it to evaluate it as such. Brogan's multiple data sets, data structures, and innovative classification scheme allowed him to see the connections between and among discourses that he would eventually draw into a time line charting the development of modern English metrical theory. It was this classification scheme and the map that would make it possible for him to write his dissertation in about a month (figure 29 and figure 30).

There are two concurrent data structures in *EVRG*. The regular table of contents shaped one approach to versification, leading us through histories of sound and rhythm before we arrive at meter. The second, more complicated cross-referencing data structure highlights the intertextual history of versification. Like the PPA, Brogan's *EVRG* exceeded the possible organizational structures of a book in order to foreground multiple and often recursive paths through literary history. His annotations make plain how, as readers and researchers, our choices about versification rely on models. In one of our interviews, he recalled how the time line emerged:

> It all arose because I had all these cards, this big clump that said "meter," and I could structure it by "theories" and by "praxis." I realized I needed the diagram, and I did the diagram, and the diagram gave me the idea for the dissertation. Everybody brings a model, and the models are largely individual. I mean there are plenty of crackpots in the field, and they make up

---

4. T. V. F. Brogan, interview with Meredith Martin.

```
                                           Citation
                                           Prefix       Page
     Introduction                                        xi
     Acknowledgments                                    xxvii
     List of Abbreviations                              xxix


                  Part 1:   MODERN ENGLISH VERSE
                            (since Wyatt)

  I.  Primary References                      A           3
      1 Histories                                         5
      2 Collections of Essays                            13
      3 Earlier Bibliographies                           15

 II.  General Studies                         B          17

III.  The Poem:  Elements and Structures                 51
      4 Sound                                 C          53
           Pronunciation                                 54
           General Studies                               57
           Alliteration, Assonance, Consonance           69
                in language                              69
                in poetry                                71
           Rhyme                                         77
                in language                              78
                in poetry                                79
           Sonal Mimesis                                 97
                in language (Phonetic Symbolism)         98
                in poetry (Onomatopoeia)                103
      5 Rhythm                                D         109
           Linguistic Rhythm                            110
                General                                 110
                Stress                                  113
                Pitch                                   119
                Timing                                  120
           Kinesthetic Rhythm                           122
           Prose Rhythm                                 125
           Poetic Rhythm                                130
      6 Meter                                 E         141
           General Studies                              144

                  (Schools of Metrists)                 164
           Quantitative Metrics                         164
           Temporal Metrics                             193
                Musical                                 209
                Acoustic                                226
```

FIGURE 29. T. V. F. Brogan, table of contents, *English Versification, 1570–1980: A Reference Guide with a Global Appendix* (Baltimore: Johns Hopkins University Press, 1981).

shit, but mostly there are models—in the nineteenth century, classical philology ran their little boats up and down; twentieth-century linguistics, eighteenth-century music, sixteenth-century music of the spheres, Middle Ages something else, old English something else, all obvious: models, largely, mostly wrong. But people used them anyway. At least to some degree they used them anyway because they were helpful.[5]

5. Brogan. Brogan's phrasing here ("all obvious: models, largely, mostly wrong. But people used them anyway. At least to some degree they used them anyway because they were helpful")

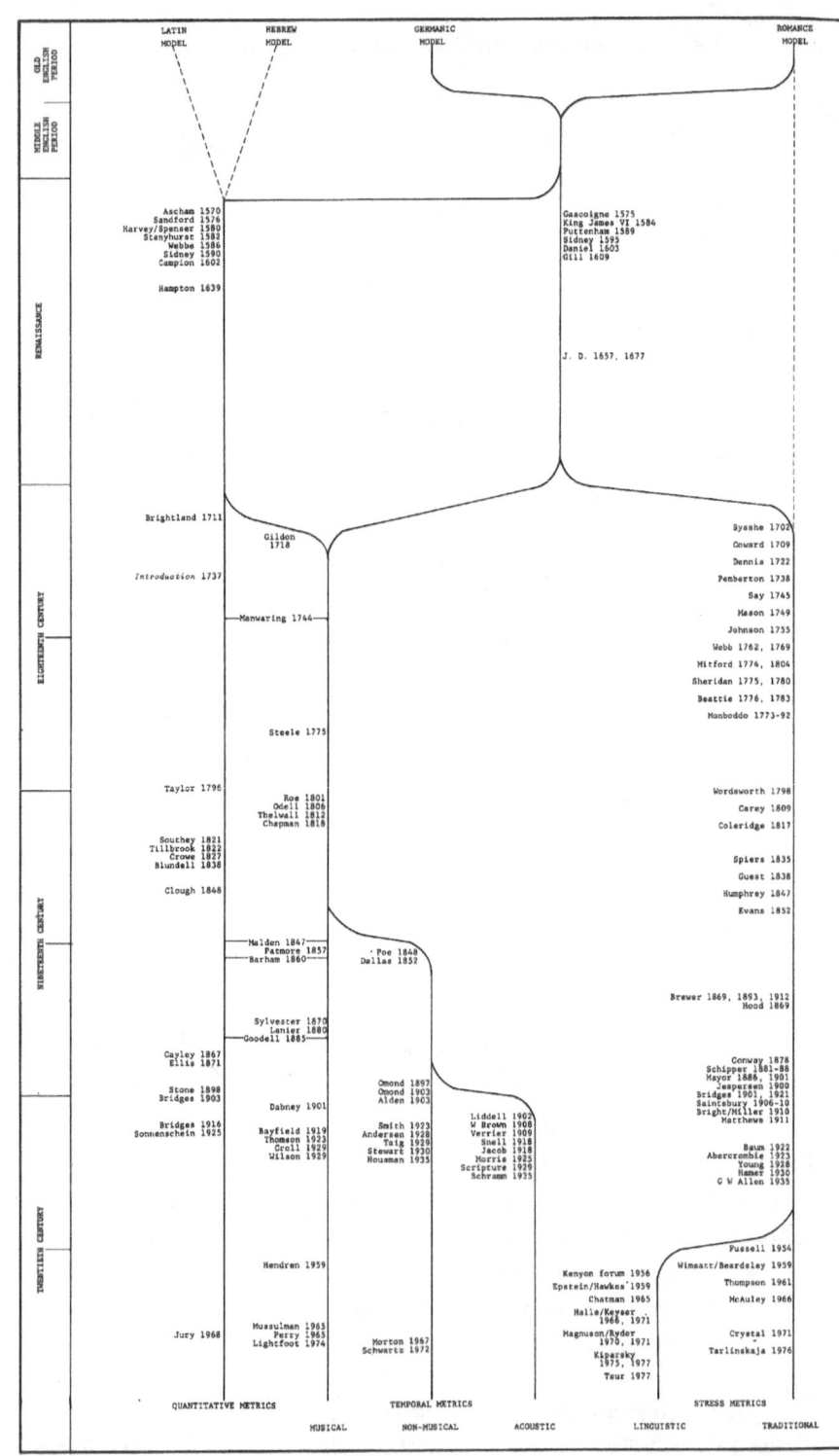

THE DEVELOPMENT OF MODERN ENGLISH METRICAL THEORY

FIGURES 30a and 30b (inset). "The Development of Modern English Metrical Theory," *English Versification, 1570–1980: A Reference Guide with a Global Appendix* (Baltimore: Johns Hopkins University Press, 1981), 142.

Thirty years prior he wrote at the end of the preface to chapter 6, section E, on meter: "No comprehensive history of English metrical theory yet exists (it will be a desiccated tome, a history of error and ignorance)."[6] Brogan understood that a scholar's choice of which archive to explore, which metrical system to follow, and how we access and cite that history profoundly impacts how that scholar reads poetry. In three different ways, *EVRG* took on what Brogan saw as the "palpable ignorance of the historical tradition of versification" in his relational text: first, by the table of contents and the guide through poetry's data; second, through his extensive, evaluative annotation; and third, in his system of cross-referencing to highlight the recursive nature of that historical tradition.[7] *English Versification* structurally presents overlapping representations—models—of the literary history of versification, which is, itself, a history full of attempts to present coherent models for how we should read poetry's data.

Brogan's table of contents was a navigational aid for the research guide, but it also argued that there was a method to understanding the complicated history of English versification: begin with the forbears, the "Primary Reference" materials (section I, A), which include "Histories, Collections, of Essays, and Earlier Bibliographies." The history of versification is a history of others trying to account for histories of versification (historical narrative as one approach to the representation of knowledge). "General Studies" (II, B), a longer section, is the justification for his exercise. There is no adequate "general study" of the problem, and so Brogan lays the groundwork necessary for someone else to write one. The book's first two sections pay homage to the prosodists who, in their own work, cite their forbears to replace them; he departs from

---

resembles the phrasing of Box ("All models are wrong," but some are useful) (Box, "Science and Statistics," 792) and has been a flashpoint in discussions of computational literary study. See So, "All Models Are Wrong." See also Katherine Bode's "Abstraction, Singularity, Textuality: The Equivalence of 'Close' and 'Distant' Reading," in Bode, *World of Fiction*, 17–36.

6. T. V. F. Brogan, *EVRG*, 143.
7. Brogan, 116.

this repeated structure of the prosody manual because he does not explicitly present his own approach to versification in *EVRG*. Rather, he developed organizational systems that focused on the component parts of the future system he hoped for, to try to ensure that future scholars did not repeat the errors of the past and to accelerate the creation of a better, more comprehensive theory of meter in the future.

Brogan wrote that "no one proceeds very far in theory without a clear sense of what is already known as well as what is missing—which avenues have widened out or else turned out to be dead ends—and so there is value in having all the known, published work searched out and listed, if not discussed and evaluated, in one location."[8] As a character in his own narrative, he justifies his task as an expert who will "search out and list" as well as evaluate his predecessors. More importantly, he will correct the contemporary ignorance that clouds what he feels should be a well-known, centuries-long discourse. But why? In the introduction to the first section, he shows that his hopes are to

> indicate the major points of interest which have become obligatory and must not be overlooked as well as those still more intriguing minor monuments located well away from the major thoroughfares of intellectual commerce which have been all but forgotten in the rush of history, but which have significance and value well beyond whatever may be suggested by their more modest facades or more obscure locations.[9]

This metanarrative of his archival recovery project ("more obscure locations") aims to reorient historians of versification toward materials that have been overlooked: if we blindly follow narratives of versification that history has laid out for us (as in the prior "Histories and General Studies"), he argues, we will simply repeat history's mistakes. The only way to avoid that path is to survey those mistakes and then to present, part by part, the elements that make up poetry's data.

Brogan chooses his data carefully and in order. Sound and rhythm are "elements and structures" crucial to the understanding of versification. Without an adequate understanding of these, any theory of meter is destined to fail.

---

8. Brogan, xi–xii.

9. Brogan, xii. He cannot help, on the next page, to insult his peers (another trope of the prosody manual): "Even though interest in versification has perhaps never been wider or keener, it has been accompanied by a very palpable ignorance of the historical tradition and resources" (xiii).

The Poem: Elements and Structures

4. Sound

>Pronunciation
>General Studies
>Alliteration, Assonance, Consonance
>>in language
>>in poetry
>
>Rhyme
>>in language
>>in poetry
>
>Sonal Mimesis
>in language (Phonetic Symbolism)
>in poetry (Onomatopoeia)

5. Rhythm

>Linguistic Rhythm
>>General
>>Stress
>>Pitch
>>Timing
>
>Kinesthetic Rhythm
>Prose Rhythm
>Poetic Rhythm[10]

Instead of beginning with meter, Brogan's foregrounds sound and rhythm (via linguistics, note "sonal mimesis" and "phonetic symbolism") in direct response to those who promoted the idea of a cohesive metrical system as a given, a universal model for understanding rhythm not only across differently perceiving and pronouncing people but across civilizations. Brogan instead focuses on the data: we do not have an agreed-on concept of how we might measure sound in language, either for pronunciation of language most generally or for patterns in language that might produce repeated sounds. For meter to be a stable pattern, we would need to describe sound adequately. Brogan turns to the linguistic concepts of segmental and suprasegmental phonemes—the smallest bits of language—but laments that even with this vocabulary,

---

10. Brogan, vii.

linguists still don't have an adequate way to describe what is happening, or what may have happened, sonically in language, despite the proliferation of systems that attempt to achieve that description within a metrical system. This deficit in our ability to classify and accurately describe sound in language prevents anyone from devising an adequate system of meter (since, for Brogan, linguistics did not yet have this capacity). These sections on history, general studies, sound, and rhythm (A–D is 140 pages and 1,007 total annotated references) make up only about a third of the total annotations in the book (section E, "Meter," is 1,554 references total). By putting sound and rhythm *before* meter—by contextualizing and demystifying these concepts—*EVRG* leads the reader through the component parts necessary to begin apprehending such a complicated and misunderstood concept.

Contrast Brogan's structure to the popular approach of his contemporary Paul Fussell. Fussell's *Poetic Meter and Poetic Form* was published in 1965 and revised and reprinted in 1979, during the time when Brogan was in graduate school and was completing his reference guide (figure 31). A twentieth-century counterpart to George Saintsbury, Fussell has done as much as anyone else to solidify the concept that metrical patterns (measured in feet) are stable and perceivable across poems with only a little practice. But the patterns, which Fussell's students are taught to mark with graphical scansion, only implicitly rely on sound. The word "sound" appears only twenty times in Fussell's handbook. Meter is based on measuring rhythm, and sound is what a student marks when following Fussell's instructions for accentual-syllabic scansion (the word appears first in the section "Technique for Scansion"): "Notice that in scanning we mark according to the sound of words, not according to their appearance on the page."[11] For Fussell, pronunciation is the only guide to scansion, though he assumes that all readers hear and pronounce words the same way: scansion's only aim is perception so as to develop critical judgment. This sort of "perception" is possible only when the critic performs a scansion that then translates "sound into visual terms."[12] But by "sound" here, Fussell only means the perception of stressed sounds that make up English meter—the patterns of meter that he abstracts out to something that every human body should naturally feel. For Fussell, then, poetry's data is not something in a poem or its component parts, but the information that the critic decides to consolidate based on Fussell's metrical model, and how adherence to or variations from that model might make meaning; his project differs al-

---

11. Fussell, *Poetic Meter*, 22–23.
12. Fussell, 34.

Contents

PART ONE / *Poetic Meter*

1 The Nature of Meter *3*
2 The Technique of Scansion *17*
3 Metrical Variations *30*
4 The Historical Dimension *62*
5 Free Verse *76*
6 Some Critical Implications of Metrical Analysis *90*

PART TWO / *Poetic Form*

7 Structural Principles: The Example of the Sonnet *109*
8 The English Stanzas *127*
9 Some Critical Implications of Stanzaic Forms *154*
10 Conventions and the Individual Talent *173*

Suggestions for Further Reading *181*

Index *183*

FIGURE 31. Table of contents, in Paul Fussell, *Poetic Meter and Poetic Form* (New York: Random House, 1965).

together from the study of linguistic data as part of poetry and marks the stark separation between the two spheres. For Brogan, the focus on phonetics is a key to understanding any system of English meter. For Fussell, a model of reading based on the individual ear and geared toward pleasure and appreciation is overlayed with authoritative-seeming descriptions of the accentual-syllabic system, named and enumerated *as if* they formed part of a coherent model, but lacking the underlying elements and structures that Brogan was careful to describe.

For both "rhythm" and "sound," Brogan refers to the complicated and understudied domain of linguistics to address a common confusion—not to present an alternative solution, but to display through the structure of his reference guide how even within linguistics there were and are contested categories of rhythm in language and poetry:

> The structure of English verse is not finally separable from the nature of the elements comprising that structure. No student of English metrics will fully understand the dimensions of the problem until he understands the current as well as the past conceptions of such key terms as "accent," or until he realizes exactly how much and how little consensus has been reached by linguists on how to demarcate discrete entities out of the flux. No metric without its phonetic: the serious metrist will have to inform himself about matters linguistic, among many.[13]

According to Brogan, no student of English metrics will fully understand meter without a full understanding of phonetics. But this scientific understanding is not what concerns Fussell; rather, the point is pleasure:

> The pleasure which universally results from foot tapping and musical time-beating does suggest that the pleasures of meter are essentially physical and as intimately connected with the rhythmic quality of our total experience as the similarly alternating and recurring phenomena of breathing, walking, or love-making.[14]

I do not fault scholars for likening abstract rhythm to dancing or even the cyclical qualities of nature, essentializing, naturalizing, and physicalizing the effects of poems as they do; the PPA contains a long history of these approaches to the teaching of poems, and Fussell and others are part of a branch of poetic pedagogy that appeals to abstract universals in order to introduce and welcome readers of poetry who might otherwise be intimidated. Children are often an example of primal or natural rhythm, as they are in Fussell, who wrote that they cannot help but to display pleasure by "foot tapping" and "head nodding."[15] This semiphysiological approach to rhythm serves to keep the complications of phonetics and linguistics—the science of language that might otherwise prove alienating—at bay. Rather than sound's variation forming a part of rhythm, sound might be just as likely to be perceived as percussive, *striking* the ear physically and tuning the body to respond to something these scholars imply the body already innately knows.[16]

13. T. V. F. Brogan, *EVRG*, 110.
14. Fussell, *Poetic Meter*, 6.
15. Fussell, 6. Cf. Martin, "'Imperfectly Civilized.'" This language also pervades late nineteenth- and early twentieth-century ethnographic discourse (see, for example, Wallaschek, *Primitive Music*) and is one that Ewan Jones discusses in his recent book *The Turn of Rhythm*.
16. For Fussell and others, I mean the body in an abstract way, not in the way that phoneti-

There are ideological dangers here that I have noted elsewhere, in which the poem's aesthetic effects are configured as an interaction between the poem and a body already coded with the alternating patterns necessary to be activated by the poem's similar, yet slightly more varied, alternations. The poetic handbook can act as an agent of insidious ideologies when it describes the poem's rhythm as if the poem itself were also a body, organized and civilized into a slightly more complicated *meter* to be read not actively by the eye and ear, but in some other place beyond perception; *the poem*, abstracted from even the sounds it is made of, creates (in this branch of interpretation) an undercurrent of understanding between a similarly organized and civilized body. The attraction of that metrical abstraction is so strong that even the science of phonetics cannot overturn it. In referring to the kymograph and oscillograph as an acoustic scansion technique, Fussell easily disregards those measuring tools in favor of his traditional, graphical system of marking the accentual-syllabic model via classical metrical feet. The kymograph "has the advantage of accuracy, especially in its representation of many of the empirical phenomena of verse when it is actually spoken aloud; its disadvantages are its complexity, its novelty, and its incapacity to deal with rhythms which no speaker enunciates but which every silent reader feels."[17] Machines that record linguistic data on graph paper cannot "deal with rhythms . . . which every silent reader feels." Of course, not every silent reader feels rhythms the way Fussell feels rhythms, and the trap of subjective interpretation is clear in the next line: "the reader first marks stressed and unstressed syllables, *not according to any preconceived pattern, but according to the degree of rhetorical emphasis residing in the syllables.*"[18] Fussell doubly emphasizes the importance of rhetorical emphasis here. Without any data about how sound works, the reader is the performer, emphasizing *emphasis* in their analysis, and therefore superimposing an individual model of interpretation—a model of reading that resides primarily in the reader as critic—*before* attempting to evaluate the poem's adherence to the accentual-syllabic metrical model Fussell promotes.

Poetry's data is made into capta by the reader's apprehending, interpretive, and evaluative process. All models are wrong, but the combination of these two models (the reader's emphasis in tension with the eventual perception of

cians were recording people reciting verses and measuring their regularity on a kymograph. Cf. "Instrumental Prosody," in Hall, *Nineteenth-Century Verse and Technology*, 207–53.

17. Fussell, *Poetic Meter*, 22.
18. Fussell, 22 (emphasis in original).

an accentual-syllabic metrical system) has proven particularly useful since it marshals enough of what looks like (and *feels* like) poetry's "linguistic" data to stake critical interpretations of metrical poetry. This pseudo-empirical approach is what rankled those, like Brogan, who believed in the science of linguistics and who felt that a different interpretive frame for the metrical grid could provide a more accurate account of how the language in poetry was activated.

Fussell appears several times in *EVRG*, for each of his entries in the 1974 *Princeton Encyclopedia of Poetry and Poetics* (entries Fussell expanded from *Poetic Meter and Poetic Form*). These entries, Brogan wrote, present "valuable review" but nonetheless make basic errors. For Fussell's *Encyclopedia* entry "English Prosody," Brogan scolds: "'Prosody' in the title is a solecism for 'Metrics.'"[19] And in his treatment of Fussell's popular handbook, Brogan is less circumspect:

> The most widely disseminated student's manual of metrics available at present, the intent of which is not so much typological as heuristic: Fussell aims to "sensitize" students to the supple flexes of poetic form. But, as paradigm of the perfect American consumer, he is more than willing to trade in precision for style, so that what this book gains in urbanity it more than loses in rigor.

He concludes, "Whatever the beginning student might learn here about 'sensitivity' cannot be valued over his learning a fundamentally licentious method."[20] Brogan developed a model for literary history that allowed for new interpretations of the past based on accumulated data about how past scholars viewed the component parts of poetry's data. Similarly to the other scholars Brogan collected, evaluated, put into relation, and indexed, Fussell performed Brogan's task in miniature, gathering poems that would serve as evidence for his own organizational model of English meter.

Brogan critiques Fussell's method as "almost purely expressionist,"[21] based on a complicated (and, in Brogan's mind, ridiculous) foot-based practice of metrical scansion that, despite the *appearance* of a kind of scientific or systematic approach, nonetheless rewards individual impressions of a poem over a deeper, more rigorous understanding of how versification might be working

---

19. T. V. F. Brogan, *EVRG*, 150.
20. Brogan, 250–51.
21. Brogan, 250.

in a longer tradition of linguistic and metrical effects. Brogan spent years collecting and annotating every book and article ever written on the history of versification, and Fussell's handbook popularizes a view that poetic meter and poetic form are separate from the complicated history of prosody (and, according to Brogan, Fussell doesn't know the difference between meter and prosody to begin with). It is as if the history Brogan knew so well was being erased, replaced by a convoluted (yet authoritative-seeming) system of foot-based scansion that replicated several of the mistakes he had already seen and was hoping to correct. Part of how he tries to correct this is by cross-referencing the scholars in the book—a model that allows for his creation of his developmental map.

Brogan's unique identifiers and cross listings show the complicated interrelations between various paths or discourses, and his chart shows how these discourses have converged or diverged over time. Not only was Brogan struggling with the complicated layering of mistaken accounts of English versification, but he was also struggling with the complicated presentation of multiple structures of information, or data structures. His annotations are also citations, links to further reading, and connections to other, perhaps more worthy, more rigorous accounts elsewhere in his guide. For instance, under the annotation to Fussell's *Poetic Meter and Poetic Form*, Brogan wrote, of the beginning student, "send him instead to Malof (E581) for information on forms, McAuley (E578) for scansion-technique, and Smith (B202) and Booth (B20) for close-reading."[22] This scholarly flex is also his way of demonstrating expertise; only Brogan had read all these materials and knew the best ways to teach and describe versification in English. Yet this cross-referencing is also demonstrating something else—something that derives from the form out of which this research first emerged. It is the evidence of the plywood box "file" that accumulated notecards, and it is also the evidence of his own categorizations of those notecards.

Each lettered section (A–N for the entire book) has a heading: A is used for "Primary Reference," B for "General Studies," C for "Sound," D for "Rhythm," E for "Meter." Within these lettered sections there are subsections (so for instance, within sound there is first "Pronunciation" and then "General Studies."); and in each subsection, entries are organized by the author's last name. Each entry is given an identifier keyed to the section, so, for instance, Raymond Macdonald Alden's *English Verse* is A1, in the "Histories" section of

---

22. Brogan, 251.

"Primary Reference." But in that entry, Brogan wrote that Alden seems most indebted to Schipper (A9—the ninth entry in section A) and Mayor (E592). Mayor's *Chapters on English Meter* is in section E (by far the largest), "Meter," where we find John Thelwall (E403), Edward Bysshe (E505), and William Gardiner (E354). Each letter is also a chapter, so "Meter" is chapter 6 of the guide, but that division is an overlay. One index is by the author's last name, the other by poet. Though not containing "every poet mentioned by every critic," the index criteria for inclusion was that "at least one distinct section of a book or article must be devoted exclusively to the poet or work cited."[23]

The reference guide undermines some of the more traditional navigational techniques of the modern codex while maintaining others, adding database features to the monograph.[24] *English Versification* illustrates how the story of versification must always be plural, and it teaches readers to question how a typical monograph (or a typical history) might build knowledge only in a progression from start to finish. What was successful about Fussell's guide was not only that it eschewed Brogan's attention to the actual data in poems, but that it disregarded the broader, more complex, and entangled history that a fuller study of the scholarship would have revealed. Fussell's model, and others like it, were too limited, too small. And Fussell could assert this teleological history and this accentual-syllabic model for reading poetry also because he wrote from a position of privilege and power—it mattered less that the system might be alienating to many readers and mattered more that it was good enough to make "right readers" out of enough students. For Brogan, the system didn't work. It would take collaborative labor across disciplines, working with linguists, knowing the data of the past, and thinking with different ways of

23. Brogan, 753. From this data, we can quickly see that Shakespeare is mentioned 186 times to Milton's 137; Alexander Pope is at 61, Hopkins 55, Tennyson 51, T. S. Eliot 47, Ezra Pound 39, Robert Browning 38, and Wordsworth 37. We'll organize these statistics by publication date for the listed references in the index so that we can measure them against what we discover as we analyze the complete data in the PPA (measuring only the references in *EVRG* for the years we include in the PPA).

24. Brogan was by no means the first scholar to attempt to present a network of relationships and influences in print form, but the model of the data that he presents coincides with the development, in 1974, of the SQL programming language by IBM researchers Raymond Boyce and Donald Chamberlin. This work was based on Codd, "Relational Model of Data for Large Shared Data Banks." The Structured English Query Language (SEQUEL), now commonly known as SQL, was developed by IBM to use the model, and it is now the standard database language. (There are now plenty of Structured Query processors and plenty of implementations of Relational Data Base Management Systems.)

approaching language to arrive at a new and more inclusive future for how we think about how poetry's data makes meaning. We live in Fussell's university and not Brogan's, for better or worse, but the influence of Brogan's thinking still permeates the authoritative print institution of the *Princeton Encyclopedia*.

Either Direction Will Work

Brogan's career in the 1980s and 1990s dramatizes the transition from traditional bibliographic library structures to our current moment of online library catalogs and multiple aggregated databases. It isn't an accident that Brogan was attracted to notecards and a plywood box. The box represented the borders of what he was trying to understand, so that at first "everything" went into the box, and then, once he understood the structure of the reference guide, he began to cross-reference, to distinguish and categorize his initial pass at collection into another structure altogether. His cross-referencing system continued in a slimmer bibliography titled *Verseform: A Comparative Bibliography* in 1989, an attempt to tell a shorter version of the story of verse form he thought students *should* know, rather than having to wade through everything he had read and annotated (all the wrong paths and wrong answers). Whereas *EVRG* set out to show the many possible paths of English meter and give a sense of how we might make sense of it, *Verseform* attempted to make sense of "English meter" by curtailing its definitional reach altogether. *Verseform* was an attempt to highlight what he felt to be "the more important work" as well as, importantly, to make the slimmer volume affordable to students. He didn't need a complicated unique identifier system for the smaller, more concise story he was trying to tell about who he thought nudged us along the right path toward the linguistic future he wanted:

> A reader who wants to know about the rhythm of French poetry, for example, can look into the chapter on "French," where the more general studies of French verse are cited and where studies of rhythm are cross-referenced to the chapter on "Rhythm"; or she can look into the latter chapter, where all the major studies of poetic rhythm are cited, some of which treat French specifically, with cross-references to more generalized studies of French prosody in the chapter which include discussion of rhythm. Either direction will work.[25]

25. T. V. F. Brogan, *Verseform*, xiv.

Either direction will work. Reviewers noted the excellent cross-referencing system. In both *EVRG* and *Verseform*, the bidirectional cross-references work only because both are highly curated data environments that he has created. This is different from the hierarchical structure of a table of contents or the flat structure of an index; though not intentionally "relational" as the relational database structure of the PPA, Brogan's project nevertheless reveals a dream of connectivity and networked knowledge, a sense, popular in the late 1980s and early 1990s, that information—and literary history, structured here as kinds of data—existed within discourse networks (prosodists taking to one another or talking about similar approaches) and citation networks. Were we able to map these connections, Brogan dreamed, we would be able to see our way through the past more clearly, and, so Brogan hoped, we could then see our way toward a better kind of knowledge in the future.

This kind of information required a different format. Would he have seen how much his maps and systems resembled the entity-relationship diagrams that went on to form the groundwork for relational databases? Could we call that different format something more akin to the structured techniques for software development that were emerging in the 1990s? What he knew, or what he learned, in assembling *EVRG* was that he was likely one of the specialized few who felt that any future prosodic system lay in the ability of linguistics to develop an adequate method of talking about sound in verse. And yet linguistics, at the very same time, was undergoing its own divisions into corpus and computational linguistics due to the same technical developments that Brogan was interested in understanding.

Brogan set out to create a forum in which linguists and literary scholars could collaborate. Shortly after *EVRG* was published, Brogan (with poet Sally Gall) began to publish a newsletter called *EIDOS: The International Prosody Bulletin*. The first issue reads, "New Bulletin Announced: With the explosive growth of interest in metrics, and other aspects of versification, a forum devoted exclusively to the efficient exchange of prosodic information has become essential." The editors note, "if you are working with computers, why not let your colleagues know? There may be some problems that are more easily solved by collaboration."[26] The editors foreground that *EIDOS* is written on an IBM personal computer, a NEC 3550 "letter quality" printer, a newly acquired word-processing program named (with a bow to Tolkien) Palantir: "Palantir compares very favorably with other dedicated word processing pro-

---

26. See T. V. F. Brogan, *EIDOS* 1, no. 1:4.

grams like MultiMate, FinalWord, and WordStar"; and the editors cite both the software company address and a favorable review of it in the December 1983 issue of *PC Magazine*. The editors justify the new software program by providing a nod to its actual creation—the physical address where the company is located, as if a scholar could make an appointment, take a tour, and learn how it worked—which opens a window to the ethos of this moment. Kirschenbaum narrates that WordStar "dominated the home computer market in the first half of the 1980s before losing out to WordPerfect, itself to be eclipsed by Microsoft Word. Initially sold through mail order (it came on a diskette in a plastic baggie), WordStar set the standard for word processing in the first generation of personal computers."[27]

EIDOS presents a history of the state of metrical theory in the mid-1980s at the same time as it makes visible the changing mechanisms for scholarship and communication. After a brief announcement about a new article on Chinese metrics, the bulletin publicizes the University Microfilm Clearinghouse: "UMI is operating a new article delivery service available through libraries or institutions affiliated with OCLC, CLASS OnTyme, and ITT Diacom. Recent articles (in general 1978 or later) published in some 7,500 periodicals can now be ordered electronically."[28] The appearance of these two announcements concurrently—how *EIDOS* is written on a computer using a particular word-processing software program and how microfilms are being made electronically available to scholars—brings to light the layered technological changes to scholarly research that occurred during the 1980s. The technologies of meter are scaffolded by new information systems and word-processing software and add to Brogan's dream of a future where scholars might truly be able to communicate—to visualize—the complicated, overlapping histories of prosody to move, across disciplines, toward a unified future for the study of poetry. For instance, Brogan offers "Chronological Guide to English Metrists" in the second volume of *EIDOS*, admitting that the analog structure of *EVRG*

---

27. Kirschenbaum, *Track Changes*, 2. Word Processing software was developed out of writing technology, merging later into computing practices. In 1964 IBM brought out the MT/ST (Magnetic Tape / Selectric Typewriter); magnetic tape was the first *reusable* storage medium for typed information. This development marked the beginning of word processing. Ivan Flores, *Word Processing Handbook* (New York: Van Nostrand Reinhold, 1983), quoted in Kunde's class project, "A Brief History of Word Processing (through 1986)." Kunde has worked for Stanford University Libraries since 1988 and was (as of 2023) the serials receiving and maintenance specialist.

28. See T. V. F. Brogan, *EIDOS* 1, no. 1:5.

might not allow for scholars to view and organize the references how they would like to:

> Scholars interested in the history of English prosody may find Brogan's *English Versification* inconvenient for identifying everything published within a certain period, or works published near a work of interest, since *EVRG* is arranged topically and alphabetically. The length of the book precluded inclusion of a chronological index, but such an index is now available separately from the author.
>
> The format is a bit uninviting—green-and-white-bar computer paper—but computerization was the only feasible method of organizing so much information at the time. The index lists author, short title, date, and EVRG citation number for every item in sections A through K of the book and runs to 3600 lines. Two formats are available—one including sections J and K (Old and Middle English), one excluding. The cost of printing and xeroxing is $5. Address: T. V. F. Brogan, 2540 Dole St. #C6, Honolulu, HI 96822.[29]

Just as with OCLC, Brogan had computerized his own resource and wanted to make it available even if the format of green-and-white-bar computer paper might not be appealing. Similarly, there are calls to form a special MLA discussion group, and to expand the annual review of publications on prosody and related areas in all the world's languages. Each new subscriber (after mailing in their SASE) would be listed in the next issue "in order to promote communication among metrists, prosodists, and versificationists of all persuasions." *EIDOS* presents this emerging moment at the border of older (yet still robust) networks for future readers and offers to mail the index (printed out as a supplement to his own structure in *EVRG*) as an analog effort at community building, showing Brogan's desire for more interoperable structures of exchange between literary and linguistic research.

Format, early computing, and advances in microfiche and information management were all part of this transitional moment; the print run of *EIDOS*, from 1984 to 1987, gives a window into some of the ways that each of these structural changes in information science impacted literary and linguistic scholarship, an impact that has been understudied and undertheorized. Both linguistics and literary scholarship were impacted by these structural changes: linguistics by the advent of accelerated corpus linguistics methods as well as

---

29. See T. V. F. Brogan, *EIDOS* 2, nos. 1 and 1:2.

the establishment of computational linguistics and NLP in the 1990s, literary studies by the digitization of research materials and the transfer of their ownership from a research library to the companies that digitized the materials from microfiche.[30] *EIDOS* was at once an analog solution to the future hopes for the field Brogan expressed in *EVRG*—to bring the linguistic study of sound together with the complex histories of English prosody—and a record of this transitional moment of mail order updates and new approaches to information management.

Broken Links

EIDOS shows an early moment of optimism for exploring complicated theoretical and methodological problems in the humanities collaboratively and bringing different fields together, even if there are setbacks (commonly referred to in the newsletter as the difficulty of getting Brogan and Gall's computers to communicate effectively with one another). Richard Cureton, Reuven Tsur, and Derek Attridge were all contributors to the newsletter. The pages included reviews and excerpts of work by M. L. Rosenthal and Marjorie Perloff, and announcements of international conferences and panels where the stated aims are to investigate prosody and verse form. In the 1980s age of the personal computer, technology held the promise of easier communication and collaboration for scholars who were not situated squarely in academic departments, but who nevertheless had expertise.[31] At the same time, the technological changes were impacting how scholars accessed information. The 1980s also saw the transition away from microfilm and microfiche into electronic

---

30. Cf. Fyfe, "Archeology of Victorian Newspapers"; Fyfe, *Digital Victorians*. Edith Rickert published *New Methods for the Study of Literature* in 1927 based on her work as a cryptographer in the Code and Cipher section of Military Intelligence in World War I; Father Busa and his team of punch-card operators worked on the *Index Thomasticus* in a partnership with IBM in 1951; Josephine Miles and her team of women graduate students created massive concordances of Dryden's poetry with the electrical engineering department at Berkeley and contracted with their computer lab and its IBM tabulating machine in 1957; the journal *Computers in the Humanities* was founded in 1966. Cf. Heffernan and Buurma, *Teaching Archive*; Buurma and Heffernan, "Search and Replace"; Pasanek, "Extreme Reading"; Nyhan, *Computation and the Humanities*; Hockey, *Guide to Computer Applications*. There is not, nor could there be, one cohesive history of humanities computing and digital humanities.

31. Behind all of this is the changing structures of financial support in the increasingly neoliberal university and the sense of professional expertise (or mastery) as a sort of commodity. Cf. Bourdieu, *Distinction*; Guillory, *Cultural Capital*.

material. It also saw the digitization of the card catalog, an ongoing response to Frederick Lancaster's 1978 book *Toward Paperless Information Systems*, and the development of both the Library of Congress's standard for machine-readable catalog (MARC) records and OCLC, a bibliographic utility intended to facilitate interlibrary loan and resource sharing.[32] The 1990s saw the advent of digitized collections available on CD-ROMs; as Ted Underwood wrote, scholars began to access information by performing full-text search and became much less reliant on those now-digitized card catalogs.[33]

The OCLC (then the Ohio College Library Center, now the OCLC Online Computer Library Center), the first major online shared cataloging system, was established in 1967. Christine Borgman wrote that shared cataloguing utilities would not have developed when they did "without the establishment of standards for exchanging bibliographic data in computer-readable form in the later 1960s. The Library of Congress began work toward the machine-readable catalog (MARC) format in 1961, conducted a pilot project from 1966 through 1968, and began the MARC II distribution service in 1968. The international exchange of records between the United States and the United Kingdom began in 1969."[34] Alan Liu discusses the parallel evolutions of information technology and literary theory and cultural criticism in the era of the personal computer and network, and he points to the social upheavals of May 1968 as a particularly crucial turning point.[35] Each field, Liu argues, "manifested a common will to decentralize or democratize the traditional understanding of literary sociality." Liu theorizes that the "core circuit" of "authors, publishers, readers (and interpreters) mediated by documents" was replaced by a more decentralized network of scholarship.[36] Those who study the history of prosody, which had not and *could not* establish the kinds of standards or "fixity" that the post-1968 era sought to destabilize, never quite fit into this model. However, the recursive model of prosodic history did map onto the collaborative, iterative method—or ongoing process—of studying prosody's history in the ever-changing technological present.[37]

---

32. Sapp, *Brief History of the Future of Libraries*.

33. Underwood, "Theorizing Research Practices." See also Drucker "Why Distant Reading Isn't," *PMLA* 2017.

34. Borgman, *Big Data, Little Data, No Data*, 221.

35. Liu, *Laws of Cool*, 4–5; Liu, *Local Transcendence*, 6.

36. Liu, "From Reading to Social Computing."

37. Malinconico and Fasana, in *Future of the Library Catalog* (which describes the benefits and detriments of MARC), contrast how a systemic catalog would bring together English phi-

> |◀ ◀ ▶ ▶| 🖑
>
> ## Navigating through the Book
>
> **Hyperlinks:**
> Unlike documentation manuals on paper, electronic documentation relies on hyperlinking to move you quickly and easily from one page to another.
> All entries in all versions of the Table of Contents—both the short and long versions—are hyperlinked. This means that in any Table of Contents, you can click on any part of any line, either text or page number, to jump to that chapter or page. Use the Go Back button on the Toolbar or command on the View Menu to return to where you were.
>
> **Scrolling:**
> Move around on a page with the Hand tool: 🖑
> Move down to a specific page by using the scrollbars on the Page window at right or the Thumbnails window at left.
>
> **Moving Back, Forward, or to the Beginning or End:**
> Navigate in the current document with the VCR-style buttons: |◀ ◀ ▶ ▶|.
> These buttons take you (left to right) to the Beginning of the current document (chapter), Back one page, Forward one page, and to the End of the document (chapter).
>
> **Going to a Specific Page:**
> On the View Menu, use the Go To Page command, or call this dialog box more directly by clicking on the leftmost box on the Status Bar at the bottom of the screen (showing as "Page xx of yyy").

FIGURE 32. T. V. F. Brogan, "Navigating through the Book," instructions, *English Versification, 1570–1980: A Reference Guide with a Global Appendix; Hypertext Version* (Baltimore: Johns Hopkins University Press, 1981, 1999).

Brogan already had the analog equivalent of a hypertext index in his earlier unique identifiers—from the index cards with which he began his research, to the microfiche-augmenting *EIDOS*-hypertext version of *EVRG* that he wrote and maintained—as a logical adjunct to the histories of versification that continued to proliferate elsewhere in print. In 1999, the online journal *Versification* hosted this version of the networked prosodic discourses that Brogan's early *EVRG* had structured. Like George Landow's *Victorian Web* (1987) and other scholar-driven online resources, *EVRG*'s hypertext version allowed scholars to navigate bidirectional cross-references in real time.[38] Though there was no other visualization accompanying the online version of *EVRG*, Brogan added a few addendums as well as instructions (figure 32 and figure 33).

---

lology, then orthography and etymology, and other items, including grammar and prosody. Under "Prosody" they list "Dramatic Poetry, Lyric Poetry, etc." (36), but this was not replicated in the OCLC records.

38. Landow's book *Hypertext*, 5–6, put Roland Barthes's theory of the "writerly" reader in conversation with digital media.

Long Table of Contents		
	Prefix	Page
Introduction		xi
Acknowledgments		xxvii
List of Abbreviations		xxix
Part I: MODERN ENGLISH VERSE (since Wyatt)		
I. Primary References (Histories, Collections, Bibls.)	A	3
II. General Studies	B	17
III. The Poem: Elements and Structures		51
Sound	C	53
Pronunciation		54
General Studies		57
Alliteration, Assonance, Consonance		69
Rhyme		77
Sonal Mimesis		97
Rhythm	D	109
Linguistic Rhythm		110
Kinesthetic Rhythm		122
Prose Rhythm		125
Poetic Rhythm		130
Meter	E	141
General Studies		144
(Schools of Metrists)		164
Quantitative Metrics		164
Temporal Metrics		193
Stress Metrics		233
Traditional		233
Linguistic		290
Structural		290
Generative		299
Systems of Metrical Organization)		319
Accentual Verse		320
Ballad and Hymn Meter		324
Sprung Rhythm		330
Syllabic Verse		337
Accentual-Syllabic Verse		339
Blank Verse		356
Couplet Verse		389
Free Verse		402
Syntax & Grammar	F	417
Stanza Structures	G	445
Visual Structures	H	463
IV. The Poem in Performance	I	469

FIGURE 33. T. V. F. Brogan, long table of contents for *English Versification, 1570–1980: A Reference Guide with a Global Appendix; Hypertext Version* ("click any row to jump"). (Baltimore: Johns Hopkins University Press, 1981, 1999).

The book's cover, replicated in the online format, links back to the "usage information." The table of contents and entries are identical to those in the analog form, except for the bright blue hyperlinks rendered here in gray scale (figure 34).

There were about three years when I could use these links.[39] We were able to replicate his bibliography by downloading the complete files of his book

---

39. Brogan sent some additional bibliographic material about medieval prosody; when I

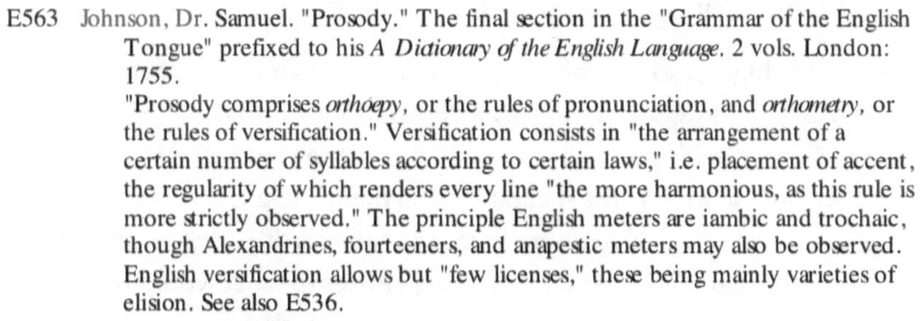

E563   Johnson, Dr. Samuel. "Prosody." The final section in the "Grammar of the English Tongue" prefixed to his *A Dictionary of the English Language*. 2 vols. London: 1755.
"Prosody comprises *orthoepy*, or the rules of pronunciation, and *orthometry*, or the rules of versification." Versification consists in "the arrangement of a certain number of syllables according to certain laws," i.e. placement of accent, the regularity of which renders every line "the more harmonious, as this rule is more strictly observed." The principle English meters are iambic and trochaic, though Alexandrines, fourteeners, and anapestic meters may also be observed. English versification allows but "few licenses," these being mainly varieties of elision. See also E536.

FIGURE 34: T. V. F. Brogan, entry on Samuel Johnson with blue hyperlink, *English Versification, 1570–1980: A Reference Guide with a Global Appendix; Hypertext Version* (Baltimore: Johns Hopkins University Press, 1981, 1999).

and then cleaning them, curating them into our own version of structured data and, using regular expressions, was how we were able to replicate his bibliography (see chapter 1, the section "counting the counters."). The OCLC and other text standards presented one way of navigating the past; Brogan presented another, supplemental way, but, like all scholar-built digital projects, it was ephemeral. We cross-checked what he had found with what was available in the HathiTrust Digital Library and then, later, in ECCO.[40] *Versification* is now defunct, and the hypertext doesn't work if you can navigate to the still-existing URL, as of this writing.[41] Brogan had hoped to create and sustain not only an online resource for prosody, but a community of literary and linguistic scholars working together. As with most dreams of the 1990s and the networked web, Brogan couldn't plan for ongoing maintenance. Without stable academic employment and without institutional backing, the hypertext version of the project, and the connections it tried to theorize, are now a series of broken links.

---

reminded him that I could download them, and *EVRG* via the *Versification* website, he wrote: "Ah yes, I'd forgotten that website, since it's so forgettable." T. V. F. Brogan, email to author, June 1, 2010.

40. We have his annotations but chose not to replicate them in the PPA. Though we may still consider replicating his hyperlinks, we have not yet worked out how that would function within the larger design. In 2015, an undergraduate thesis advisee of Professor Brian Kernighan named Capella Yee wrote a thesis re-creating a social network of prosodists who referred to one another using his cross-references—she called the project Social Scholar (Yee, "Digital Interactions for the Modern Scholar"). She went on to work at Google and in 2022 became head of Operations and Business Development at Sun at Six.

41. *Versification: An Electronic Journal of Literary Prosody*, http://arsversificandi.info/resources/index.html. Though the links are broken, that doesn't mean his work is lost; I have the files downloaded with annotations, as do many scholars.

The Princeton Encyclopedia of Poetry and Poetics (PEPP)

In the April–July 1985 issue of *EIDOS*, we find the announcement of *PEPP*'s editors, Alex Preminger and Brogan, with associate editors O. B. Hardison and Frank J. Warnke, with publication tentatively set for 1990. They solicited suggestions from "scholars and specialists, particularly in the areas of prosody, rhetoric, and genre, but also on movements, schools of criticism, and national poetries."[42] Brogan had been contributing entries to what would become the 1986 *Princeton Handbook of Poetic Terms*, a spinoff of the second, enlarged edition of *The Princeton Encyclopedia of Poetry and Poetics*, as soon as it was announced, and as its title indicates, it features "a Select Reading List by T. V. F. Brogan." Brogan was known at that time for his work on *EVRG* as well as for *EIDOS*. Members of Princeton University Press met on September 9, 1984, with the editor of the third edition, Preminger, and his two associate editors, Hardison and Warnke. In a letter from Loren Hoekzema (editor at Princeton UP) reporting on the meeting, which covered both the forthcoming handbook and what it should include as well as the proposal to revise *PEPP*, she wrote,

> it was very important to meet with Preminger, Hardison, and Warnke, and all three made good contributions to the meeting. Before I met Preminger, I was worried about his ability to handle the project. His health is not good, and he seems to be waiting for the Press's decision before he selected the terms.... I think Preminger wants to discuss plans for transferring control to T. V. F. Brogan. Perhaps now is the time to make that transition.[43]

Within a month (October 7, 1984), Preminger contacted Brogan in Hawaii to invite him to serve as an editor. Brogan replied on October 15, 1984:

> I believe I can offer you the energy, perseverance, breadth of knowledge, and attention to detail which are requisite to the task before us. I have worked hard over the years to keep my readings in poetics and metrics as wide as possible.... I shall give the *Encyclopedia* my wholehearted energy and attention.

However, he continues,

> Given the distance and the slowness of the mail to and from Hawaii, I cannot easily imagine an effective collaboration on a major project so long as

---

42. See T. V. F. Brogan, *EIDOS* 2, nos. 1 and 2:1.
43. Princeton University Press Records, CO728, box 41, Manuscripts Division, Department of Special Collections, Princeton University Library.

I remain here.... If there are good prospects for a grant for the work on the revised *PEPP* that would very much enhance our prospects for relocation, for in that event my wife might well find a position at a good place, the grant then freeing me entirely for editorial work. The alternative is for me to take a position with the understanding that in the near future I would take a leave of absence for the project. All of this comes to mind now because I have just yesterday read the MLA job list for the coming year.... In any event it is essential to my wife and I that our next move be the last one for a long while: I want to be at a place where my work on the *PEPP* will be considered an advancement [rather than] a digression from my career.[44]

He then mentions that he "just missed the deadline for applying to the National Humanities Center in North Carolina." When Herbert Bailey at the press learned this, he put in a call to the assistant director of the National Humanities Center. Brogan sent his application on October 28, but he didn't receive that fellowship. Without any assurance that his work on *PEPP* would be "considered an advancement" and not a "digression" from his career, he quickly applied for an NEH grant to work on the project for the following several years. The first grant was not successful, and the press archives contain detailed back-and-forth about whether the design of the proposed *PEPP* third edition should be altered to match the concerns of the first round of NEH reviewers. Hoekzema received a letter from Preminger on June 26, 1986, expressing that "the loss of NEH funds concerns all the editors but it is crucial for Terry Brogan." She and everyone else at the press spent a great deal of time worrying about Brogan's funding. I just want to reiterate here that the funding was "crucial" for Brogan because both he and his wife left jobs at Hawaii to move to South Bend, but only his wife got a job at Notre Dame, and Brogan was never offered the job he reports he was promised before relocating.[45]

In another letter from Hoekzema on September 9, 1985, Bailey wrote, "I've looked into Terry's grant proposal, and I'm impressed with his knowledge of computers." The proposal submitted in September 1986 for $387,000 covered the costs of computers, assistants, and reduction of his course load. Though this initial grant was not approved, they appealed, and the project received two years of funding and an extension in 1988. His application supported his own salary and supported the training of graduate student workers in the technical

44. Princeton University Press Records.
45. From T. V. F. Brogan, interview with Meredith Martin: "They said they would give us both jobs, but they lied about that; they really only needed more female faculty—hire the couple, trash the husband. Great, ugly stories in there."

project of encoding the encyclopedia. In each of the grants, the intellectual justification included the need to expand and modernize, as "issues of interpretation, history, gender, culture, and the nature of literature as an entity now dominate the crucial scene which were largely unknown in 1965." Brogan includes developments in various national poetries, and the need to treat theory and criticism (deconstruction, New Historicism, feminism and gender studies, reception theory). He also spends a paragraph enumerating the growth in "much older fields":

> Prosody, traditionally a bywater of English poetics . . . witnessed a veritable explosion of interest in the years following 1966: from 1880 to 1960, publications on prosody averaged only about twenty per year, or 200 per decade. But from 1966 to 1970 alone nearly 500 books and articles appeared on this subject, and from 1970 to 1980 another 800 more. In the light of this extraordinary swell of new research in the field, much of the prosodic matter of *PEPP*, written prior to 1963, now seems distinctly inadequate.[46]

Brogan argues for a wider, more comparative frame and the need to update the volume because of what he knew was happening in other fields: conversations in which poetry and poetics had been participating, but for which the largely conservative new critical edition of 1963 (and enlarged 1974 edition) did not account. In addition to widening and modernizing the scope of the approaches in the proposed third edition, he argues for a new methodology for its construction, which includes "a reduction of production costs":

> the rationale for federal support of our work is that it permits us to assemble the manuscript of the third edition of the *Encyclopedia* on computer by a fulltime staff in a timely fashion. The immediate and specific benefits of having the manuscript in electronic form are manifold: revisions and proofreading corrections are expedited, typesetting codes can later be inserted by the publisher to reduce printing costs significantly, and in future years revision of the manuscript for subsequent editions is greatly expedited. Too, the manuscript becomes available for dissemination in other electronic forms.[47]

Again, at that time, he was a part-time lecturer at Notre Dame University, where his wife had secured a position. Brogan was essentially the only full edi-

---

46. Princeton University Press Records, CO728, NEH grant, 6–7. That studies of prosody would explode as scholars began to adopt humanities computing is a chapter for another book.

47. Princeton University Press Records, 8.

tor: Preminger, who had been the only original editor from the first (1965) edition, had to withdraw because of declining health (he moved to Daytona Beach, Florida, and died in 1996). Warnke was hit by a truck in Antwerp at age sixty-two in 1988,[48] and Hardison died of cancer at sixty-one in 1990.[49] The third edition of *PEPP*, titled *The New Princeton Encyclopedia of Poetry and Poetics* was published in 1993, yet Preminger's name comes before Brogan's. I emphasize here both Brogan's wishes to have *NPEPP* exist in electronic form so that it would be easier to update, and his desire to support a full-time staff of graduate students whom he would train to help code the text, all while acting as an underpaid and sole editor of another enormous undertaking. In his marginal position, adjacent to the profession, funded by grants he was writing rather than a stable income, he wrote and assembled the reference guide that would nevertheless position his work as the authority in poetry and poetics for at least two decades. His literary authority was also matched by his technical savvy: he wrote the custom Adobe PostScript program the encyclopedia was designed in and so became the main vendor of the system that enabled Princeton University Press to undertake the production of the *NPEPP*.

The Princeton University Press Archives contain numerous letters back and forth about the complicated typesetting for marks of scansion and how Brogan would set the diacritical marks and the foreign languages; it is clear in these letters that the press staff is baffled by his development of new software that will enable the accelerated editing and printing of these models. This caused no end of headache for the press. Brogan typeset *NPEPP* electronically. He taught the graduate students he hired his custom Adobe Postscript program to accommodate the seventeen languages: "they had no mechanism to print those characters," he reported. "I hired a staff and trained people to do custom PostScript—the language all electronic laser printers ran in the 90s."[50] Postscript essentially translates documents into print; invented in 1984 as Adobe's "founding technology," it was the first device-independent page description language (PDL), and it was also a programming language. Brogan introduced this language to the press and compelled them to embrace what has since been called the desktop publishing revolution: the moment when publishing moved from photo publication to in-house desktop publication, or DTP. It wasn't only Adobe, but a combination of Adobe, Hewlett-Packard, Apple (and its

48. "Frank J. Warnke, Educator, 62."
49. Blau, "O. B. Hardison Jr. Is Dead at 61."
50. T. V. F. Brogan, interview with Meredith Martin.

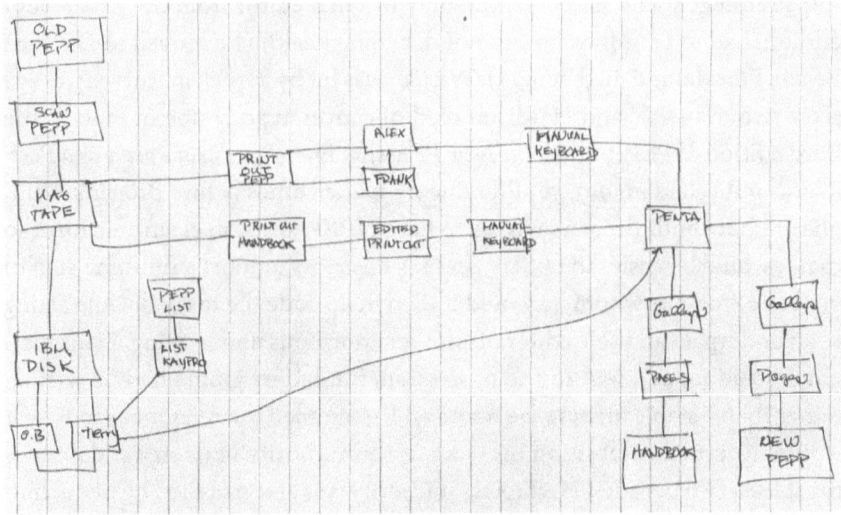

FIGURE 35. T. V. F. Brogan, workflow for updating and extracting entries for Alex Preminger and T. V. F. Brogan, eds., *The New Princeton Encyclopedia of Poetry and Poetics* (Princeton, NJ: Princeton University Press, 1993), and *The New Princeton Handbook of Poetic Terms*, edited by T. V. F. Brogan (Princeton, NJ: Princeton University Press, 1994).

Graphical User Interface), and Aldus (PageMaker) that combined to create the metaphor that we now know so well—the desktop, the ability to think about the computer screen as a page. In addition to managing the entries and editorial oversight, Brogan was managing the operations by which *NPEPP* would be printed, its technical apparatus.

The press archives contain the drawing in figure 35 of the workflow for *The New Princeton Encyclopedia of Poetry and Poetics* as well as *The New Princeton Handbook of Poetic Terms*, which, along with the *Princeton Handbook of Multicultural Poetries*, he would go on to edit. The "Old PEPP" is the second edition, which, according to the workflow, will be scanned, then put onto magnetic tape. He will share a printout with Alex and Frank, and then they'll edit it in analog form. Hardison and Brogan will read it via disk, and Brogan will check the old list of entries with the new list on a different floppy disk (Kaypro). Brogan will then deliver these files over to the print shop (Penta), which will proceed to print them. This entire process was new to Princeton University Press. Brogan's earlier understanding of *EVRG* as a relational data structure allowed him to imagine how *PEPP*, though not hyperlinked or relational, could nevertheless use the affordances of magnetic tape to save time and to expedite revisions to the project. He was a self-taught programmer and, like many in the profession now, taught himself programming only when it was necessary for him to solve a research problem: in this case, how do you use technology to revise and publish the technical histories of poetry?

In 2010, Brogan told me that between 1984 and 1991 there were some years when he didn't work on the encyclopedia very hard and some years where he had an office and a staff of five people and worked on it night and day (that's how his second ex-wife, Jaqui, described it in a 2020 interview as well):[51]

> One day the editor came to me and said that everyone had died and they needed the money; how soon can it be done. I had about five articles left, and I said I could do it in one month but I'd like two. "Poetry" was the last article written. "Prosody," "Sound." The big ones last. "Meter" was done, "Rhyme" done. I wanted to save the ones that were best [for] last.[52]

Looking at the projects for which he is most well known, or most often cited, *The New Princeton Encyclopedia of Poetry and Poetics* (*NPEPP*, 1993, coedited with Preminger), the related *New Princeton Handbook of Poetic Terms* (1994), and *The Princeton Handbook of Multicultural Poetries* (1996), you can see the evidence of the prior research he undertook for *EVRG*. His biography in *NPEPP* lists him as "visiting assistant professor of English at Indiana University at South Bend."[53] Press archives show that they were required to rely on his technical expertise as a vendor. The contracts he signed for the "client" Princeton University Press indicate that "Leximetrics, Inc" was to "furnish electronic design and typesetting services, editorial services, and proofreading services ... one complete set of printed comps for the work as well as one final copy in electronic format, specifically Postscript files, on CD-ROM." Because he already had these files in PostScript, after creating *PEPP* in the same way, it makes sense that he would need two contracts, but there is a good deal of confusion on the press side about how this work was going to be transmitted.[54] I can only conjecture that there is some connection between his status as a vendor and the odd introduction, titled "pre(Till We Have Faces) face: Culture, Poetry, the Other, 'Sexy Ideas,' 'Clerical Work,' and Genuine

---

51. J. Brogan, interview with Meredith Martin.
52. T. V. F. Brogan, interview with Meredith Martin.
53. Preminger and Brogan, *New Princeton Encyclopedia of Poetry and Poetics*.
54. In a letter on February 23, 1995, Debbie Tegarden wrote, "We aren't sure about handling your software."

Savagery," for the *Handbook of Multicultural Poetries*. It is a meandering, unhinged rant, displaying entitlement, disillusionment, and a fixation with method over ideology.[55] After reading it, I understood why Roland Greene pulled me aside in 2013 to recommend that I rename the collection "Original Bibliography" instead of "Brogan."

When I first spoke with Brogan, he was cantankerous and grumpy about the planned revisions to his third edition, which had taken a decade of his life. He was not pleased that the editors were widening the list of contributors to so many distinct voices—he felt that it made the fourth edition, as he put it, "more cultural and less technical" and that they'd "probably have typesetting issues—they'll lay it out in Quark, and it will probably stay in the same font." But he knew what he had done, and how much influence he had had:

> I know that for the better part of a generation everybody and every graduate student in America who wanted to come through poetry came through me. And now they will come through other people, and that's fine; I've got no rub with that. I've said what I've had to say. People can use it or not. I tried to be fair. I did try to be fair. I don't think it always shows.

For the better part of a generation, it was Brogan's definition of English meter, poetry, prosody, and sound, what he called "the big ones," that were the formative definitions in the authoritative encyclopedia about poetry and poetics. Whether Fussell's abstractions or Brogan's pathways through his data won the larger prosody war is unclear, but I can only imagine that Brogan relished replacing Fussell's earlier entries on meter in the third edition, of which Brogan wrote 138 of the entries himself. The most recent, fourth version still bears the traces of Brogan's labor: in it, he is cited 181 times and is often listed as a coauthor.[56]

---

55. Early in the pandemic I reached out to Jaqui Brogan, now emeritus from Notre Dame. She lamented that he "never ever wrote a single piece of interpretive insight. Not a single critical article on what he had learned." She reported that he was fired from twenty-two jobs—"He just got fired and fired and fired"—and that he was "super smart, totally self-trained; that's why he went to work for Accenture, totally brilliant, just not good with people at all. And that shows in the encyclopedia." She equates him, in his time editing the *NPEPP*, to "the guy who worked for the *Oxford English Dictionary*" and called him a "brilliant, mechanical, maniacal mind." J. Brogan, interview with Meredith Martin.

56. I spoke with and corresponded with Jodi Brogan, with whom he was living when he died, about how I might help her go through his half-finished manuscript on Robert Bridges (which we were planning to write together as we were both huge Bridges fans), and his seven-

Nearly all the English-language texts Brogan referenced in *EVRG* are now searchable in the PPA, and the blue accent color of the PPA's design story recalls the 1999 hyperlinks in his hypertext edition of *EVRG*, of the multiple stories that his structures wanted to tell. Coincidentally, the press sold their printing plant in Lawrenceville in 1993 (when they acquired it, back in 1963, it had been announced with fanfare). When I interviewed Brogan on August 25, 2010, he quipped,

> Also they wanted the whole fucking thing in New Baskerville, so I said okay, I'll generate the whole bloody thing in New Baskerville. And when I was done I bought one of the very first CD Rom versions, 4500, and downloaded the entire PostScript file and burned it and put it in a box and shipped it to them. They called and said, "What is this?" And I said, "It's a CD; don't you have a drive?" So they went out to Best Buy or whatever and bought a drive and put it into the network, and when they printed the first page they almost fell over.

This distinctive voice is, if you read for it, all over the entries he wrote for *NPEPP*. I assume that the press almost fell over because they were impressed by his technological accomplishment, but of course we could also conjecture that they fell over because they were dealing with a personality who had

---

teen bins of boxes, which I was hoping contained some of the harder-to-find materials I wanted to include in my database. There is another story there about how difficult it was for me, as a then assistant professor, to find funding to travel to Indiana and go through the books, or to facilitate the hire of an appraiser who might help me catalog them so that I could see if my library would want to purchase them. Princeton University Library subject specialist John Logan tried to help by suggesting a nearby appraiser (since, after all, the library already owned quite a few things that he had in his collection, though I wanted the rest—notes, hard drives, marginalia). As Logan pointed out, Brogan wasn't famous enough to justify the creation of a collection in his name. He didn't have an institutional affiliation—he was a so-called independent scholar, not a tenured professor. For all Logan knew, Brogan had ended up as a hobbyist who was in the right place at the right time. Alex Preminger's papers would be interesting, I remember Logan saying, or maybe if Brogan had rare materials relating to Slavic prosody, but it was not going to be easy to simply move the boxes, and I'd need to convince our Slavic subject specialist to sponsor my interest. I would also need to coordinate everything myself—the funding, the cataloguing, the coordination of the graduate student or appraiser to visit Indiana and go through the boxes. It was overwhelming, and I messed it up—or rather, I thought I had more time to figure it out. Logan was helpful and supportive, but at that time I certainly didn't understand how to navigate obtaining those seventeen boxes, which would have been transformative for my research.

convinced them to use—and purchase—a system that they did not quite understand.[57]

I could tell the story of how he was misunderstood and contingent and directed that ire and frustration into his obsessive quests to draw parallels between the technical aspects of poetry and some antecedent in the data structures and technologies he taught himself. But the connections between the truth of poetry, or his feeling that poetry could be something purely technical, and the technical aspects of his development as a programmer in the 1990s and early 2000s, are less interesting to me than the fact that he moved his authority away from poetry and into databases. I do not want my fate to mirror his, but I cannot help but see the parallels. His career spanned the move from microfiche to scanned, searchable materials; he both witnessed and helped nudge along this development of information systems for libraries that would restructure how we research and gather information. And in the end, he was valued as a vendor, a technical provider of services, and not as a researcher or author. I fear that putting "digital humanities" in the title of this book, or even the word "data" next to the word "poetry," will cause others to view my work with the same disdain. Why did we let the theorization and construction of the way we research sit in the hands of so few scholars? Why didn't we, why don't we, intervene in the research infrastructures of our universities as these infrastructures became—and become—more and more opaque? Now, when we attempt to go back and present a genealogy of this field that we might call "digital humanities," these moments are a flash in a much larger narrative about the changing nature of research and humanities in the digital age. The project of using technology to display the various arguments and pathways is still valued less than a single, authoritative account of research in a monograph, even if anyone doing research on a scholarly monograph is relying on technology to access and organize their sources. These processes are also methods, and they have several fields attached to them that theorize the interpretive data work necessary to conduct research responsibly in the digital age. By valuing the monograph over these collaborative fields, over the labor of assembling and maintaining new technological infrastructures and the people who build and maintain them, we also—as a profession—refuse to understand or even to face how technologically mediated all aspects of our scholarly research and information environment are by corporations outside of the university. I had

---

57. He then added, "They were very good editors. I respected them." T. V. F. Brogan, interview with Meredith Martin.

to embrace the technical to try to display the cultural record of poetry's data, and I wrote this book because the technical project of the Princeton Prosody Archive, like Brogan's work before mine, does not count and is not legible to or properly valued by the very people who might use the PPA, people who assume that it is a service and not scholarship, who might learn from it without recognizing the interpretive labor that went into its creation, a resource and not a decade's worth of research. There are hundreds—thousands, even—of densely argued, intensely theorized research projects like mine that have changed and are changing what we think we know about the literary past. This book offers an argument against our single-minded emphasis on scholarly models that do not acknowledge our embeddedness in the collaborative structures, technologies, and stories that undergird literary knowledge. I'm not interested in the technical truth of poetry. But the cultural stories that the obsession with poetry's data teaches me to read have helped me understand how much our profession has yet to learn.

6

Coda [How to Cite]

> Computerization was the only feasible method of
> organizing so much information at the time.
>
> T. V. F. BROGAN, *EIDOS* 1, NO. 2 (JULY 1984): 12

NO ONE COULD TELL me how to contact T. V. F. Brogan at first, but eventually, after two emails bounced back, I wrote a letter to a postal address in Indiana and received an email reply. He was diagnosed with esophageal cancer in August 2010, which he mentioned when we first spoke, and he passed away October 23, only two weeks after our last conversation. From our August interview, I learned the story of his coeditorship of *The New Princeton Encyclopedia of Poetry and Poetics* (NPEPP), and of how much work he had done to create the program that could print the various kinds of typescripts necessary to convey the book's many languages. Though my questions were mostly about why he structured *EVRG* the way he did, I could tell he considered his editorial work on *PEPP* his true life's work. The third edition of *PEPP* occupied him obsessively from 1983 to 1991. He was never employed as a tenure-track professor; he wrote and received grants to support his editorial work on *PEPP*. It was in this information environment that he tried to forge a path for himself, participating on the side of navigating and creating resources, and yet never with acknowledgment or credit within the modern research university.

As with the creation of a hyperlinked *EVRG*, he saw the limitations of academic publishing during the moment of the "desktop revolution" and designed the system that would allow Princeton University Press to accurately represent the seventeen languages appearing in *PEPP*. After realizing that he'd never fit in academia once he finished the work on *PEPP*, he moved into the quickly growing field of database design and became a technical manager. He narrated:

> I had NEH grants for three or four years to work on the encyclopedia; then I realized after that this was never going to translate into a career for me because I didn't come up in the formal system in the formal way. I had chosen to do unusual things, and as a result of those choices they were just never going to hire me. I trained myself to be a programmer pretty quickly and then to be a database programmer and then to be a technical manager, and I got a series of jobs very quickly. The market was really good, and the money was really good, and I was good at it, and I could do it, and the reason I was good at it was because of the *PEPP*.[1]

"I didn't come up in the formal system in the formal way" means that he took a job as a partner hire (after leaving one job at the University of Hawaii) so that he could follow his partner to a tenure-track job at Notre Dame, where he had hoped he would be hired (that did not happen, and his sense of entitlement and frustration about that broken promise seeps into his writing). The exhaustive and intense labor of editing and creating the technological infrastructure for *The New Princeton Encyclopedia of Poetry and Poetics* prepared him for his eventual dual career—as a programmer and as a manager—and facilitated his departure from academia, with its overvaluation of single-author monographs and its inability to see his labor as labor worth counting. As I try to write something about citation in a monograph that proves inadequate to the task of collaboration, I am reminded of how the recognized authority of a literary scholar was always just out of reach for Brogan in academia, but it was available to him as a scholar of information, data, and, eventually, computer programming. In all these connections between prosody and technology that Brogan's career brings to light, we also witness ongoing and, I would suggest, limiting tensions within the academy between individual and collaborative scholarship in the humanities, and authority and contingency in the profession.

This monograph is also a result of that limiting tension: I pause here to reflect that I received tenure in 2012, and the work that I undertook on the PPA has relied on a series of internally funded grants and only two externally funded awards. For most of my colleagues in digital humanities, this is unheard of. I have never had to rely on grant support to buy my own time out of

---

1. Brogan.

teaching, and because a course release is my main compensation for my directorship of the Center for Digital Humanities, I seldom teach more than three classes total per academic year. I also have not had to rely on grant funding to pay the full-time, noncontingent staff we hired to build out the Center for Digital Humanities (which had been how most software developers on humanities projects were paid at digital humanities centers across the country). This financial stability is not the situation of most of my colleagues in the profession, and that contingency is one of the reasons that the system from which I benefit is imploding: because I benefit and others do not; because my labor counts, and others' does not; because a monograph counts, but a collaborative project does not.[2] I am narrating my understanding of how those of us in these positions of privilege undervalue the collaborative labor—the invisible labor—of nearly all work in "the humanities."[3]

I am ambivalent about my use of the first-person point of view in this monograph since the Princeton Prosody Archive is the result of collaborative labor. I cannot possibly list all the people and things that contributed to that work: the conversations, design reviews, GitHub issues, user stories, job descriptions, interviews, space planning, performance evaluations, funding proposals, grant reports, and Slack channels; the undergraduate researchers, graduate students researchers, project managers, UX/UI designers, postdoctoral fellows, and research software engineers; and Mary Naydan, project manager and colleague, who read every word of the manuscript for this book more than once. I am immensely proud of having built a center that employs so

---

2. Cf. Nyhan and Duke-Williams, "Joint and Multi-authored Publication Patterns." Coauthorship does not necessarily mean collaboration, and we do not have standards for contribution types in collaborative humanities scholarship.

3. I know that there are structures of security and promotion for many knowledge and cultural heritage workers in libraries and information science; their structures of credit are different from ours, but there are few models where collaborators across a university are compensated equally for collaborative labor. Librarianship is scholarly, not (as it is often counted) merely service oriented. See Sample, "When Does Service Become Scholarship?"; Starkman, "What 'Counts'?"; and "Closing the Evaluation Gap," a special issue of *Journal of Digital Humanities* 1, no. 4 (Fall 2012). Though the new MLA guidelines for evaluating digital scholarship should be released by the time this book is in print, they will make little difference if universities don't adopt them. See also "Fair Cite," an initiative meant to rethink citational practices in the humanities: https://faircite.wordpress.com/. At the CDH, we adhere to the "Collaborators' Bill of Rights." Tanya Clement, Douglas Reside, Brian Croxall, Julia Flanders, Neil Freistat, Steve Jones, Matt Kirschenbaum, Suzanne Lodato, Laura Mandell, Paul Marty, David Miller, Bethany Nowviskie, Stephen Olsen, Tom Scheinfeldt, David Seaman, Mark Tebeau, John Unsworth, and Kay Walter, "Collaborators' Bill of Rights," in Clement and Reside, *Off the Tracks*, 9–10.

many outstanding, intelligent, exciting scholars within a landscape that values humanities scholarship less and less. But yes, I resent that few people see this work as scholarly labor, that a monograph means more than our collective accomplishments, means more than our databases, data sets, projects, coauthored research articles, countless meetings introducing faculty and graduate students to these processes, and contributions to the ongoing conversations about humanities and technology. This book is the reason I am now a full professor, and yet I am writing it about a project that was, in large part, built by Rebecca Koeser, Nick Budak, Meagan Wilson, Xinyi Li, Gissoo Doroudian, Mary Naydan, and, in its earlier phases, Grant Wythoff. Citing the PPA, of which I am an editor, when I cite the material objects that I access through the PPA is one way to give these other people credit for that work.

To paraphrase Sara Ahmed, citational structures can form what we call disciplines.[4] In this book, I try to create citations that welcome scholars into the vast and yet very differentiated set of conversations that make up the disciplines of digital humanities. It is not one field with a field statement; and because our concept of "digital" shifts and changes with new media technologies and our concept of "humanities" shifts and changes with institutional restructuring and with political meddling, those of us who work with or on technology are often describing the history of a field at the same time as we are trying to describe our methodologies (which vary from scholar to scholar). The citations in this book cannot cover the entire history of "digital humanities" just as they do not cover the entire history of thinking about "prosody" or even the entire history of recent work that looks at poetry's data computationally. What the citations attempt is to foreground a series of ongoing conversations about scholarly practice and to give some orientation in the several distinct fields that inform my approach to digital humanities, including critical archival studies, critical data studies, bibliography, book history, critical code studies, software studies, science and technology studies, history of science, history of computing, information studies, and media studies, media history, and media archeology.

Jonathan Blaney and Judith Siefring explore "the resistance to citing digital sources that is still widespread in the humanities." They wrote: "we have found

---

4. Feminist Killjoys Blog, "Making Feminist Points," September 11, 2013, https://feministkilljoys.com/2013/09/11/making-feminist-points/. On the politics of citation more broadly, see the excellent issue of *Diacritics* 48, no. 3 (2020), "Citation, Otherwise." For an overview of citational justice work in DH in particular, see Earhart, Risam, and Bruno, "Citational Politics."

this resistance is particularly prevalent where a print version of the source also exists."[5] Each of the historical sources in this book comes from the Princeton Prosody Archive, which is built with images and data from HathiTrust and ECCO.

Of the PPA, we state on the website, "This project is the product of intense and ongoing collaboration, which makes any attempt to assign authorship in a citation a problematic endeavor.... Because our collection uses digitized works from HathiTrust or Gale, please use HathiTrust or Gale's recommended citation *and* cite the Princeton Prosody Archive."

To cite the PPA, the following information may be added to the end of your standard MLA or Chicago bibliography entry or note citation:

> Accessed [date] via *Princeton Prosody Archive*, edited by Meredith Martin et al., Center for Digital Humanities Princeton University.

If you wish to include a single bibliography entry for this resource, the following may be used:

> *Princeton Prosody Archive*. Version 3.12.1. Center for Digital Humanities at Princeton, 2018. http//prosody.princeton.edu. Accessed June 4, 2024.

And if your style guide insists on author names, for bibliography entries:

> Martin, Meredith, Meagan Wilson, Mary Naydan, and Rebecca Sutton Koeser, eds. *Princeton Prosody Archive*. Version 3.12.1. Center for Digital Humanities at Princeton, 2018. http//prosody.princeton.edu. Accessed June 4, 2024.

Or for full citations in endnotes or in footnotes:

> Meredith Martin, Meagan Wilson, Mary Naydan, and Rebecca Sutton Koeser, eds., *Princeton Prosody Archive*, version 3.12.1, Center for Digital Humanities at Princeton, 2018, http//prosody.princeton.edu, accessed June 4, 2024.

These citations are not pleasant to look at in print form, and we will not maintain the PPA for as long as this book will last. As a compromise, I have put full citation information (recommended on the PPA "how to cite" page) in the appendix of this book for each of the reproduced images in the figures. In the bibliography, you will find the shorter file path from the PPA rather than the

---

5. Blaney and Siefring, "Culture of Non-citation." Roman Bleier posits the use of persistent identifiers and permalink strategies in "How to Cite This Digital Edition." See also McDaytor, "Tagging the Faces behind the Code."

full citation. The file paths will work as long as the PPA is maintained, but even when they break you will see, there, the traces of where and how I accessed these sources, and how their assembly in the database helped me to assemble the arguments I make in this book. They use long links with confusing characters. Looking at them in print is uncomfortable and off-putting, as if someone must have made a mistake. They are not tidy. But they are citing the labor, otherwise invisible, that we and others expended to create the database that allowed the researcher to access that particular source, while also citing the provenance of that work, giving a media archeology in miniature of how the researcher was able to access the digitized historical page (via our data work and APIs and architecture, then via the digitization process at the library that scanned the book for Google and that was then ingested by HathiTrust or, in the case of ECCO, digitized from microfiche). In some small way, then, these citations try to show that this monograph is not a product of my own research interests in isolation, but the result of a process of learning about the knowledge structures I took for granted and did not understand. By citing the Center for Digital Humanities in addition to the PPA, I am acknowledging that the larger mission of our research center was the product of some of those processes, and I reevaluate what those mean for the PPA (which will end, but also become an experiment in thinking about ending) and for all our collaborative research and teaching.[6] I imagine all citational practices will undergo changes in the coming years as we continue to shift our relationship to and understanding of the technological remediations of culture we access on our computers. Even when the links I provide in this book break, and they will, we can read these numbers as the mark of how we found and how we read poetry's historical data in the first quarter of the twenty-first century. And I hope they will be read, also, as a trace of the important, collaborative labor of building new knowledge in the humanities.

6. For more on process over product and fair labor practices in DH, see Ross and Pilsch, "Labor, Alienation, and the Digital Humanities."

APPENDIX: FULL CITATION INFORMATION
FOR PPA SOURCES

Figure 1. Goold Brown, *The Grammar of English Grammars* (New York: Samuel S. and William Wood, 1851), HathiTrust, https://babel.hathitrust.org/cgi/pt?id=nyp.33433069256851&seq=15, accessed June 4, 2024, via *Princeton Prosody Archive*, edited by Meredith Martin et al., Center for Digital Humanities, Princeton University, https://prosody.princeton.edu/archive/nyp.33433069256851/.

Figure 2. Goold Brown, *The Grammar of English Grammars* (New York: Samuel S. and William Wood, 1884), 827, HathiTrust, https://babel.hathitrust.org/cgi/pt?id=wu.89099427403&seq=834&view=1up, accessed June 4, 2024, via *Princeton Prosody Archive*, edited by Meredith Martin et al., Center for Digital Humanities, Princeton University, https://prosody.princeton.edu/archive/wu.89099427403/.

Figure 3. Goold Brown, *The Grammar of English Grammars* (New York: Samuel S. and William Wood, 1884), 828, HathiTrust, https://babel.hathitrust.org/cgi/pt?id=wu.89099427403&seq=834&view=1up, accessed June 4, 2024, via *Princeton Prosody Archive*, edited by Meredith Martin et al., Center for Digital Humanities, Princeton University, https://prosody.princeton.edu/archive/wu.89099427403/.

Figure 6. Edward Bysshe, *The Art of English Poetry Containing, I. Rules for Making Verses. II A Dictionary of Rhymes. III. A Collection of the Most Natural, Agreeable, and Notable Thoughts, Viz. Allusions, Similes, Descriptions, and Characters, of Persons and Things, That Are to Be Found in the Best English Poets* (London: R. Knaplock at the Angel in St. Paul's Church-Yard; E. Castle next Scotland-Yard-Gate by White-Hall; and B. Tooke at the Middle-Temple-Gate in Fleet Street, 1702), HathiTrust, https://babel.hathitrust.org/cgi/pt?id=uc1.31175035204380&seq=5, accessed May 24, 2024, via *Princeton Prosody Archive*, edited by Meredith Martin et al., Center for Digital Humanities, Princeton University, https://prosody.princeton.edu/archive/uc1.31175035204380/.

Figure 10. "A Tabular View of the Science of Elocution," in S. S. Hamill, *The Science of Elocution* (New York: Nelson and Philips, 1872), 20, HathiTrust, https://babel.hathitrust.org/cgi/pt?id=nnc1.cu58274898&seq=26, accessed June 4, 2024, via *Princeton Prosody Archive*, edited by Meredith Martin et al., Center for Digital Humanities, Princeton University, https://prosody.princeton.edu/archive/nnc1.cu58274898/.

Figure 12. From William Gardiner, *The Music of Nature; or, Attempt to Prove That What Is Passionate and Pleasing in the Art of Singing, Speaking, and Performing upon Musical Instruments, Is Derived from the Sounds of the Animated World; With Curious and Interesting Illustrations* (London: Rees, Orme, Brown, Green, and Longham, 1832), 156, HathiTrust, https://babel.hathitrust.org/cgi/pt?id=hvd.ml14ed&seq=172, accessed June 4, 2024, via *Princeton Prosody Archive*, edited by Meredith Martin et al., Center for Digital Humanities, Princeton University, https://prosody.princeton.edu/archive/hvd.ml14ed/.

Figure 13. William Gardiner, *The Music of Nature; or, Attempt to Prove That What Is Passionate and Pleasing in the Art of Singing, Speaking, and Performing upon Musical Instruments, Is Derived from the Sounds of the Animated World; With Curious and Interesting Illustrations* (London: Rees, Orme, Brown, Green, and Longham, 1832), 39, HathiTrust, https://babel.hathitrust.org/cgi/pt?id=hvd.ml14ed&seq=55, accessed June 4, 2024, via *Princeton Prosody Archive*, edited by Meredith Martin et al., Center for Digital Humanities, Princeton University, https://prosody.princeton.edu/archive/hvd.ml14ed/.

Figure 14. George Saintsbury, *A History of English Prosody from the Twelfth Century to the Present Day*, vol. 2 (London: Macmillan, 1908), 548, HathiTrust, https://babel.hathitrust.org/cgi/pt?id=uc1.$b792864&seq=560, accessed June 4, 2024, via *Princeton Prosody Archive*, edited by Meredith Martin et al., Center for Digital Humanities, Princeton University, https://prosody.princeton.edu/archive/uc1.b3515213/.

Figure 15. John Thelwall, *Selections for the Illustration of a Course of Instructions on the Rhythmus and Utterance of the English Language: With an Introductory Essay on the Application of Rhythmical Science to the Treatment of Impediments, and the Improvement of Our National Oratory; And an Elementary Analysis of the Science and Practice of Elocution, Composition, &c.* (J. M'Creery, Black-Horse-Court; and Sold by Messrs. Arch, Cornhill; Ridgeway, Piccadilly; Kent, Holborn: and Harwood, Great Russell-Street, 1812), xlix, HathiTrust, https://babel.hathitrust.org/cgi/pt?id=nnc1.1002383080&view=1up&seq=57, accessed June 4, 2024, via *Princeton Prosody Archive*, edited by Meredith Martin et al., Center for Digital Humanities, Princeton University, https://prosody.princeton.edu/archive/nnc1.1002383080/.

Figure 16. Alexander Ellis, *The Essentials of Phonetics* (London: F. Pitman, 1848), 77, HathiTrust, https://babel.hathitrust.org/cgi/pt?id=nyp.33433082 185335&seq=99, accessed June 4, 2024, via *Princeton Prosody Archive*, edited by Meredith Martin et al., Center for Digital Humanities, Princeton University, https://prosody.princeton.edu/archive/nyp.33433082185335/.

Figure 17. Raymond Alden, *English Verse: Specimens Illustrating Its Principles and History* (New York: H. Holt, 1903), 4, HathiTrust, https://babel.hathitrust.org/cgi/pt?id=uc1.$b252798&seq=24, accessed June 4, 2024, via *Princeton Prosody Archive*, edited by Meredith Martin et al., Center for Digital Humanities, Princeton University, https://prosody.princeton.edu/archive/uc1.$b252798/.

Figure 18. William Thomson, *The Basis of English Rhythm* (Glasgow: W. & R. Holmes, 1904), 54, HathiTrust, https://babel.hathitrust.org/cgi/pt?id=wu.89099904617&seq=56, accessed June 4, 2024, via *Princeton Prosody Archive*, edited by Meredith Martin et al., Center for Digital Humanities, Princeton University, https://prosody.princeton.edu/archive/wu.89099904617/.

Figure 23. Adelaide Crapsey, from *A Study in English Metrics* (New York: Alfred A. Knopf, 1918), 21, HathiTrust, https://babel.hathitrust.org/cgi/pt?id=mdp.39015030934858&seq=25, accessed June 4, 2024, via *Princeton Prosody Archive*, edited by Meredith Martin et al., Center for Digital Humanities, Princeton University. https://prosody.princeton.edu/archive/mdp.39015030934858/.

Figure 24. L. T. Weeks, "The Order of Rimes in the English Sonnet," *Modern Language Notes* 25, no. 6 (1910): 179, HathiTrust, https://babel.hathitrust.org/cgi/pt?id=mdp.39015060429357&view=1up&seq=210, accessed June 4, 2024, via *Princeton Prosody Archive*, edited by Meredith Martin et al., Center for Digital Humanities, Princeton University, https://prosody.princeton.edu/archive/mdp.39015060429357-p176/?query=.

Figure 27. John Thelwall, *Selections for the Illustration for a Course of Instructions on the Rhythmus and Utterance of the English Language: With an Introductory Essay on the Application of Rhythmical Science to the Treatment of Impediments, the Improvement of Our National Oratory; And an Elementary Analysis of the Science and Practice of Elocution, Composition, &c.* (London: J. M. M'Creery, 1812), xlvii, HathiTrust, https://babel.hathitrust.org/cgi/pt?id=mdp.390150

21952943&seq=65, accessed June 4, 2024, via *Princeton Prosody Archive*, edited by Meredith Martin et al., Center for Digital Humanities, Princeton University, https://prosody.princeton.edu/archive/mdp.39015021952943/.

Figure 28. Joshua Steele, *Prosodia Rationalis: Or an Essay toward Establishing the Melody and Measure of Speech, to Be Expressed and Perpetuated by Peculiar Symbols* (London: J. Nichols, 1779), 28, Eighteenth Century Collections Online, https://go-gale-com.ezproxy.princeton.edu/ps/i.do?p=ECCO&u=prin77918&id=GALE|CW0113075673&v=2.1&it=r&sid=gale_api&sPage=46&asid=948a3eca, accessed June 4, 2024, via *Princeton Prosody Archive*, edited by Meredith Martin et al., Center for Digital Humanities, Princeton University, https://prosody.princeton.edu/archive/CW0113075673/.

ACKNOWLEDGMENTS

The Center for Digital Humanities (CDH) research community is the best possible place I could imagine working. I am so proud of what we do and how we do it. From our humble beginnings when it was just an old psych lab to our current extended family, every person who has come through our doors has taught me something. The CDH and the PPA grew in tandem, so I will start with my earliest collaborators on both projects: Grant Wythoff, Ben Johnston, David Mimno, Clifford Wulfman, Jean Bauer, and Travis Brown. Thank you, Nick Budak, Gissoo Doroudian, Meg Hicks, Xinyi Li, and Kevin McElwee for transforming the project in 2018. Former graduate students Yan Che, Catilin Crandell, Colette Johnson, Gregory Londe, Liora Selinger, John Schulz, and Amelia Worsley all have thought through and with the data in the PPA. Meagan Wilson, you are one of a kind; I would have given up many times if it weren't for your determination. The PPA exists because of you. Undergraduate researchers Armani Aguiar, Caroline Bailey, Eve Fleisig, Christian Fryer-Davis, Carlos Giron, Selena Hostetler, Gavin Keasler, Margaret King, Teddy Leane, Elizabeth Macksey, Andrew Matos, Anthony Nathan, Sydney Peng, Cecilia Quirk, Sally Root, Olivia Roslansky, Paul Schorin, Molly Taylor, Sylvie Thode, Claire Thornton, Andrew Tye, Vinicius Wagner, Capella Yee, and James Zhang have all contributed interpretive data work, original research, or editorial insight to this project. Rebecca Sutton Koeser has been thinking with me about poetry's data for years, and has patiently taught me so much about this work. Ryan Heuser, thank you particularly for your help reading early drafts. Laure Thompson and Wouter Haverals, it is thanks to you both that we are finally discovering all that we knew we could learn from this data. Jim Casey and Sierra Eckert, you are all over these pages; thank you for your belief in me and this project. Historical poetics reading group, this is for you, because of you, and about you: Max Cavitch, Michael Cohen, Ben Friedlander, Mary Ellis Gibson, Erin Kappeler, Charles Laporte, Naomi Levine, Tricia Lootens, Yopie Prins, Jason Rudy, Alex Socarides, and Carolyn Williams. To graduate students past and current: Veronica Alfano, Jessica Brofsky, Chelsea Clark, Tammuz Frankel, Madeleine Joelson, Urvi Kumbhat, Diana Little, Emily Lobb, Tenisha McDonald, Gabriel Medina, Lottie Page, Arush Pande, Mary Shelley Reid, Lewis Roberts, Isabelle Stuart, and Pasquale Toscano—thank you for thinking about poetry's data and poetic form with me.

I have benefited from the enthusiasm and support of several friends and colleagues who have read, heard me talk about, or have otherwise helped me shape aspects of the PPA and this book: Amelia Acker, Mark Algee-Hewitt, Ruha Benjamin, Alison Booth, Happy Buzaaba, Alison Chapman, Tanya Clement, Annemarie Drury, Christiane Fellbaum, Dino Felluga, Frances Ferguson, Paul Fyfe, Ben Glaser, Jackie Goldsby, Roland Greene, Natalie Houston, Anne Jarvis, Simon Jarvis, Andrew Jewell, Zoe LeBlanc, Casie LeGette, John Logan, Shannon Mattern, Emily McGinn, Lisa Moore, James Mulholland, Brad Pasanek, John Plotz, Leah Price, Rita Raley, Christine Roughan, Jesse Sheidlower, Courtney Weiss Smith, David Smith, Daniel Snelson, Andrew Stauffer, Dustin Stewart, Jeff Strabone, Jon Stroop, Dennis Tenen, Toma Tomasovic, Kyla Wazana Tompkins and Ted Underwood. My collaborators on the Collective of Data Collectives and the Nineteenth-Century Data Collective have helped me imagine shared knowledge infrastructures: Anthie Georgiadi, Gabriel Hankins, Laura McGrath, Anna Preus, Sarah Reif-Connell, Dan Sinykin, Melanie Walsh, Megan Ward, and Mi Yu. I presented earliest versions of parts of this book at UC-Irvine in January 2020 with Harris Feinsod, Caleb Smith, and Juliana Spahr; and those discussions were crucial to thinking about the archive of prosody. Early conversations with Sara Mesle and Tey Meadow helped me get up the courage to put myself in the story. Talia Schaffer, mentor extraordinaire, first suggested that I put the other book aside and just write this one, so I did. Susan Stewart asked me early on why I hadn't written a book about the PPA. Bill Gleason has always believed in its contribution, and in me. Brian Kernighan, in addition to being an excellent proofreader, is also a pretty decent programmer and I am grateful to have taught with him and learned from him. I could not have done that writing without the guiding enthusiasm of Michelle Nieman. Andrew Piper helped me imagine how to conceptualize the invisible labor of field building. Nathan Hensley cheered me on when I needed it most. Sarah Osment, thank you for hopping on to help at the frenetic end.

As I wrote this book, I worked with Zoe LeBlanc on a series of interviews for our coauthored project, *Data Work in the Humanities*. Though I do not cite any of those conversations directly in this book, I know that by sheer osmosis this book is stronger because of what I learned from those conversations, and so I cite and thank them here: Ruth Ahnert, Laurie Allen, Maria Antoniak, Kath Bode, Ryan Cordell, Gimena del Rio Riande, Quinn Dombrowski, Miguel Escobar Varela, Lorena Gautherau, Alex Gil, Jo Guldi, Lauren Klein, Jessica Marie Johnson, Benjamin Germaine Lee, Trevor Owens, Marisa Parham, Miriam Posner, Sylvia Fernández Quintanilla, Roopika Risam, Ben Schmidt, Melissa Terras, Lauren Tilton, Gabriela Baeza Ventura, Carolina Villaroel, Scott Weingart, and Bryan Winston.

I am grateful for the collaboration of Anne Savarese and the incredible team at Princeton University Press. Kathleen Kageff is a phenomenal copyeditor. Theresa Liu is an amazing production editor. Thank you also to Christie Henry, Eric Crahan, Matt Rohal, James Collier, Lauren Reese, Dimitri Karetnikov, Karl Spurzem (for the cover), and William Pagdatoon (for publicity).

Other friends and colleagues whose love and support I feel include Tanya Agathoclaous, Helena Alexander, Miriam Allersma, Ruha Benjamin, Susan Blumenthal, Kathy Brodhag, Martha Carlson, Margaret Carr, Allison Carruth, Zahid Chaudhary, Janice Clear, Sean Cotter, Molly Crockett, Kathleen Crown, Jeff Dolven, Jay Dominick, Aaron Dunn, Eric Foster, Matt Hopkins, Matthew Jones, Lani Kawamoto, Janine Konkel, John Lacombe, Danny Lavery, Grace Lavery, Wendy Anne Lee, Dana Linane, Meg Lynch, Tricia McElroy, Indra Mukhopadhyay, Lindsay Nordell, Forrest Perry, Justin Read, Anne Reader, Neile Rissmiller, Jess Roberts, Carrie Ruddick, Marina Rustow, Charles Sabatos, Gayle Salamon, Elizabeth Samios, Starry Schor, Jean Shaver, Eve Sorum, Kate Stanton, Justin Steinhouse, Brandon Stewart, Tamara Thatcher, Mary Thiel, Sarah Thody, Valerie Kouras Walker, John Whittier-Ferguson, Jeri Wieringa, Vivica Williams, Siona Wilson, Mana Winter, Tamsen Wolff, Autumn Womack, Christine Woodruff, Tricia York, and Jon, Sarah, and Eva Zames. Emily Chester, thank you for taking such good care of Ada. Sydney Cummings, thank you for helping me show up for myself. Thank you to First Ascent Coffee. Virginia Jackson and Meredith McGill have made this a better book with every conversation and edit. Thank you to the anonymous reviewers and to all readers and interlocutors and audiences with whom I have workshopped these ideas over the past several years.

Erik Schneiderhan, Virginia Ferguson, and Glenda Musoba, you have been a part of this book since the start. I have so much gratitude for our support system and for each of you.

Natasha Ermolaev, thank you for being my external hard drive, my cheerleader, my editor, my anchor, and my dear, dear friend. Mary Naydan, you have transformed the CDH, the PPA, and this book; you are the person with whom I have thought most about these arguments over the past six years, and you have made both the PPA and *Poetry's Data* possible. I am so grateful that you are a part of my life and that you took on the project of editing this book into its final form.

I lost three friends during the writing of this book. Will Noel, I am still stunned that you are gone. Rebecca Munson, you are all over these pages, and your presence is stitched into the fabric of what we do at the CDH. Stewart Coleman, my first best friend, I feel your belief in me and your love for me, and I miss you so damn much.

Books take people away from their families, yet I am lucky that I have been able to see my family so often over the past four years. Thanks to our large and loving family: Bonnie Smith, Oliver Martin, Owen Smith, Bear Smith, Jan Smith, Bill Smith, Laura Smith, Pete Febrarro, Sarah Smith, Ryan Krzos, Izzy Smith, and Matt Johnson. Thank you, Donna Murphy, Gardner Murphy, and Mannie Murphy. I owe my obsession with early computing to long conversations during my commute with my father, Dr. Robert Martin IV, whose dissertation is titled "Why Software Projects Fail." I owe my obsession with language to my mother, Mary Martin, Montessori expert and literacy pioneer. I owe my commitment to writing and reading to my brother, Robert Martin V, my first editor and my favorite writer. Joe, you are the best one, the sun shining on the pines; thank you for all that you sacrificed so that I could finish this book. Ada, I love you more than all the books in the world and all the stars in the sky.

BIBLIOGRAPHY

Adler, Melissa. *Cruising the Library: Perversities in the Organization of Knowledge*. New York: Fordham University Press, 2017.

Adler, Melissa, and Greg Nightingale. "Books and Imaginary Being(s): The Monstrosity of Library Classifications." *Proceedings from the 2020 Annual Meeting of the Document Academy* 7, no. 6 (2020): 1–9.

Alden, Raymond Macdonald. *English Verse: Specimens Illustrating Its Principles and History*. New York: H. Holt, 1903. https://prosody.princeton.edu/archive/uc1.$b252798/.

Alfano, Veronica Rose, and Andrew Stauffer, eds. *Virtual Victorians: Networks, Connections, Technologies*. New York: Palgrave Macmillan, 2015.

Altick, Richard, and John J. Fenstermaker. *The Art of Literary Research*. New York: Norton, 1963.

Arafat, Sachi, and Elham Ashoori. *Search Foundations*. Cambridge, MA: MIT Press, 2019.

Aruffo, David. *A Rational Guide to Verse: Scansion Made Simple*. Gainesville, FL: Acoustic Learning, 2013.

———. *A Rational Guide to Verse: Scansion Made Simple Workbook*. Gainesville, FL: Acoustic Learning, 2014.

Attridge, Derek. *Poetic Rhythm*. Cambridge: Cambridge University Press, 1996.

Battles, Matthew. *Library: An Unquiet History*. New York: W. W. Norton, 2003.

Berman, Sanford. *Prejudices and Antipathies: A Tract on LC Subject Heads concerning People*. Metuchen, NJ: Scarecrow, 1971.

Bernard, Stephen Jarrod. "Edward Bysshe and 'The Art of English Poetry': Reading Writing in the Eighteenth Century." *Eighteenth-Century Studies* 46, no. 1 (2012): 113–29.

Berry, Dorothy. "The House Archives Built." Up//root, June 22, 2021. https://www.uproot.space/features/thehouse-archives-built. Accessed June 24, 2024.

Bervin, Jen. "The Dickinson Composites Series." https://www.jenbervin.com/projects/the-dickinson-composites-series#2. Accessed January 24, 2024.

Binder, Jeffrey. *Language and the Rise of the Algorithm*. Chicago: University of Chicago Press, 2022.

Birkerts, Sven. *The Gutenberg Elegies*. New York: Farrar, Straus and Giroux, 2006.

Blair, Ann M. *Too Much to Know: Managing Scholarly Information before the Modern Age*. New Haven, CT: Yale University Press, 2010.

Blair, Hugh. *Abridgment of Lectures on Rhetoric by Hugh Blair*. Edited by "A Teacher of Philadelphia." 1832. https://prosody.princeton.edu/archive/nyp.33433082515648/.

Blaney, Jonathan, Sarah Milligan, Marty Steer, and Jane Winters. *Doing Digital History*. Manchester: Manchester University Press, 2021.

Blaney, Jonathan, and Judith Siefring. "A Culture of Non-citation: Assessing the Digital Impact of British History Online and the Early English Books Online Text Creation Partnership." *Digital Humanities Quarterly* 11, no. 1 (2011). https://www.digitalhumanities.org/dhq/vol/11/1/000282/000282.html.

Blau, Eleanor. "O. B. Hardison Jr. Is Dead at 61; Author and Folger Library Head." *New York Times*, August 7, 1990, 6.

Bleier, Roman. "How to Cite This Digital Edition." *Digital Humanities Quarterly* 15, no. 3 (2021). https://www.digitalhumanities.org/dhq/vol/15/3/000561/000561.html.

Bode, Katherine. "What's the Matter with Computational Literary Studies?" *Critical Inquiry* 49, no. 4 (2023): 507–29.

———. *A World of Fiction: Digital Collections and the Future of Literary History*. Ann Arbor: University of Michigan Press, 2018.

Booth, Alison. "Mid-range Reading: Not a Manifesto." *PLMA* 132, no. 2 (2017): 620–27.

Borgman, Christine L. *Big Data, Little Data, No Data: Scholarship in the Networked World*. Cambridge, MA: MIT Press, 2015.

———. "From Acting Locally to Thinking Globally: A Brief History of Library Automation." *Library Quarterly: Information, Community, Policy* 67, no. 3 (1997): 3–32.

Bories, Anne-Sophie, Petr Plecháč, and Pablo Ruiz. *Computational Stylistics in Poetry, Prose, and Drama*. Berlin: De Gruyter, 2023.

Bories, Anne-Sophie, Gérald Purnelle, and Hugues Marchal, eds. *Plotting Poetry*. Liège: Presses Universitaires de Liège, 2021.

Bourdieu, Pierre. *Distinction: A Social Critique of the Judgement of Taste*. Translated by Richard Nice. Cambridge, MA: Harvard University Press, 1984.

Bowker, Geoffrey, Karen Baker, Florence Miller, and, and David Ribes. "Toward Information Infrastructure Studies: Ways of Knowing in a Network Environment." In *International Handbook of Internet Research*, edited by Jeremy Hunsinger et al., 71–117. Dordrecht: Springer Nature, 2010.

Bowker, Geoffrey, and Susan Leigh Star. *Sorting Things Out: Classification and Its Consequences*. Cambridge, MA: MIT Press, 1999.

Box, George E. P. "Science and Statistics." *Journal of the American Statistical Association* 71, no. 356 (December 1976): 791–99.

Boyd, James. *Elements of English Composition, Grammatical, Rhetorical, and Practical*. New York: A. S. Barnes and Burr, 1860.

Brandt, Richard L. *The Google Guys*. New York: Penguin, 2011.

Brin, Sergey, and Lawrence Page. "The Anatomy of a Large-Scale Hypertextual Web Search Engine." *Computer Networks and ISDN Systems* 30 (1998): 107–17.

Brogan, Jaqui. Interview with Meredith Martin. April 2020.

Brogan, T. V. F., ed. *EIDOS: The International Prosody Bulletin* 1, no. 1 (April 1984).

———, ed. *EIDOS: The International Prosody Bulletin* 1, no. 2 (July 1984).

———, ed. *EIDOS: The International Prosody Bulletin* 2, nos. 1 and 2 (April–July 1985).

———. *English Versification, 1570–1980: A Reference Guide with a Global Appendix*. Baltimore: Johns Hopkins University Press, 1981.

———. *English Versification, 1570–1980: A Reference Guide with a Global Appendix; Hypertext Version*. Baltimore: Johns Hopkins University Press, 1981, 1999.

———. Interview with Meredith Martin. August 10–25, 2010.

———, ed. *The New Princeton Handbook of Poetic Terms*. Princeton, NJ: Princeton University Press, 1994.

———, ed. *The Princeton Handbook of Multicultural Poetries*. Princeton, NJ: Princeton University Press, 1996.

———. *Verseform: A Comparative Bibliography*. Baltimore: Johns Hopkins University Press, 1989.

Brooks, Sarah Warner. *English Poetry and Poets*. Boston: Estes and Lauriat, 1890. https://prosody.princeton.edu/archive/nyp.33433074834866/.

Broussard, Meredith. *Artificial Unintelligence: How Computers Misunderstand the World*. Cambridge, MA: MIT Press, 2019.

———. *More Than a Glitch: Confronting Race, Gender, and Ability Bias in Tech*. Cambridge, MA: MIT Press, 2023.

Brown, Goold. *The Grammar of English Grammars*. New York: Samuel S. and William Wood, 1851. https://prosody.princeton.edu/archive/nyp.33433069256851/.

Brown, Susan, Patricia Clemens, and Isobel Grundy, eds. *The Orlando Project*. htttps://www.artsrn.ualberta.ca/Orlando. Accessed September 26, 2024.

Buurma, Rachel, and Laura Heffernan. "Search and Replace: Josephine Miles and the Origins of Distant Reading." *Modernism/Modernity* 3, no. 1 (2018): 1–9.

Bysshe, Edward. *The Art of English Poetry Containing, I. Rules for Making Verses. II A Dictionary of Rhymes. III. A Collection of the Most Natural, Agreeable, and Notable Thoughts, Viz. Allusions, Similes, Descriptions, and Characters, of Persons and Things, That Are to Be Found in the Best English Poets*. London: R. Knaplock at the Angel in St. Paul's Church-Yard; E. Castle next Scotland-Yard-Gate by White-Hall; and B. Tooke at the Middle-Temple-Gate in Fleet Street, 1702. https://prosody.princeton.edu/archive/ucl.31175035204380/.

———. *The Art of English Poetry: The Second Edition Corrected and Improved*. London: Sam Buckley, 1705. https://prosody.princeton.edu/archive/CW0110721087/.

Camlot, Jason. *Phono-poetics: The Making of Early Literary Recordings*. Palo Alto, CA: Stanford University Press, 2019.

Campbell-Kelly, Martin. *I.C.L.: A Business and Technical History*. Oxford: Clarendon, 1989.

Carlson, Julia. *Romantic Marks and Measures: Wordsworth's Poetry and Fields of Print*. Philadelphia: University of Pennsylvania Press, 2016.

Carper, Thomas. *Meter and Meaning: An Introduction to Rhythm in Poetry*. New York: Routledge, 2003.

Caswell, Michelle. "'The Archive' Is Not Archives: On Acknowledging the Intellectual Contributions of Archival Studies." *Reconstruction* 16, no. 1 (2016). https://escholarship.org/uc/item/7bn4v1fk.

———. *Urgent Archives*. New York: Routledge, 2021.

Caswell, Michelle, Ricardo Punzalan, and T-Kay Sangwand. "Critical Archival Studies: An Introduction." *Journal of Library and Information Studies* 1, no. 2 (2017): 1–8.

Chadwyck-Healey, Charles. "Personal Interview, Part 1 of 2." YouTube, Professor Alan McFarlane-Ayababa, November 4, 2009. https://www.youtube.com/watch?v=2W8RoMFP5ps&ab_channel=ProfAlanMacfarlane-Ayabaya. 55:51:01–1:09:41:12.

———. *Publishing for Libraries at the Dawn of the Digital Age*. London: Bloomsbury Books, 2021.

Chapman, Alison. "Digital Studies." In *Blackwell Encyclopedia of Victorian Literature, 1840–1870*, edited by Dino Franco Felluga, Pamela K. Gilbert, and Linda K. Hughes, 434–43. London: Wiley-Blackwell, 2015.
———. "Digital Victorian Periodical Poetry." *Digital Victorian Periodical Poetry Project.* https://dvpp.uvic.ca/. Accessed June 24, 2024.
———. "Transatlantic Mediations: Teaching Victorian Poetry in the New Print Media." In *Teaching Transatlanticism: Resources for Teaching Anglo-American Nineteenth-Century Print Culture*, edited by Linda K. Hughes and Sarah R. Robbins, 211–24. Edinburgh: Edinburgh University Press, 2018.
———. "Virtual Victorian Poetry." *Virtual Victorians: Networks, Connections, Technologies*, edited by Veronica Rose Alfano and Andrew Stauffer, 145–66. London: Palgrave Macmillan, 2015.
Chatterjee, Ronjaunee, Alicia Mireles Christoff, and Amy R. Wong, "Undisciplining Victorian Studies." *Los Angeles Review of Books*, July 10, 2020. https://lareviewofbooks.org/article/undisciplining-victorian-studies/.
Chun, Wendy Hui Kyong Chun, and Thomas Keenen, eds. *New Media, Old Media: A History and Theory Reader.* New York: Routledge, 2006.
Clement, Tanya. *Dissonant Records: Close Listening to Literary Archives.* Boston: MIT Press, 2024.
Clement, Tanya E., and Douglas Reside. *Off the Tracks: Laying New Lines for Digital Humanities Scholars.* College Park, MD: Maryland Institute of Technology in the Humanities, 2011.
Clement, Tanya, Sara Steger, John Unsworth, and Kirsten Uskhalo. "How Not to Read a Million Books." October 2008. https://people.brandeis.edu/~unsworth/hownot2read.rutgers.html.
Cobb, Lyman. *Cobb's New Spelling Book.* New York: Andrus, McChain, 1842. https://prosody.princeton.edu/archive/nyp.33433069253171/.
Codd, E. F. "A Relational Model of Data for Large Shared Data Banks." *Communications of the ACM* 14, no. 6 (June 1970): 377–87.
Cohen, Dan. *Searching for the Victorians* (blog). October 4, 2010. http://dancohen.org.
Cohen, Dan, and Frederick Gibbs. "A Conversation with Data: Prospecting Victorian Words and Ideas." *Victorian Studies* 54, no. 1 (Autumn 2011): 69–77.
Cohen, Patricia. "Analyzing Literature by Words and Numbers." *New York Times*, December 3, 2010. https://www.nytimes.com/2010/12/04/books/04victorian.html.
Cordell, Ryan. " 'Q I-jtb the Raven.' " *Book History* 20 (2017): 188–225.
———. "Viral Textuality in Nineteenth-Century U.S. Newspaper Exchanges." In *Virtual Victorians: Networks, Connections, Technologies*, edited by Veronica Rose Alfano and Andrew Stauffer, 29–52: London: Palgrave Macmillan, 2015.
Cordell, Ryan, and Abby Mullen. "Fugitive Verses: The Circulation of Poems in Nineteenth-Century American Newspapers." *American Periodicals* 27, no. 1 (Spring 2017): 29–52.
Cordell, Ryan, and David Smith. *Viral Texts: Mapping Networks of Reprinting in 19th-Century Newspapers and Magazines.* 2022. http://viraltexts.org.
Cordell, Ryan, David Smith, and Abby Mullen. "Computational Methods for Uncovering Reprinted Texts in Antebellum Newspapers." *American Literary History* 27, no. 3 (August 2015): E1–E15.
———. "Reprinting, Circulation, and the Network Author in Antebellum Newspapers." *American Literary History* 27, no. 3 (August 2015): 417–45.
Couch, Arthur Quiller, ed. *The Oxford Book of English Verse.* Oxford: Oxford University Press, 1901. https://prosody.princeton.edu/archive/mdp.39015009203343/.

Crane, Gregory. "What Do You Do with a Million Books?" *D-Lib Magazine* 12, no. 3 (March 2006). https://www.dlib.org/dlib/march06/crane/03crane.html.

Crapsey, Adelaide. *A Study in English Metrics*. New York: Alfred A. Knopf, 1918. https://prosody.princeton.edu/archive/mdp.39015030934858/.

Crowther, Stefania, Ethan Jordan, Jacqueline Wernimont, and Hillary Nunn. "New Scholarship, New Pedagogies: Views from the 'EEBO Generation.'" *Early Modern Literary Studies* 14, no. 2 (2008) https://extra.shu.ac.uk/emls/14-2/crjowenu.html.

Culler, Dwight. "Edward Bysshe and the Poet's Handbook." *PMLA* 63, no. 3 (September 1948): 858–85.

Culler, Jonathan. *Theory of the Lyric*. Cambridge, MA: Harvard University Press, 2015.

Daston, Lorraine, ed. *Science in the Archives*. Chicago: University of Chicago Press, 2017.

The Data-Sitters Club. datasittersclub.github.io. Accessed June 24, 2024.

David, Emilia. "Google Books Reportedly Indexing Bad AI-Written Works." *Verge*, April 5, 2024. https://www.theverge.com/2024/4/5/24122077/google-books-ai-indexing-ngram.

Day, Ronald E. *Documentarity: Evidence, Ontology, and Inscription*. Cambridge, MA: MIT Press, 2019.

———. *Indexing It All: The Subject in the Age of Documentation, Information, and Data*. Cambridge, MA: MIT Press, 2014.

Desrochers, Nadine, and Patricia Tomaszek. "Bridging the Unknown: An Interdisciplinary Case Study of Paratext in Electronic Literature." In *Examining Paratextual Theory and Its Applications in Digital Culture*, edited by Nadine Desrochers and Daniel Apollon, 160–89. Hershey, PA: IGI Global, 2014.

Dotzler, Bernhard, and Henning Schmidgen. *Foucault, Digital*. Lüneberg: Meson, 2022.

Dotzler, Bernhard, Henning Schmidgen, and Benno Stein. "From the Archive to the Computer: Michel Foucault and the Digital Humanities." *Journal of Cultural Analytics* 7, no. 4 (March 2023). https://doi.org/10.22148/001c.55795.

Drabinksi, Emily. "Queering the Catalog: Queer Theory and the Politics of Correction." *Library Quarterly* 82, no. 3 (April 2013): 94–111.

Drouin, Jeffrey. "Close- and Distant-Reading Modernism: Network Analysis, Text Mining, and Teaching *The Little Review*." *Journal of Modern Periodical Studies* 5, no. 1 (2014): 110–35.

Drucker, Johanna. *The Digital Humanities Coursebook: An Introduction to Digital Methods for Research and Scholarship*. Oxford: Routledge, 2021.

———. "Performative Materiality and Theoretical Approaches to Interface." *Digital Humanities Quarterly* 7, no. 1 (2013). http://digitalhumanities.org:8081/dhq/vol/7/1/000143/000143.html.

———. *Visualization and Interpretation: Humanistic Approaches to Display*. Cambridge, MA: MIT Press, 2020.

———. "Why Distant Reading Isn't." *PMLA* 132, no. 3 (May 2017): 628–635.

Duchan, Judith Felton. "A History of Speech-Language Pathology." Revised May 29, 2023. https://www.acsu.buffalo.edu/~duchan/new_history/overview.html.

Dworkin, Craig. *The Consequences of Innovation: 21st Century Poetics*. New York: Roof Books, 2008.

———. *Dictionary Poetics: Toward a Radical Lexicography*. New York: Fordham University Press, 2020.

———. *No Medium*. Cambridge, MA: MIT Press, 2013.

Dworkin, Craig. *The Radium of the World: A Poetics of Materiality*. Chicago: Chicago University Press, 2020.

———. *Reading the Illegible*. Evanston, IL: Northwestern University Press, 2003.

Eagleton, Terry. *The Function of Criticism*. London: Verso, 1985.

Earhart, Amy. *Traces of the Old, Uses of the New: The Emergence of Digital Literary Studies*. Ann Arbor: University of Michigan Press, 2015.

Earhart, Amy E., Roopika Risam, and Matthew Bruno. "Citational Politics: Quantifying the Influence of Gender on Citation in Digital Scholarship in the Humanities." *Digital Scholarship in the Humanities* 36, no. 3 (September 2021): 581–94.

Edmond, Jennifer, Nicola Horsley, Jorg Lehmann, and Mike Priddy. *The Trouble with Big Data*. London: Bloomsbury Academic, 2022.

Elam, Michele. "Poetry Will Not Optimize, or, What Is Literature to AI." *American Literature* 95, no. 2 (June 2023): 281–303.

Ellis, Alexander John. *The Essentials of Phonetics: Containing a Theory of a Universal Alphabet*. London: F. Pitman, 1848. https://prosody.princeton.edu/archive/nyp.33433082185335/.

———. *On Early English Pronunciation*. London: Philological Society by Asher; for the Early English Text Society and the Chaucer Society by Trübner, 1869. https://prosody.princeton.edu/archive/mdp.39015078118786/.

Emerson, Lori. *The Lab Book*. Minneapolis: University of Minnesota Press, 2022.

———. *Reading Writing Interfaces*. Minneapolis: University of Minnesota Press, 2014.

Ernst, Wolfgang. *Digital Memory and the Archive*. Edited by Jussi Parikka. Minneapolis: University of Minnesota Press, 2013.

———. "Radically De-historicising the Archive: Decolonising Archival Memory from the Supremacy of Historical Discourse." *Decolonising Archives: L'Internationale Online*. 2016. https://www.internationaleonline.org/media/files/03-decolonisingarchives.pdf.

Faber, Liz W. *The Computer's Voice: From Star Trek to Siri*. Minneapolis: University of Minnesota Press, 2020.

Felluga, Dino. "Addressed to the nines: The Victorian Archive and the Disappearance of the Book." *Victorian Studies* 48, no. 2 (Winter 2006): 305–19.

———. "branching Out: Victorian Studies and the Digital Humanities." *Critical Inquiry* 55, no. 1 (April 2013): 43–56.

———. "The Eventuality of the Digital." *19: Interdisciplinary Studies in the Long Nineteenth Century* (2015): 21. https://doi.org/10.16995/ntn.742.

Finch, Annie. "Scansion Marks." In *A Poet's Craft: A Comprehensive Guide to Making and Sharing Your Poetry*. Ann Arbor: University of Michigan Press, 2012.

Fish, Stanley. "The Digital Humanities and the Transcending of Mortality." *New York Times*, January 9, 2012. https://archive.nytimes.com/opinionator.blogs.nytimes.com/2012/01/09/the-digital-humanities-and-the-transcending-of-mortality/.

———. "Mind Your P's and B's: The Digital Humanities and Interpretation," *New York Times*, January 23, 2012. https://archive.nytimes.com/opinionator.blogs.nytimes.com/2012/01/23/mind-your-ps-and-bs-the-digital-humanities-and-interpretation/.

Fisher, Anne. *An Accurate New Spelling Dictionary, and Expositor of the English Language*. London, 1773. https://prosody.princeton.edu/archive/CB0127785659/.

Fitzpatrick, Kathleen. "Do 'the Risky Thing' in Digital Humanities." *Chronicle of Higher Educa-

tion, September 25, 2011. https://www.chronicle.com/article/do-the-risky-thing-in-digital-humanities/.

Flanders, Julia. "Women Writers Project." wwp.northeastern.edu. June 24, 2024.

Flood, Alison. "Robot Artist to Perform AI Generated Poetry in Response to Dante." *Guardian*, November 2021. https://www.theguardian.com/books/2021/nov/26/robot-artist-to-perform-ai-generated-poetry-in-response-to-dante.

Folsom, Ed. "Database as Genre: The Epic Transformation of Archives." *PMLA* 122, no. 5 (October 2007): 1571–79.

Forsythe, R. S. "Modern Imitations of the Popular Ballad." *Journal of English and Germanic Philology* 13 (1914): 88–97.

Foucault, Michel. *The Order of Things: An Archeology of the Human Sciences*. New York: Pantheon Books, 1970.

"Frank J. Warnke, Educator, 62." *New York Times*, June 29, 1988, sec. D, "Obituaries," 25.

Freedgood, Elaine. "Divination." *PMLA* 128, no. 1 (January 2013): 221–25.

Funkhouser, C. T. *New Directions in Digital Poetry*. New York: Continuum Books, 2012.

———. *Prehistoric Digital Poetry: An Archeology of Forms, 1959–1995*. Tuscaloosa: University of Alabama Press, 2007.

Fussell, Paul. *Poetic Meter and Poetic Form*. New York: McGraw Hill, 1965.

Fyfe, Paul. "Access, Computational Analysis, and Fair Use in the Digitized Nineteenth-Century Press." *Victorian Periodicals Review* 51, no. 4 (Winter 2018): 716–37.

———. "An Archeology of Victorian Newspapers." *Victorian Periodicals Review* 49, no. 4 (Winter 2016): 546–77.

———. *Digital Victorians: From Nineteenth-Century Media to Digital Humanities*. Stanford, CA: Stanford University Press, 2024.

Gabrielson, Arvid. *Rime as a Criterion of the Pronunciation of Spenser, Pope, Byron, and Swinburne: A Contribution to the History of the Present English Stressed Vowels*. Uppsala, Sweden: Almquist, Wiksells Boktryckeri, 1909. https://prosody.princeton.edu/archive/mdp.39015030924255/.

Gallon, Kim. "Making a Case for the Black Digital Humanities." In *Debates in the Digital Humanities*, edited by Matthew K. Gold and Lauren F. Klein, 42–49. Minneapolis: University of Minnesota Press, 2016.

Garber, Marjorie. *Loaded Words*. New York: Fordham University Press, 2012.

Gardiner, William. *The Music of Nature; or, An Attempt to Prove That What Is Passionate and Pleasing in the Art of Singing, Speaking, and Performing upon Musical Instruments, Is Derived from the Sounds of the Animated World; With Curious and Interesting Illustrations*. London: Rees, Orme, Brown, Green, and Longham, 1832. https://prosody.princeton.edu/archive/hvd.ml14ed/.

Garth, John. *Secrets of "The Hydra": How Tolkien Research Uncovered Lost Wilfred Owen Magazines* (blog). June 17, 2014. https://johngarth.wordpress.com/2014/06/17/secrets-of-the-hydra-how-tolkien-research-uncovered-lost-wilfred-owen-magazines/.

Gildon, Charles. *The Complete Art of Poetry*. Vol. 1. London, 1718. https://prosody.princeton.edu/archive/mdp.39015031594768/.

———. *The Laws of Poetry*. London, 1721. https://prosody.princeton.edu/archive/CW0112397329/.

Gitelman, Lisa. *Paper Knowledge*. Durham, NC: Duke University Press, 2014.

———, ed. *"Raw Data" Is an Oxymoron*. Cambridge, MA: MIT Press, 2013.

Gitelman, Lisa. *Scripts, Grooves and Writing Machines*. Stanford, CA: Stanford University Press, 2000.

———. "Searching and Thinking about Searching JSTOR." *Representations* 127, no. 1 (Summer 2014): 73–82.

Glaser, Ben. *Modernism's Metronome*. Baltimore: Johns Hopkins University Press, 2020.

———. "White Things: Form, Formalization, and the Use of Prosody." *New Literary History* 54, no. 4 (2024): 1547–72.

Golston, Michael. *Rhythm and Race in Modernist Poetry and Science*. New York: Columbia University Press, 2007.

"Google Books History." Google Books, https://books.google.com/googlebooks/about/history.html. Accessed June 24, 2024.

Gordin, Michael. *A Well-Ordered Thing*. Princeton, NJ: Princeton University Press, 2019.

Graff, Gerald. *Professing Literature: An Institutional History*. Chicago: University of Chicago Press, 1987.

Graff, Gerald, and Michael Warner, eds. *The Origins of Literary Studies in America: A Documentary Anthology*. New York: Routledge, 1989.

Griffiths, Eric. *The Printed Voice of Victorian Poetry*. Oxford: Oxford University Press, 1989.

Grobe, Christopher. "Can the Computer Speak?" *American Literature* 95, no. 2 (2020): 439–43.

Gross, Harvey. *Sound and Form in Modern Poetry*. Ann Arbor: University of Michigan Press, 1964.

Guillory, John. *Cultural Capital: The Problem of Literary Canon Formation*. Chicago: University of Chicago Press, 1993.

———. *Professing Criticism: Essays on the Organization of Literary Study*. Chicago: University of Chicago Press, 2022.

Gummere, Frances Barton. *A Handbook of Poetics for Students of English Verse*. Boston: Ginn, 1886. https://prosody.princeton.edu/archive/hvd.hwkax9/.

Gupta, Anshul, et al. "Automatic Assessment of OCR Quality in Historical Documents." In *Proceedings of the Twenty-Ninth AAAI Conference on Artificial Intelligence*, 1735–41. Austin, TX: Association for the Advancement of Artificial Intelligence, 2015.

Guthrie, K. M. "JSTOR and the University of Michigan: An Evolving Collaboration." *Library Hi Tech* 16, no. 1 (1998): 9–14.

Hall, Jason David. *Nineteenth-Century Verse and Technology: Machines of Meter*. New York: Palgrave, 2017.

Hamill, S. S. *The New Science of Elocution*. New York: Nelson and Philips, 1886.

———. *The Science of Elocution*. New York: Nelson and Philips, 1872.

Hartman, Charles O. *The Scandroid Manual*. Version 1.1. http://cherry.concoll.edu/cohar/Programs.

Hayles, N. Katherine. *How We Became Posthuman*. Chicago: University of Chicago Press, 1999.

———. *How We Think*. Chicago: University of Chicago Press, 2012.

———. *My Mother Was a Computer*. Chicago: University of Chicago Press, 2005.

———. *Postprint*. New York: Columbia University Press, 2021.

Hayot, Eric, Anatoly Detwyler, and Lea Pao, eds. *Information: A Reader*. New York: Columbia University Press, 2022.

Heffernan, Laura, and Rachel Sagner Buurma. *The Teaching Archive: A New History for Literary Study*. Chicago: University of Chicago Press, 2021.

Heil, Jacon, and Todd Samuelson. "Book History in the Early Modern OCR Project, or, Bringing Balance to the Force." *Journal for Early Modern Cultural Studies* 13, no. 4 (2013): 90–103.

Helton, Laura. "On Decimals, Catalogs, and Racial Imaginaries of Reading," *PMLA* 134, no. 1 (2019): 99–120.

Hering, Katherine, Michael Kramer, Joshua Sternfield, and Kate Theimer. "Digital Historiography and the Archives." *Journal of Digital Humanities* 3, no. 2 (Summer 2014). http://journalofdigitalhumanities.org/3-2/digital-historiography-and-the-archives/.

Heuser, Ryan, and Long Le-Khac. "Learning to Read Data: Bringing Out the Humanistic in the Digital Humanities." *Victorian Studies* 54, no. 1 (Autumn 2011): 79–86.

Hill, Mark J., and Simon Hencghen. "Quantifying the Impact of Dirty OCR on Historical Text Analysis: Eighteenth Century Collections Online as a Case Study." *Digital Scholarship in the Humanities* 34, no. 4 (2019): 825–43.

Hockey, Susan. *A Guide to Computer Applications in the Humanities*. London: Duckworth; Baltimore: Johns Hopkins University Press, 1980.

Hofmeyr, Isabel. "Colonial Copyright, Customs, and Port Cities: Material Histories and Intellectual Property." *Comparative Literature* 70, no. 3 (2018): 264–77.

Hood, Thomas. *Practical Guide for English Versification . . . to Which Are Added Bysshe's "Rules for Making English Verse."* London: J. Hogg, 1877. https://prosody.princeton.edu/archive/mdp.39015030934841/.

———. *The Rhymester: Or, the Rules of Rhyme*. New York: D. Appleton, 1882, 1911, 1916. https://prosody.princeton.edu/archive/mdp.39015010528647/.

———. *The Rules of Rhyme: A Guide to English Versification*. London: J. Hogg, 1869. https://prosody.princeton.edu/archive/njp.32101072898222/.

Houston, Natalie. "Distant Reading and Victorian Women's Poetry." in *The Cambridge Companion to Victorian Women's Poetry*, edited by Linda K. Hughes, 249–65. Cambridge: Cambridge University Press, 2019.

———. "Exploring the Idiom of Victorian Rhyme through Applied Historical Poetics." In *Plotting Poetry: On Mechanically-Enhanced Reading*, edited by Anne-Sophie Bories, Gérald Purnelle, and Hugues Marchal, 41–55. Liège: Presses Universitaires de Liège, 2021.

———. "Modeling the Poem on the Page: Encoding the Database Schema for the *Periodical Poetry Index*." *Victorian Periodicals Review* 52, no. 3 (Fall 2019): 626–35.

———. "The Periodical Poetry Index." https://www.periodicalpoetry.org. Accessed June 24, 2024.

———. "Reading the Visual Page in the Digital Archive." In *Research Methods for Reading Digital Data in the Digital Humanities*, edited by Gabriele Griffin and Matthew Hayler, 36–50. Edinburgh: Edinburgh University Press, 2016.

———. "Re:Search Technologies: A Counterfactual Exploration of *The Wellesley Index*." *Victorian Periodicals Review* 54, no. 2 (Summer 2021): 304–26.

———. "Toward a Computational Analysis of Victorian Poetics." *Victorian Studies* 56, no. 3 (Spring 2014): 498–510.

Howell, Wilbur Samuel. "Sources of the Elocutionary Movement in England: 1700–1748." *Quarterly Journal of Speech* 45, no. 1 (February 1959): 1–18.

Jackson, Virginia. *Before Modernism: The Invention of American Poetry*. Princeton, NJ: Princeton University Press, 2023.

Jackson, Virginia. "Historical Poetics and the Dream of Interpretation: A Response to Paul Fry." *MLQ* 81 (September 2020): 289–318.

———. "Poe's Common Meter." In *The Oxford Handbook of Edgar Allan Poe*, edited by Gerald Kennedy, Scott Peeples, and Caleb Doen, 121–38. New York: Oxford University Press, 2019.

Jackson, Virginia, and Yopie Prins. "Lyrical Studies." *Victorian Literature and Culture* 27, no. 2 (1999): 521–30.

———. *The Lyric Theory Reader: A Critical Anthology*. Baltimore: Johns Hopkins University Press, 2014.

Jones, Ewan. *The Turn of Rhythm: How Victorian Poetry Shaped a New Concept*. Charlottesville: University of Virginia Press, 2023.

Jones, Matthew. "Querying the Archive: Data Mining from Apriori to PageRank." In *Science in the Archives*, edited by Lorraine Daston, 311–27. Chicago: University of Chicago Press, 2017.

Karlin, Daniel. "Victorian Poetry and the English Poetry Full-Text Database: A Case Study." *Chadwyck-Healey Literature Collections: About the Literature Collections*. http://collections.chadwyck.co.uk/marketing/products/karlin.jsp. Accessed June 24, 2024.

Kernighan, Brian. "A Regular Expression Matcher." In *Beautiful Code: Leading Programmers Explain How They Think*, edited by Andy Oram and Greg Wilson, 1–9. Sebastopol, CA: O'Reilly Media, 2007.

Kim, Annabel. "The Politics of Citation." *Diacritics* 48, no. 3 (2020): 4–9.

King, Anne Mills, and Sandra Kurtinitis. *Being and Becoming: An Introduction to Literature*. New York: Random House, 1987.

Kinzie, Mary. *A Poet's Guide to Poetry*. Chicago: University of Chicago Press, 2013.

Kirschenbaum, Matthew. "Again Theory: A Forum on Language, Meaning, and Intent in a Time of Stochastic Parrots." *In the Moment (Critical Inquiry* blog). June 27, 2023. https://critinq.wordpress.com/2023/06/27/again-theory-a-forum-on-language-meaning-and-intent-in-the-time-of-stochastic-parrots-2/.

———. *Bitstreams*. Philadelphia: University of Pennsylvania Press, 2021.

———. "Editor's Introduction." In "Image-Based Humanities Computing." Special issue, *Computers and the Humanities* 36, no. 1 (2002): 3–6.

———. *Mechanisms: New Media and the Forensic Imagination*. Cambridge, MA: MIT Press, 2008.

———. "Prepare for the Textpocalypse." *Atlantic*, March 8, 2023. https://www.theatlantic.com/technology/archive/2023/03/ai-chatgpt-writing-language-models/673318/.

———. *Track Changes*. Cambridge, MA: Harvard University Press, 2016.

———. "The .txtual Condition: Digital Humanities, Born-Digital Archives, and the Future Literary." *Digital Humanities Quarterly* 7, no. 1 (2013). http://digitalhumanities.org:8081/dhq/vol/7/1/000151/000151.html.

Kirschenbaum, Matthew, and Sarah Werner. "Digital Scholarship and Digital Studies: The State of the Discipline." *Book History* 17 (2014): 406–58.

Knapp, Steven, and Walter Benn Michaels. "Against Theory." *Critical Inquiry* 8, no. 4 (Summer 1982): 723–42.

Köbis, Nils, and D. Luca Mossink. "Artificial Intelligence versus Maya Angelou: Experimental Evidence That People Cannot Differentiate AI-Generated from Human-Written Poetry." *Computers in Human Behaviour* 114 (2021). https://doi.org/10.1016/j.chb.2020.106553.

Krajewski, Markus. *Paper Machines: About Cards and Catalogs, 1548–1929*. Cambridge, MA: MIT Press, 2011.

Kunde, Brian. "A Brief History of Word Processing (through 1986)." https://web.stanford.edu/~bkunde/fb-press/articles/wdprhist.html#FL; and published via his own Fleabonnet Press online platform. Accessed June 24, 2024.

Labbe, Jacqueline. "Poetics." In *A Handbook of Romanticism Studies*, edited by Joel Faflak and Julia M. Wright, 143–58. Chichester: Wiley-Blackwell, 2012.

Lamborn, E. A. *Expression in Speech and Writing*. Oxford: Clarendon, 1922. https://prosody.princeton.edu/archive/mdp.39015031040986/.

Lancaster, Frederick *Toward Paperless Information Systems*. Ann Arbor, MI: Academic, 1978.

Lancelot, Claude. *Quatre traitez de poësies, latine, françoise, italienne, et espagnole*. Paris: Pierre Le Petit, 1663.

Landow, George. *Hypertext: The Convergence of Contemporary Critical Theory and Technology*. Baltimore: Johns Hopkins University Press, 1992.

———. *Victorian Web*. 1987. http://www.victorianweb.org/.

Lee, Maurice. *Overwhelmed: Literature, Aesthetics, and the Nineteenth-Century Information Revolution*. Princeton, NJ: Princeton University Press, 2019.

Leighton, Angela. *Hearing Things*. Cambridge, MA: Belknap Press of Harvard University Press, 2019.

Lemercier, Clair, and Clair Zalc, eds. *Quantitative Methods in the Humanities: An Introduction*. Translated by Arthur Goldhammer. Charlottesville: University of Virginia Press, 2019.

Leung, Sofia Y., and Jorge R. López-McKnight, eds. *Knowledge Justice: Disrupting Library and Information Science through Critical Race Theory*. Cambridge, MA: MIT Press, 2021.

Lewi, Hanna, Wally Smith, Dirk vom Lehn, and Steven Cooke. *The Routledge International Handbook of New Digital Library Practices in Galleries, Libraries, Archives, Museums and Heritage Sites*. London: Routledge, 2019.

Liu, Alan. "From Reading to Social Computing." *Literary Studies in the Digital Age: An Evolving Anthology*. MLA Commons, 2013. https://doi.org/10.1632/lsda.2013.0.

———. *The Laws of Cool: Knowledge Work and the Culture of Information*. Chicago: University of Chicago Press, 2004.

———. *Local Transcendence: Essays on Postmodern Historicism and the Database*. Chicago: University of Chicago Press, 2008.

Long, Hoyt, and Richard Jean So. "Literary Pattern Recognition: Modernism between Close Reading and Machine Learning." *Critical Inquiry* 42, no. 2 (Winter 2016): 235–67.

Loukissas, Yanni Alexander. *All Data Are Local: Thinking Critically in a Data-Driven Society*. Cambridge, MA: MIT Press, 2019.

MacArthur, Marit, J. Howard Rambsy II, Xiaoliu Wu, Qin Ding, and Lee M. Miller. "101 Black Women Poets in Mainly White and Mainly Black Rooms." *LARB*, August 27, 2002. https://lareviewofbooks.org/article/101-black-women-poets-in-mainly-white-and-mainly-black-rooms/.

MacArthur, Marit, Georgia Zellou, and Lee M. Miller, "Beyond Poet Voice: Sampling the (Non) Performance Styles of 100 American Poets." *Journal of Cultural Analytics* 3, no. 1 (2018). https://doi.org/10.22148/16.022.

Mak, Bonnie. *How the Page Matters*. Toronto: University of Toronto Press, 2011.

Malinconico, Michael, and Paul J. Fasana. *The Future of the Library Catalog: The Library's Choices*. White Plains, NY: Knowledge Industry, 1979.

Mandell, Laura. *Breaking the Book: Print Humanities in the Digital Age*. Chichester: Wiley-Blackwell, 2015.

———. "Digitizing the Archive: The Necessity of an 'Early Modern' Period." *Journal for Early Modern Cultural Studies* 13, no. 2 (2013): 83–92.

———. "Marking Texts in Many Dimensions." In *A Companion to Digital Humanities*, edited by Susan Schreibman, Ray Siemens, and John Unsworth, 198–217. Oxford: Blackwell, 2004.

Mandell, Laura, et al. "Navigating the Storm: IMPACT, eMOP, and Agile Steering Standards." *Digital Scholarship in the Humanities* 32, no. 1 (2015): 189–94.

Manovich, Lev. *The Language of New Media*. Cambridge, MA: MIT Press, 2001.

Marsh, George. *Lectures on the English Language*. New York: C. Scribner, 1860.

Martens, Gunther. "Literature, Digital Humanities, and the Age of the Encyclopedia." *CLCWeb: Comparative Literature and Culture* 15, no. 3 (2013). https://doi.org/10.7771/1481-4374.2241.

Martin, Meredith. "'Imperfectly Civilized': Ballads, Nations, and Histories of Form." *ELH* 82, no. 2 (Summer 2015): 345–63.

———. "Prosody." In *The Cambridge Companion to Victorian Women's Poetry*, edited by Linda K. Hughes, 28–44. Cambridge: Cambridge University Press, 2019.

———. "Prosody and Meter: Early Modern to 19th Century." In *Oxford Bibliographies in British and Irish Literature*, edited by Andrew Hadfield. Oxford: Oxford University Press, 2009. https://doi.org/10.1093/OBO/9780199846719-0172.

———. *The Rise and Fall of Meter*. Princeton, NJ: Princeton University Press, 2012.

———. "The Writing of Sound." In *The Sound of Writing*, edited by Christopher Cannon and Steven Justice, 127–50. Baltimore: Johns Hopkins University Press, 2023.

Martin, Meredith, and Ryan Heuser. "Historical Prosody and Mechanical Form." Paper presented at the American Comparative Literature Association Annual Conference, 2024, panel AI and/as Form.

Matthews, Brian. "Millions of Sources: The Disruption of History and the Humanities?" *Chronicle of Higher Education*, January 12, 2015. https://www-chronicle-com.ezproxy.princeton.edu/blognetwork/theubiquitouslibrarian/millions-of-sources-the-disruption-of-history-and-the-humanities.

McCurdy, Nina, Julie Lein, Katharine Coles, and Miriah Meyer. "Poemage: Visualizing the Sonic Topology of a Poem." *IEEE Transactions on Visualization and Computer Graphics* 22, no. 1 (2016): 439–48.

McDaytor, Mark. "Tagging the Faces behind the Code: Why DH Projects Need to Acknowledge All Contributors." *Click Here* (blog). January 18, 2012. https://clickherefordigitalhumanities.wordpress.com/2012/01/18/tagging-the-faces-behind-the-code-why-dh-projects-need-to-acknowledge-all-contributors/.

McGann, Jerome. "Culture and Technology: The Way We Live Now, What Is to Be Done?" *New Literary History* 36 (Winter 2005): 71–82.

———. "Database, Interface, and Archival Fever." *PMLA* 122, no. 5 (October 2007): 1588–92.

———. "Dialogue and Interpretation at the Interface of Man and Machine: Reflections on Textuality and a Proposal for an Experiment in Machine Reading." *Computers and the Humanities* 36 (2002): 95–107.

---. "Literary Scholarship and the Digital Future." *Chronicle of Higher Education*, sec. 2, "Chronicle Review," December 13, 2002, B7–B9.

---. *Radiant Textuality: Literature after the World Wide Web*. New York: Palgrave, Macmillan, 2001.

---. "The Rationale of Hypertext." Institute for Advanced Technology in the Humanities. https://www2.iath.virginia.edu/public/jjm2f/rationale.html. Accessed June 24, 2024.

---. "What Is Text?" In *Marking the Text: The Presentation of Meaning on the Digital Page*, edited by Joe Bray, Miriam Handley, and Anne C. Henry, 329–34. Ashgate: Aldershot, 2000.

---. "Who's Carving Up the Nineteenth-Century?" *PMLA* 116, no. 5 (October 2001): 1415–21.

McGann, Jerome, and Johanna Drucker. "Images as the Text: Pictographs and Pictographic Rhetoric." *Information Design Journal* 10, no. 2 (2000/2001): 95–106.

McGill, Meredith. *American Literature and the Culture of Reprinting 1834–1853*. Philadelphia: University of Pennsylvania Press, 2003.

---. "Copyright and Intellectual Property: The State of the Discipline." *Book History* 16 (2013): 387–427.

---. "Format." *Early American Studies* 16, no. 4 (Fall 2018): 671–77.

---. "Literary History, Book History, and Media Studies." In *Turns of Event: American Literary Studies in Motion*, edited by Hester Blum, 23–39. Philadelphia: University of Pennsylvania Press, 2016.

---. *Traffic in Poems: Nineteenth-Century Poetry and Transatlantic Exchange*. New Brunswick, NJ: Rutgers University Press, 2008.

McGill, Meredith, and Andrew Parker. "The Future of the Literary Past." *PMLA* 125, no. 4 (October 2010): 959–67.

McPherson, Tara. "Why Are the Digital Humanities So White? Or Thinking Histories of Race and Computation." In *Debates in Digital Humanities*, edited Matthew K. Gold, 139–60. Minneapolis: University of Minnesota Press, 2012.

McSherry, Corynne. "Big Win for Fair Use in Google Books Lawsuit." *Electronic Frontier Foundation*, October 16, 2015. https://www.eff.org/deeplinks/2015/10/big-win-fair-use-google-books-lawsuit.

Mead, William Edward. *The Versification of Pope in Its Relations to the Seventeenth Century*. Leipzig: Frankenstein and Wagner, 1880.

Metahaven. "Peripheral Forces: On the Relevance of Marginality." *Future Non Stop*. http://future-nonstop.org/c/3ede167767497be7eb99cf5da0c6a4e6. Accessed June 24, 2024.

Miller, J. Hillis. "Graphic or Verbal: A Dilemma." *Electronic Book Review*, January 1, 1998. http://electronicbookreview.com/essay/graphic-or-verbal-a-dilemma/.

Milligan, Ian. "Illusionary Order: Online Databases, Optical Character Recognition, and Canadian History, 1997–2010." *Canadian Historical Review* 94, no. 4 (2013): 540–69.

Mimno, David. "Computational Historiography: Data Mining in a Century of Classics Journals." *ACM Journal on Computing and Cultural Heritage* 5, no. 1 (April 2012): 1–19. https://doi.org/10.1145/2160165.2160168.

Mitford, William. *An Inquiry into the Principles of Harmony in Language and the Mechanism of Verse, Modern and Antient*. London: T. Cadell and W. Davies, 1804.

Momma, Haruko. *From Philology to English Studies: Language and Culture in the Nineteenth Century*. Cambridge: Cambridge University Press, 2013.

Monluzin, Emily Lorraine de. "The Poetry of the *Gentleman's Magazine* 1731–1800: An Electronic Database of Titles, Authors, and First Lines." gmpoetrydatabase.org/db. Accessed June 24, 2024.

Montfort, Nick, et al. *10 PRINT CHR$(205.5+RND(1));: GOTO 10*. Cambridge, MA: MIT Press, 2012.

Moretti, Franco. *Distant Reading*. London: Verso, 2013.

———. *Graphs, Maps, Trees*. New York: Verso, 2005.

Muehlberger, Guenter, et al. "Transforming Scholarship in the Archives through Handwritten Text Recognition: Transkribus as a Case Study." *Journal of Documentation* 75, no. 5 (2019): 954–76.

Mustazza, Chris. "Machine-Aided Close Listening: Prosthetic Synaesthesia and the 3D Phonotext." *DHQ* 12, no. 3 (2018). https://www.digitalhumanities.org/dhq/vol/12/3/000397/000397.html.

The National Cyclopedia of American Biography. New York: James T. White, 1898.

Neave, Nick, et al. "Digital Hoarding Behaviours: Measurement and Evaluation." *Computers in Human Behavior* 96 (July 2019): 72–77.

Newcomer, Alphonso G. "License in English Rhyme." *Nation* 68 (February 2, 1899). https://prosody.princeton.edu/archive/pst.000068744151-p63/.

Nims, John Frederick, and David Mason. "A Note on Scansion." In *Western Wind: An Introduction to Poetry*, 5th ed., edited by John Frederick Nims and David Mason, 210–20. Boston: McGraw Hill, 2006.

Noble, Safiya [Umoja]. *Algorithms of Oppression: How Search Engines Reinforce Racism*. New York: New York University Press, 2018.

———. "A Future for Intersectional Black Feminist Technology Studies." *Scholar and Feminist Online* 13, no. 3–14, no. 1 (2016). http://sfonline.barnard.edu/traversing-technologies/safiya-umojanoble-a-future-for-intersectional-black-feminist-technology-studies/.

Noel, Roden. *Essays on Poetry and Poets*. London: Kegan Paul, Trench, 1886.

Norman, Jeremy. *History of Information*. historyofinformation.com. Accessed June 24, 2024.

Noviskie, Bethany. "Speculative Collections and the Emancipatory Library." In *Routledge International Handbook of New Digital Library Practices in Galleries, Libraries, Archives, Museums and Heritage Sites*, edited by Hanna Lewi et al., 92–102. London: Routledge, 2019.

Nyhan, Julianne. *Computation and the Humanities: Towards an Oral History of Digital Humanities*. Cham: Springer Open Access, 2016.

Nyhan, Julianne, and Oliver Duke-Williams." Joint and Multi-authored Publication Patterns in the Digital Humanities." *Literary and Linguistic Computing* 29, no. 3 (September 2014): 387–99.

O'Neil, Cathy. *Weapons of Math Destruction: How Big Data Increases Inequality and Threatens Democracy*. New York: Crown, 2016.

Owens, Trevor. "What Do You Mean by Archive? Genres of Usage for Digital Preservers." *The Signal: Digital Happenings at the Library of Congress* (blog). February 27, 2014. https://blogs.loc.gov/thesignal/2014/02/what-do-you-mean-by-archive-genres-of-usage-for-digital-preservers/.

Pannapacker, William. "On 'The Dark Side of the Digital Humanities.'" *Chronicle of Higher Education*, January 5, 2013. https://www.chronicle.com/blogs/conversation/on-the-dark-side-of-the-digital-humanities.

Pasanek, Brad. "Extreme Reading: Josephine Miles and the Scale of the Pre-digital Digital Humanities." *ELH* 86, no. 2 (2019): 355–85.

Pasanek, Brad, and D. Sculley. "Mining Millions of Metaphors." *Literary and Linguistic Computing* 23, no. 3 (2008): 345–60.

Pechenick, Eitan Adam, Christopher Danforth, Peter Sheridan Dodds. "Characterizing the Google Books Corpus: Strong Limits to Inferences of Socio-Cultural and Linguistic Evolution." *PLOS One* 10.10 (2015): https://doi.org/10.1371/journal.pone.0137041.

Perloff, Marjorie. *Infrathin: An Experiment in Micropoetics*. Chicago: University of Chicago Press, 2021.

Perlow, Seth. *The Poem Electric: Technology and the American Lyric*. Minneapolis: University of Minnesota Press, 2018.

Pinney, Thomas, ed. *The Letters of Rudyard Kipling*. Vol. 4, *1911–1919*. Iowa City: University of Iowa Press, 1999.

Piper, Andrew. *Enumerations: Data and Literary Study*. Chicago: University of Chicago Press, 2018.

Plecháč, Petr, Robert Kolár, Anne-Sophie Bories, and Jakub Říha, eds. *Tackling the Toolkit: Plotting Poetry through Computational Literary Studies*. Prague: Institute of Czech Literature of the Czech Academy of Sciences, 2021.

Pollock, Sheldon, Benjamin A. Elman, and Ku-ming Kevin Chang, eds. *World Philology*. Cambridge, MA: Harvard University Press, 2015.

Poole, Joshua. *English Parnassus: Or, a Helpe to English Poesie*. London: Printed for Tho. Johnson, 1657. https://prosody.princeton.edu/archive/A55357-pnp/.

Preminger, Alex, ed. *Encyclopedia of Poetry and Poetics*. Princeton, NJ, Princeton University Press, 1965.

———, ed. *Princeton Encyclopedia of Poetry and Poetics*. Princeton, NJ: Princeton University Press, 1974.

———, ed. *The Princeton Handbook of Poetic Terms with a Select Reading List by T. V. F. Brogan*. Princeton, NJ: Princeton University Press, 1986.

Preminger, Alex, and T. V. F. Brogan, eds. *The New Princeton Encyclopedia of Poetry and Poetics*. Princeton, NJ: Princeton University Press, 1993.

Price, Leah. *The Anthology and the Rise of the Novel: From Richardson to George Eliot*. Cambridge: Cambridge University Press, 2000.

———. *What We Talk about When We Talk about Books*. New York: Basic Books, 2019.

Prins, Yopie. "'Break, Break, Break' into Song." In *Meter Matters: Verse Cultures of the Long Nineteenth Century*, edited by Jason David Hall, 124–54. Athens: Ohio University Press, 2011.

———. "Historical Poetics, Dysprosody, and the Science of English Verse." *PMLA* 123, no. 1 (2008): 229–34.

———. "Metrical Translation: Nineteenth-Century Homers and the Hexameter Mania." In *Nation, Language and the Ethics of Translation*, edited by Sandra Bermann and Michael Wood, 229–56. Princeton, NJ: Princeton University Press, 2005.

———. "Robert Browning, Transported by Meter." In *The Traffic in Poems: Nineteenth-Century Poetry and Transatlantic Exchange*, edited by Meredith McGill, 205–30. New Brunswick, NJ: Rutgers University Press, 2008.

Prins, Yopie. "Victorian Meters." In *The Cambridge Companion to Victorian Poetry*, edited by Joseph Bristow, 89–113. Cambridge: Cambridge University Press, 2000.
———. "Voice Inverse." *Victorian Poetry* 42, no. 1 (2004): 43–60.
———. "What Is Historical Poetics?" *Modern Language Quarterly* 77 no. 1 (2016): 13–40.
The Programming Historian. programminghistorian.org. Accessed June 24, 2024.
"Publications Received." *American* 5, no. 117 (November 4, 1882): 60.
Putnam, Lara. "The Transnational and the Text-Searchable: Digitized Sources and the Shadows They Cast." *American Historical Review* 121, no. 2 (April 2016): 377–402.
Raley, Rita. *Tactical Media*. Minneapolis: University of Minnesota Press, 2009.
Ramsey, Stephen. *Reading Machines: Toward an Algorithmic Criticism*. Urbana: University of Illinois Press, 2011.
Redding, Anna Crowley. *Google It: A History of Google*. New York: Feiwel and Friends, 2018.
Reed, Brian. "Idea Eater: The Conceptual Lyric as an Emergent Literary Form." *Mosaic: An Interdisciplinary Critical Journal* 49, no. 2 (June 2016): 1–18.
"Review of *The Grammar of English Grammars* by Goold Brown." *Saturday Review*, October 24, 1868, 568.
Rickert, Edith. *New Methods for the Study of Literature*. Chicago: University of Chicago Press, 1927. https://prosody.princeton.edu/archive/mdp.39015031011748/.
Risam, Roopika. *New Digital Worlds: Postcolonial Digital Humanities in Theory, Praxis, and Pedagogy*. Evanston, IL: Northwestern University Press, 2019.
———. "Revising History and Re-authoring the Left in the Post-colonial Digital Archive." *Left History* 18, no. 2 (2015): 35–46.
Risam, Roopika, and Kelly Baker Josephs, eds. *The Digital Black Atlantic*. Minneapolis: University of Minnesota Press, 2021.
Robson, Catherine. "How We Search Now: New and Old Ways of Digging Up Wolfe's 'Sir John Moore.'" In *Virtual Victorians*, edited by Veronica Rose Alfano and Andrew Stauffer, 11–28. New York: Palgrave Macmillan, 2015.
Rockey, Denyse. "John Thelwall and the Origins of British Speech Therapy." *Medical History* 23, no. 2 (April 1979): 156–75.
Rockwell, Geoffrey, and Stéfan Sinclair. *Hermeneutica: Computer Assisted Interpretation in the Humanities*. Cambridge, MA: MIT Press, 2016.
Roe, Nicholas. *Wordsworth and Coleridge: The Radical Years*. Oxford: Oxford University Press, 1990.
Rosenberg, Daniel. "An Archive of Words." In *Science in the Archives*, edited by Lorraine Daston, 271–310. Chicago: University of Chicago Press, 2017.
———. "Search." In *Information: A Historical Companion*, edited by Ann Blair, Paul Duguid, Anja-Silvia Goeng, and Anthony Grafton, 259–84. Princeton, NJ: Princeton University Press, 2021.
Ross, Shawna, and Andrew Pilsch. "Labor, Alienation, and the Digital Humanities." In *The Bloomsbury Handbook to the Digital Humanities*, edited by James O'Sullivan, 335–45. New York Bloomsbury Academic, 2022.
Saint Amour, Paul. *The Copyrights: Intellectual Property and the Literary Imagination*. Cornell, NY: Cornell University Press, 2010.
Saintsbury, George. "The Danger of Phonetics." *Athenaeum*, no. 4674 (November 28, 1919): 1257–58.

———. *History of English Criticism.* New York: Dodd, Mead, 1911. https://prosody.princeton.edu/archive/nyp.33433082538830/.

———. *A History of English Prosody from the Twelfth Century to the Present Day.* Vol. 2. London: Macmillan, 1908. https://prosody.princeton.edu/archive/uc1.b3515213/.

Sample, Mark. "When Does Service Become Scholarship?" *Sample Reality* (blog). February 8, 2013. https://samplereality.com/2013/02/08/when-does-service-become-scholarship/.

Samuels, Lisa, and Jerome McGann. "Deformance and Interpretation." *New Literary History* 30 (Winter 1999): 25–56.

Sapp, Gregg. *A Brief History of the Future of Libraries: An Annotated Bibliography.* London: Scarecrow, 2022.

Sayers, Jentery, ed. *The Routledge Companion to Media Studies and Digital Humanities.* Routledge: London, 2018.

Schipper, Jakob. *A History of English Versification.* Oxford: Clarendon Press, 1910. https://prosody.princeton.edu/archive/mdp.39015005179513/.

Schmidt, Benjamin. *Creating Data: The Invention of Information in the American State, 1850–1950.* 2019. https://benschmidt.org/publication/schmidt_creating_2019/.

———. "Words Alone: Dismantling Topic Models in the Humanities." *Digital Humanities Quarterly* 2, no. 1 (Winter 2012). https://journalofdigitalhumanities.org/2-1/words-alone-by-benjamin-m-schmidt/.

Schoen, Jenna, and Gianmarco E. Saretto. "Optical Character Recognition (OCR) and Medieval Manuscripts: Reconsidering Transcriptions in the Digital Age." *Digital Philology* 11, no. 1 (2022): 174–206.

Schwartz, Joan M., and Terry Cook. "Archives, Records and Power: The Making of Modern Memory." *Archival Science* 2 (2002): 1–19.

Scripture, E. W. *The Elements of Experimental Phonetics.* New York: Scribner's Sons, 1902. https://prosody.princeton.edu/archive/mdp.39015026437072/.

Sculley, David, and Brad Pasanek. "Meaning and Mining: The Impact of Implicit Assumptions in Data Mining for the Humanities." *Literary and Linguistic Computing* 23, no. 4 (December 2008): 409–24.

Shah, Chirag, and Emily Bender. "Situating Search." In *CHIIR '22: Proceedings of the 2022 Conference on Human Information Interaction and Retrieval* (Regensberg, Germany, March 2022), 221–32. https://doi.org/10.1145/3498366.3505816.

Shechtman, Anna. "Matthew Kirschenbaum, *Bitstreams: The Future of Digital Literary Heritage.*" *American Literary History* 35, no. 2 (Summer 2023): 1086–89.

Siemans, Ray, and Susan Schreibman, eds. *A Companion to Digital Literary Studies.* West Sussex: Wiley Blackwell, 2013.

Singh, Shubman. "ChatGPT Amazes Twitter Users with Shakespearean-Style Poem on Climate Change." *Business Today,* March 19, 2023. https://www.businesstoday.in/latest/trends/story/chatgpt-amazes-twitter-users-with-shakespearean-style-poem-on-climate-change-374009-2023-03-19.

Slater, Avery. "Post-automation Poetics: Or, How Cold-War Computers Discovered Poetry." *American Literature* 95, no. 2 (June 2023): 205–27.

Smith, Abby. *Strategies for Building Digitized Collections.* Washington, DC: Digital Library Federation (DLF), 2001.

Smith, Courtney Weiss. *Empiricist Devotions: Science, Religion, and Poetry in Early Eighteenth-Century England.* Charlottesville: University of Virginia Press, 2016.

Smith, David, and Ryan Cordell. "A Research Agenda for Historical and Multilingual Optical Character Recognition." Northeastern University Library, 2018. https://repository.library.northeastern.edu/files/neu:fl881m03S.

Sneha, Puthiya Purayil. "Alternative Histories of Digital Humanities: Tracing the Archival Turn." In *Global Debates in the Digital Humanities*, edited by Domenico Fiormonte, Sukanta Chaudhuri, and Paola Ricuarte, 15–27. Minneapolis: University of Minnesota Press, 2022.

So, Richard Jean. "All Models Are Wrong." *PMLA* 13, no. 3 (2017): 668–73.

Starkman, Ruth. "What 'Counts'?" *Chronicle of Higher Education*, February 19, 2013. www.insidehighered.com/advice/2013/02/20/essay-issues-related-what-digital-scholarship-counts-tenure-and-promotion.

Stauffer, Andrew. *Book Traces*. Philadelphia: University of Pennsylvania Press, 2021.

———. "Introduction: Searching Engines, Reading Machines." *Victorian Studies* 54, no. 1 (Autumn 2011): 63–68.

———. "The Nineteenth-Century Archive in the Digital Age." *European Romantic Review* 23, no. 3 (June 2012): 335–41.

Steedman, Carolyn. *Dust: The Archive and Cultural History*. New Brunswick, NJ: Rutgers University Press, 2002.

Steele, Joshua. *An Essay toward Establishing the Melody and Measure of Speech to Be Expressed and Perpetuated by Peculiar Symbols*. London: W. Bowyer and J. Nichols; for J. Almon, in Piccadilly, 1775. https://prosody.princeton.edu/archive/uc2.ark:/13960/t9m333p7m/.

———. *Prosodia Rationalis: Or an Essay towards Establishing the Melody and Measure of Speech*. London: J. Nichols, 1779. https://prosody.princeton.edu/archive/CW0113075673/.

Stephens, Paul. *The Poetics of Information Overload*. Minneapolis: University of Minnesota Press, 2014.

Stevenson, Burton Egbert. *The Home Book of Verse: American and English*. New York: Henry Holt, 1915. https://prosody.princeton.edu/archive/wu.89099138968/.

Stoler, Ann Laura. *Along the Archival Grain: Epistemic Anxieties and Colonial Common Sense*. Princeton, NJ: Princeton University Press, 2009.

Sweet, Henry. *Collected Papers of Henry Sweet*. Oxford: Clarendon Press, 1913.

———. *The Sounds of English*. Oxford: Clarendon, 1908.

Sweeten, George, et al. "Digital Hoarding Behaviours: Underlying Motivations and Potential Negative Consequences." *Computers in Human Behavior* 85 (August 2018): 54–60.

Swidzinski, Joshua. "Poetic Numbers: Measurement and the Formation of Literary Criticism in Enlightenment England." PhD diss., Columbia University, 2015.

———. "Uncouth Rhymes: Thomas Gray, Prosody, and Literary History." *Studies in Philology* 112, no. 4 (Fall 2015): 837–61.

Tanner, William. *Composition and Rhetoric*. Boston: Ginn, 1922. https://babel.hathitrust.org/cgi/pt?id=ucl.$b307985&seq=22.

Tenen, Dennis. *Plain Text: The Poetics of Computation*. Stanford, CA: Stanford University Press, 2017.

Thelwall, John. *Illustrations of English Rhythmus*. London: McCreery, 1812. https://prosody.princeton.edu/archive/nnc1.1002383080/.

———. *Poems Written in Close Confinement in the Tower and Newgate, under a Charge of High Treason*. London: For the Author, 1795.

———. *Selections for the Illustration of a Course of Instructions on the Rhythmus and Utterance of the English Language: With an Introductory Essay on the Application of Rhythmical Science to the Treatment of Impediments, and the Improvement of Our National Oratory; And an Elementary Analysis of the Science and Practice of Elocution, Composition, &c*. J. M'Creery, Black-Horse-Court; and Sold by Messrs. Arch, Cornhill; Ridgeway, Piccadilly; Kent, Holborn: and Harwood, Great Russell-Street, 1812. https://prosody.princeton.edu/archive/mdp.39015021952943/.

Thiemer, Kate. "Archives in Context and as Context." *Journal of Digital Humanities* 1, no. 2 (Spring 2012). https://journalofdigitalhumanities.org/1-2/archives-in-context-and-as-context-by-kate-theimer/.

Thompson, Judith. *John Thelwall in the Wordsworth Circle: The Silenced Partner*. Basingstoke: Palgrave Macmillan, 2012.

———. *John Thelwall: Selected Poetry and Poetics*. New York: Palgrave Macmillan, 2015.

Thomson, William. *The Basis of English Rhythm*. Glasgow: W. and R. Holmes, 1904. https://prosody.princeton.edu/archive/ucl.$b31655/.

Torabi, Katayoun, Jessica Durgan, and Bryan Tarpley. "Early Modern OCR Project (eMOP) at Texas A&M University: Using Aletheia to Train Tesseract." In *Proceedings of the 2013 ACM Symposium on Documents Editing*, 23–26. New York: ACM, 2013. https://doi.org/10.1145/2494266.2494304.

Trettien, Whitney. *Cut/Copy/Paste*. Minneapolis: University of Minnesota Press, 2021.

Trouillot, Michel-Rolph. *Silencing the Past: Power and the Production of History*. Boston: Beacon, 1995.

Trumpener, Katie. "Critical Response I: Paratext and Genre System; A Response to Franco Moretti." In *Critical Inquiry* 36, no. 1 (Autumn 2009): 159–71.

Turner, James. *Philology: The Forgotten Origins of the Modern Humanities*. Princeton, NJ: Princeton University Press, 2014.

Underwood, Ted. *Distant Horizons: Digital Evidence and Literary Change*. Chicago: University of Chicago Press, 2019.

———. "Distant Reading and Representativeness." *Stone and the Shell*, April 1, 2013. https://tedunderwood.com/2013/04/01/distant-reading-and-representativeness/.

———. "A Genealogy of Distant Reading." *Digital Humanities Quarterly* 11, no. 2 (2017). http://digitalhumanities.org/dhq/vol/11/2/000317/000317.html.

———. "Theorizing Research Practices We Forgot to Theorize Twenty Years Ago." *Representations* 127, no. 1 (August 2014): 64–72.

———. "We Don't Already Understand the Broad Outlines of Literary History." February 8, 2013. https://tedunderwood.com/2013/02/08/we-dont-already-know-the-broad-outlines-of-literary-history/.

US Copyright Office Fair Use Index. https://www.copyright.gov/fair-use/index.html. Accessed June 24, 2024.

Walker, John. *A Critical Pronouncing Dictionary and Expositor of the English Language*. London, 1822. https://prosody.princeton.edu/archive/hvd.32044055313134/.

———. *A Rhyming Dictionary*. London: T. Cadell and W. Davies, 1819. https://prosody.princeton.edu/archive/nyp.33433069239584/.

Wallaschek, Richard. *Primitive Music*. London: Longmans Green, 1893. https://prosody.princeton.edu/archive/inu.39000005918987/.

Wallin, Wallace. "Experimental Studies of Rhythm and Time." *Psychological Review* 19 (1912): 271–98. https://prosody.princeton.edu/archive/hvd.32044103001111-p271/.

Walsh, Melanie, Anna Preus, and Maria Antoniak. "Sonnet or Not, Bot? Poetry Evaluation for Large Models and Datasets. In *ArXiv: Computation and Language*. https://doi.org/10.48550/arXiv.2406.18906. Accessed June 27, 2024.

Walt Whitman Archive. Matt Cohen, Ed Folsom, and Kenneth Price, gen. eds. https://whitmanarchive.org/. Accessed May 22, 2024.

Ward, Thomas. *The English Poets*. Vol. 4. London: Macmillan, 1880. https://prosody.princeton.edu/archive/uc1.b3310826/.

Wardrip-Fruin, Noah. *Expressive Processing: Digital Fictions, Computer Games, and Software Studies*. Boston: MIT Press, 2012.

Warner, Julia. *Human Information Retrieval*. Cambridge, MA: MIT Press, 2010.

Watts, Isaac. *The Art of Reading and Writing English: Or, the Chief Principles and Rules of Pronouncing the Mother-Tongue*. 1721. London, 1722. https://prosody.princeton.edu/archive/CW0111540239/.

———. *Watts's Compleat Spelling-Book*. London: James Williams, at No. 5, in Skinner-Row 1737. https://prosody.princeton.edu/archive/CW0114598583/.

Weeks, L. T. "The Order of Rimes in the English Sonnet." *Modern Language Notes* 25, no. 6 (1910): 176–80. https://prosody.princeton.edu/archive/mdp.39015060429357-p176/.

Wickenden, Alice. "Things to Know before Beginning, or: Why Provenance Matters in the Library." *Inscription: The Journal of Material Text—Theory, Practice, History*, June 21, 2020. https://inscriptionjournal.com/2020/06/21/things-to-know-before-beginning-or-why-provenance-matters-in-the-library/.

Williams, Abigail. "Digital Miscellanies Index." https://www.digitalmiscellaniesindex.org. Accessed June 24, 2024.

Wilson, Meagan, and Mary Naydan. "Deduplicating the Archive." In *Princeton Prosody Archive*, version 3.12.1. Princeton, NJ: Center for Digital Humanities at Princeton. http://prosody.princeton.edu. Accessed June 14, 2024.

Winslow, Horatio. *Rhymes and Meters: A Practical Manual for Versifiers*. Ridgewood: Editor, 1914.

Wolfson, Susan. *Romantic Interactions: Social Being and the Turns of Literary Action*. Baltimore: Johns Hopkins University Press, 2010.

Wright, Alex. *Cataloging the World: Paul Otlet and the Birth of the Information Age*. Oxford: Oxford University Press, 2014.

Wythoff, Grant. "Tacit Computing and Method in the Humanities." Alliance of Digital Humanities Organizations conference, June 26–29, 2018, on panel "Mid-range Reading: Manifesto Edition."

Yee, Capella. "Digital Interactions for the Modern Scholar: A Case Study on the Field of Prosody." Undergraduate thesis, Princeton University, 2015.

Yokoyama, Setsuko. "Digital Technologies for Exploring Prosody: A Brief Historical Overview." Arcade. https://shc.stanford.edu/arcade/interventions/digital-technologies-exploring-prosody-brief-historical-overview. Accessed June 24, 2024.

INDEX

Page numbers in *italics* refer to illustrations.

Abridgment of Lectures on Rhetoric, An (Blair), 84, 85
Academy of American Poets, 65n20
accent, 56–59, 94
Accurate New Spelling Dictionary, An (Fisher), 57
Agbabi, Patience, 115
Ahmed, Sara, 171
Alden, Raymond Macdonald, 99, 147–48
Algee-Hewitt, Mark, 64
alliteration, 56, 114
Analytic Elocution (Zachos), 116, *117*
anthologies, 32n6
aphasia, 78
API (application programming interface), 120
appendixes, 8
Aquinas, Thomas, Saint, 40n22
archival studies, 29, 33, 66
archiving, 9
artificial intelligence (AI), 5–6n4, 128
Art of English Poetry, The (Bysshe), 50, 54
Art of Reading and Writing in English, The (Watts), 53, 59
Ascham, Roger, 135
Attridge, Derek, 153

Bailey, Herbert, 159
ballads, 39
Barnes, William, 106
Barthes, Roland, 155n38

Bartleby.com, 65n22
Beattie, James, 93
Bell, Alexander Melville, 78–79
bibliography, 29, 33, 134–67
Bitstreams (Kirschenbaum), 20n20
Blair, Hugh, 79, 84, 93
Blake, William, 53, 63
Blaney, Jonathan, 171–72
blank verse, 89
Blei, David, 71
book history, 29, 33, 109, 110
Book Traces (crowd-sourced project), 120
Booth, Alison, 89
Borgman, Christine, 12, 154
Bourdieu, Pierre, 23n2
Bowker, Geoffrey, 89
Boyce, Raymond, 148n24
Bridges, Robert, 43, 46, 164–65n56
Brin, Sergey, 73–74n37
British Periodicals (ProQuest collection), 42, 43, 46
British Poetry 1780–1910 (hypertext archive), 35
Brogan, Jacqui, 163, 164n55
Brogan, T. V. F., 46; career path of, 135, 168–69; as compiler, 150–57; *EVRG*'s shortcomings conceded by, 151–52; Fussell disparaged by, 146–47; on "genius," 103n16; linguistics viewed by, 13, 141–44, 146, 149, 150, 153; on meter and rhythm, 2, 136, 140–42, 149; *Princeton Encyclopedia of*

203

Brogan, T. V. F. (*cont.*)
  Poetry and Poetics and, 158–68; thoroughness of, 81; as traditionalist, 149; on versification, 9, 37–43, 80, 88, 134, 137, 139–40, 146–48, 152, 156, 157
Broussard, Meredith, 74
Brown, Goold, 22–27, 131
Brown, Susan, 67
Browning, Robert, 148n23
Busa, Roberto, 40n22, 153n30
Buurma, Rachel Sagner, 15
Bysshe, Edward, 50, 51–52, 53, 131, 148

Cable, Tom, 40
caesura, 63
capitalization, 112
Chadwyck-Healey, Charles, 64n18
Chadwyck-Healey poetry collection, 64–66, 118
Chamberlin, Donald, 148n24
Chapman, Alison, 66
Chapters on English Meter (Mayor), 148
ChatGPT, 128
circulation, of poetry, 4, 6, 17, 29, 30, 39
Clark, John, 125
classification: academic depreciation of, 91, 135–36; Dewey decimal, 90; by Library of Congress, 81, 82, 89, 154; in PPA, 83–89
close reading, 5, 14–15, 30, 60, 63, 66, 87, 88, 107
Cobb, Lyman, 57
Cobb's New Spelling Book, 57
Cohen, Dan, 103–4, 105
Cohen, Patricia, 105
Coleridge, Samuel Taylor, 130
Colored Conventions Project, 68
Combe, William, 69–71
Compleat Spelling-Book (Watts), 59
Complete Art of Poetry (Gildon), 51–52
Composition and Rhetoric (Tanner), 84
computational humanities, 2, 11–14, 44, 46, 62, 64, 66, 122, 125–28, 171
computational linguistics, 150, 152–53
Comstock, Andrew, 78

Comstock's Elocution, 24
copyright, 96, 111, 121
Cordell, Ryan, 44n25, 109, 112, 119
corpora, 46, 64
couplets, 53
Crapsey, Adelaide, 122–23
critical archival studies, 29, 33, 36
Critical Pronouncing Dictionary, A (Walker), 57
cross-references, 40, 42, 135–36, 149–50, 155
Culler, Dwight, 51, 52–53
Culler, Jonathan, 114–15
Cureton, Richard, 153

"Danger of Phonetics, The" (Saintsbury), 46, 47
deconstruction, 160
Dennis, Scott, 203–4n16
Dewey, Melvil, 90
diacritical marks, 57, 100–102, 110, 111, 115
dialect, 94, 106–7, 110–11, 113, 122
Dickinson, Emily, 63, 102n15
dictionaries, 24, 60–62; of rhymes, 51, 53–57
digital hoarding, 43n24
digital humanities (DH), 2, 9, 11–15, 29; funding of, 169–70; multiple meanings of, 12
distant reading, 10, 39, 62, 63, 104, 107–8, 118, 122
Distant Reading (Moretti), 45
Dr. Syntax (racehorse), 69–71, 73, 74
Dotzler, Bernhard, 23n2
Dryden, John, 153
Dunbar, Paul Laurence, 106, 107
duplication, in data, 85
Dworkin, Craig, 47–48n30, 107n46
dysprosody, 78

Early English Books Online (EEBO), 8, 36
Early Modern OCR Project (eMOP), 108
Education Act (1870), 69
EIDOS: The International Prosody Bulletin, 150–53

Eighteenth Century Collections Online (ECCO), 8, 36, 52, 87, 157
Eighteenth-Century Poetry Archive, 64–65n19
Elam, Michele, 128
Eliot, T. S., 148n23
elocution, 78–79, 81, 84, 88, 97, 98, 106, 113–17
Ellis, Alexander John, 56, 98, 99
emphasis, 10, 56, 58–59
Endnote (software), 42
Enfield, William, 78
English Full-Text Poetry Database, 65
English Parnassus (Poole), 51
English Poetry (archive), 65
English Verse (Alden), 147–48
English Versification, 1570–1980 (EVRG; Brogan), 37, 42, 80, 88, 138–39, 140, 148, 155, 157; cross-references in, 150; Fussell criticized in, 146; as manifesto, 135; PPA linked to, 165; as relational data structure, 162; shortcomings of, 51–52; table of contents of, 156; writing and publication of, 40n22, 134–37, 139
eScriptorium, 109
"Essay on Criticism" (Pope), 58
Essentials of Phonetics (Ellis), 98
expressive use, 19–20, 110–11

fair use, 111n35, 121
"false" rhymes, 56
Feist v. Rural Telephone Services Company (1991), 121
Felluga, Dino, 118–19
feminism, 160
First Lines of English Grammar (Brown), 22
Fisher, Anne, 57
Flanders, Julia, 66
Folsom, Ed, 45n27
"For Better for Verse" (Tucker), 125–26
Foucault, Digital (Dotzler and Schmidgen), 23n2
Foucault, Michel, 23n2, 30n3
Freedgood, Elaine, 62n14

From Philology to English Studies (Momma), 28n1
front matter, 8
Fussell, Paul, 142–46, 148, 164
Fyfe, Paul, 109

Gabrielson, Arvid, 57
Gall, Sally, 150, 153
Gardiner, William, 92, 93–95, 148
Garth, John, 34–35n10
gender studies, 160
Gildon, Charles, 51–52, 131
Godwin, William, 130
Google, 121
Google Books, 8, 11, 39, 69–70, 72–74, 81, 97, 103–4n16
Google Ngram Viewer, 69, 73, 103–4
grammar books, 1, 4, 6, 21–27
Grammar of English Grammars, The (Brown), 21–27, 131
Greene, Roland, 164
Griffiths, Eric, 115
Guest, Edwin, 56
Guillory, John, 30n4, 48n31
Gummere, Frances Barton, 48

Habermas, Jürgen, 23n2
Hall, Jason, 125
Hamill, S. S., 77, 78–79
Hamilton, James, 106
handwritten text recognition (HTR), 108–9
Hansen, Kristin, 126
Hardison, O. B., 158, 161, 162
Hartman, Charles, 126
HathiTrust Digital Library, 8, 39, 52, 80–82, 85, 116, 120–21, 157
Heffernan, Laura, 15
Helton, Laura, 89–90
heroic verse, 53
Heuser, Ryan, 64, 126, 128
"hexameter mania," 42, 69
Historical Poetics project, 16
History of English Criticism (Saintsbury), 51

History of English Prosody (Saintsbury), 51, 97
Hoekzema, Loren, 158, 159
Hollerith, Herman, 64
Homer, 69
Hood, Thomas, 54, 131
Hopkins, Gerard Manley, 114, 148n23
Houston, Natalie, 66
Hughes, Langston, 115
Human Computer Interaction (HCI), 69n34, 113n38
humanism, 31n5
Hydra, The (anthology), 34
hypertext, 41, 155

iamb, 116
indentation, 108, 112
Index Thomasticus, 40n22
information science, 29
Information Seeking Systems (ISS), 69n34
inscriptions, 29
Institutes of English Grammar (Brown), 22
International Phonetic Alphabet (IPA), 85, 94
"Introductory Lecture" (Thelwall), 130–31

Jackson, Virginia, 16n18, 115
Jespersen, Otto, 12–13n14
Jockers, Matthew, 72–73n36
Johnson, Samuel, 85, 157
Johnston, Ben, 41, 118
Joint Information Systems Committee, 34
Jones, Daniel, 46
Jones, William, 56
JTAP (Technical Applications Program), 34–35n10

Karlin, Daniel, 65
keyword searching, 18, 55, 131–32
Kiparsky, Paul, 126
Kipling, Rudyard, 54
Kirschenbaum, Matthew, 20n20, 75–76, 107n26, 112, 151

Kittler, Friedrich, 23n2
kymograph, 145

Labbe, Jacqueline, 53
Lamborn, E. A., 113
Lancaster, Frederick, 154
Lancelot, Claude, 52, 131
Landow, George, 36, 155
Lanier, Sidney, 48
large language models (LLMs), 76
Latent Dirichlet Allocation (LDA), 72n36
Layne-Worthey, Glenn, 64
Leighton, Angela, 114–15
Levy, Amy, 65
Library of Congress (LOC) classifications, 81, 82, 89, 154
linguistics, 2, 93, 114; in Brogan's writings, 13, 141–44, 146, 149, 150, 153; literary studies vs., 5, 28; technological impact on, 152
literary criticism, 19, 28, 47
literary studies, 5, 28–29
Liu, Alan, 154
Logan, John, 164–65n56
Lowell, James Russell, 106
Luhman, Nicklas, 23n2

Mandell, Laura, 108, 119
Manovich, Lev, 45
Manwaring, Edward, 52
MARC (machine-readable catalog) system, 82–83n3, 154
markup language, 63, 112
Marsh, George, 56
Mason, John, 52
Matthews, Brander, 54, 56
Mayer, Marissa, 203–4n16
Mayor, Joseph B., 148
McGann, Jerome, 9, 33, 35, 63
McGill, Meredith, 16n18, 106, 111n35
McKay, Claude, 63
media studies, 29
mediation, 3–5, 17, 30; data and archives as, 9, 12

melodrama, 106
metadata, 8, 10, 19, 46, 79–80, 83–89, 112, 120, 132
Metahaven, 75n39
meter, 5, 11, 63, 89, 122
Microsoft Word, 151
Miles, Josephine, 153
Miller, J. Hillis, 35
Milton, John, 97–98, 148n23
Mimno, David, 71–73
Momma, Haruko, 28n1, 30n3
Monboddo, James Burnett, Lord, 93
Moretti, Franco, 45
music, 92–95
Music of Nature, The (Gardiner), 92, 93–95

Naydan, Mary, 86
New Cambridge Bibliography, The, 65
Newcomer, Alphonso, 56
New English Dictionary, 79
New Historicism, 160
New Princeton Encyclopedia of Poetry and Poetics (NPEPP, 1993), 134, 135, 161–63, 168, 169
n-grams, 69, 73, 103–4
NLP (natural language processing), 153
Noble, Safiyah, 74
"Notes upon English Verse" (Poe), 25
novels, 35, 53, 62

OCLC (Online Computer Library Center), 39, 151, 154
Omond, T. S., 97
O'Neill, Vathy, 74
On English Homophones (Bridges), 46
optical character recognition (OCR), 6, 44n25, 108–12, 121
"Order of Rimes in the English Sonnet, The" (Weeks), 124
orthoepy, 78
Orwant, John, 105
oscillograph, 145
Osmond, T. S., 40

Otlet, Paul, 40n22
Owen Collection, 34–35n10

Page, Lawrence, 73–74n37, 103–4n16
page description language (PDL), 161
Parikka, Jussi, 23n2
Parker, Andrew, 106
Patmore, Coventry, 48, 131
Penguin Book of Victorian Verse (1997), 65
performance, 78–79
Perloff, Marjorie, 153
philology, 12n14
phonemes, 10
phonetics, 55, 98, 123, 145; in Brogan's writings, 143, 144; development of, 84, 87, 98, 125; opponents of, 46, 47
phonetic speech, 58
phonology, 12–13n14
Piper, Andrew, 28, 31n5
Pitman, Isaac, 78–79
Plotting Poetry (research group), 63–64n17
Poe, Edgar Allen, 24, 25
Poetic Meter and Poetic Form (Fussell), 142–43, 146, 147
poetry handbooks, 16
Poetry Magazine, 64–65n19
Poole, Joshua, 51
Pope, Alexander, 58, 148n23
Porter, Dorothy, 90
Porter, Ebenezer, 78
PostScript (software), 161
Pound, Ezra, 148n23
Practical Guide for English Versification (Hood), 54
prefaces, 8
Preminger, Alex, 158, 159, 161, 162
Priestley, Joseph, 93
Princeton Encyclopedia of Poetry and Poetics (PEPP), 146, 149, 158–68; *New Princeton Encyclopedia of Poetry and Poetics* (NPEPP, 1993), 134, 135, 161–63, 168, 169
Princeton Handbook of Multicultural Poetries, 162, 163–64

Princeton Handbook of Poetic Terms, 158, 162, 163
Princeton Prosody Archive (PPA), 2, 3, *101*; in the academy, 28, 135, 167; aims of, 90; classifications in, 83–89; deselection in, 61–62; how to cite, 172; human-textual interface structured by, 113, 121–22; methodology for, 10; origins of, 14; outlook for, 18, 172, 173; scope of, 6–9, 94; searching in, 19, 132–33; theory vs. practice in, 12
Prins, Yopie, 16n18
print culture, 106
Project Gutenberg, 44, 64–65n19
pronunciation, 5, 7, 44, 46, 53, 55–59, 78, 113, 122, 142
ProQuest, 42, 44, 64n18, 80, 106
Prosodia Rationalis (Steele), 97, 132
Prosodic (program), 126
prosodists, 39, 100, 104, 139, 150
prosody: in Brown's grammar books, 22; classification and, 82–83, 87–88; historical, 5, 10, 11, 15–17, 31–33, 37, 60–61, 119, 122, 128, 147, 151–54; judgment and interpretation linked in, 48–49; in literary studies vs. linguistics, 5, 7; prosodic discourse and, 18–19; renewed interest in, 152, 160; speech therapy and, 78; as versification and pronunciation, 7; versification vs., 40
Prosody (racehorse), 69–71, 73
provenance, 7, 44, 49, 65, 83, 85, 87, 173
Puttenham, George, 56
Pygmalion (Shaw), 113

Quatre traitez de poësies, latine, françoise, italienne, et espagnole (Lancelot), 52

reception theory, 160
recitation, 59, 84–85, 88, 113–14
reprinting, 6, 39, 61, 85, 106, 131
Research Collection and Preservation (ReCAP) consortium, 86
rhetoric, 12–13n14, 76, 113
Rhymes and Meters (Winslow), 55

rhyming dictionaries, 51, 53–57
Rhyming Dictionary (Walker), 56, 57–59
rhythm, 5, 78, *98*, *99*, 122; "Anglo-Saxon," 102; in Brogan's writings, 136, 140–42, 149; in Brown's *Grammar*, 24–25; contested meanings of, 128; meter equated with, 101n13; "natural," 114, 144; physicality of, 144–45; racial ideologies of, 125; Thomson's view of, 99–100; Watts's view of, 59
Richards, I. A., 75
Richardson, Samuel, 53
Rickard, Edith, 153n30
Riley, James Whitcomb, 106
Rime as a Criterion of the Pronunciation of Spenser, Pope, Byron, and Swinburne (Gabrielson), 57
Risam, Roopika, 65–66
Rise and Fall of Meter, The (Martin), 9, 38
Romanticism, 130, 131
Romantic Period Poetry Archive, 64–65n18
Rosenthal, M. L., 153
Rossetti Archive, 35
Rossetti, Dante Gabriel, 63
Rowland, Thomas, 69–71
Rules for Rhyme (Hood), 54, 131
Rush, James, 78

Saintsbury, George, 37, 43, 46–49, 51, 97, 142
Saussure, Ferdinand de, 12–13n14
Say, Samuel, 52
Scandroid (program), 126, 127
scansion, 31, *99*, 123, 145–47; computational, 125; didactic, 101, 111, 126; differing views of, 97–98; interpretive, 39; in modern classroom, 101, 102; subjectivity of, 103, 110; typography and, 115–18, 122, 142, 161
Schipper, Jakob, 148
Schmidgen, Henning, 23n2
Schmidt, Benjamin, 72–73n36
Scholemaster, The (Ascham), 135
searching, 19, 49; finding aid use distinguished from, 68; interfaces for, 69n34;

by keyword, 18, 55, 131–32; researching vs., 69–71
Second Tour of Dr. Syntax in Search of Consolation, The (Combe), 69
Shakespeare, William, 148n23
Shechtman, Anna, 20n20
Siefring, Judith, 171–72
"Slumber Did My Spirit Seal, A" (Wordsworth), 32n6
Smith, Abby, 35–36
Smith, Courtney Weiss, 130
Smith, David, 109, 119
Society for Pure English (SPE), 44, 46
songs, 29
sonnets, 122, 124, 126
spacing, 63, 112
spelling reform, 57, 94
SQL (structured query language), 148n24
stammering, 78
stanzas, 63
Star, Susan Leigh, 89
statistics, 17
Stauffer, Andrew, 118, 120
Steedman, Carolyn, 65
Steele, Joshua, 52, 97, 131, 132
Stein, Benno, 23n2
Stoler, Ann Laura, 65
Study in English Metrics, A (Crapsey), 123
Study of Metre, A (Osmond), 40
Study of Versification (Matthews), 54
Sweet, Henry, 12–13n14, 78–79
Swidzinski, Joshua, 130
syllabification, 19, 24–25, 52

tagging, 63
Tanner, William, 84
Teaching Archive (Heffernan and Buurma), 15
Technical Applications Program (JTAP), 34–35n10
Tennyson, Alfred Tennyson, baron, 148n23
Terras, Melissa, 108–9
Text-Encoding Initiative (TEI), 45, 63
textual criticism, 33

Thelwall, John, 78, 97–98, 129, 130–31, 148
Third Tour of Dr. Syntax in Search of a Wife, The (Combe), 69–70
Thomson, William, 99–100
Tooke, Horne, 130
topic modeling, 71
Tour of Doctor Syntax in Search of the Picturesque, The (Combe), 69, 70, 71
Toward Paperless Information Systems (Lancaster), 154
Transkribus, 108
Trouillot, Michel-Rolph, 65
Tsur, Reuven, 153
Tucker, Herbert, 125
typography, 7, 19, 72–73n36, 96–128

Underwood, Ted, 11, 68, 105n18, 154
Unicode, 7, 19
Universal Bibliography, 40n22
University Microfilms (UMI), 151

van Leeuwen, Steven H., 65n22
Verseform (Brogan), 149–50
versification, 4, 9, 10, 13, 51, 54, 84, 114, 122; in Brogan's writings, 9, 37–43, 80, 88, 134, 139–40, 146–48, 152, 156, 157; in Brown's grammar books, 22–25; differing approaches to, 40–41, 43, 94, 102; in elocution movement, 78; history of, 29, 31, 32–33, 40, 87, 139, 147, 155; measurement of, 37; prosody distinguished from, 40; prosody equated with, 5, 7
Versification (journal), 37, 155, 157
Victorian Web, 36, 155

Walker, John, 53–59
Warnke, Frank J., 158, 161, 162
Watson, Thomas, Sr., 40n22, 64n18
Watts, Isaac, 53, 59
Weber, Max, 23n2
Webster, Augusta, 65
Webster's Dictionary, 24
Weeks, L. T., 123, 124
Whitman, Walt, 63, 65n22

Wickenden, Alice, 44n25
Wilson, Meagan, 85
Winslow, Horatio, 55
word lists, 19, 53, 55–57, 60–62, 67, 70, 86
WordPerfect, 151
WordStar (software), 151
Wordsworth, William, 32n6, 130, 148n23

Works of the Poets (Johnson), 85
Wythoff, Grant, 80, 89

Yee, Capella, 157n40
Yokoyama, Setsuko, 126

Zotero (software), 42

A NOTE ON THE TYPE

This book has been composed in Arno, an Old-style serif typeface in the classic Venetian tradition, designed by Robert Slimbach at Adobe.

GPSR Authorized Representative: Easy Access System Europe - Mustamäe tee 50, 10621 Tallinn, Estonia, gpsr.requests@easproject.com

www.ingramcontent.com/pod-product-compliance
Lightning Source LLC
Chambersburg PA
CBHW030622230426
43661CB00053B/2107